Foreign Language
and
Mother Tongue

Foreign Language and Mother Tongue

ISTVAN KECSKES
TÜNDE PAPP
State University of New York, Albany

LAWRENCE ERLBAUM ASSOCIATES, PUBLISHERS
2000   Mahwah, New Jersey   London

Copyright © 2000 by Lawrence Erlbaum Associates, Inc.
All rights reserved. No part of this book may be reproduced in any form, by photostat, microfilm, retrieval system, or any other means, without prior written permission of the publisher.

Lawrence Erlbaum Associates, Inc., Publishers
10 Industrial Avenue
Mahwah, NJ 07430

Cover design by Kathryn Houghtaling Lacey

Library of Congress Cataloging-in-Publication Data

Kecskes, Istvan.
Foreign language and mother tongue / Istvan Kecskes, Tünde Papp.
    p. cm.
  Includes bibliographical references and index.
ISBN 0-8058-2759-5 (alk. paper)
1. Multilingualism. 2. Native language. 3. Second language acquisition.
    4. Language transfer (Language learning). 5. Language awareness.
  I. Papp, Tünde. II. Title.
P115 .K43 2000
404'.2—dc21   00-028841
                                                              CIP

Books published by Lawrence Erlbaum Associates are printed on acid-free paper, and their bindings are chosen for strength and durability.

Printed in the United States of America
10 9 8 7 6 5 4 3 2 1

To our children András and Tünde, whose multilingual development helped us understand the processes we discussed in this book.

Contents

Preface ix

1. MOTHER TONGUE AND SUBSEQUENT LANGUAGES 1
   Mother Tongue *1*
   Foreign Language *2*
   FL Versus L2 *3*
   Summary *13*

2. FOREIGN LANGUAGE INFLUENCE ON WRITTEN L1 15
   The L2 → L1 Effect *15*
   Written Speech *16*
   Hypotheses *20*
   The Experiment *20*
   Discussion *25*
   Principal Findings of the Experiment *29*
   Summary *31*
   Appendix *33*

3. LANGUAGE PROCESSING DEVICE OF MULTILINGUALS 37
   Language Processing in Bilinguals *37*
   Speech Production Models *39*
   The Common Underlying Conceptual Base *47*
   Summary *53*

4. THOUGHT AND WORD 55
   The Conceptual–Linguistic Interface *55*
   Concept and Word in Linguistic Theory *58*
   Development of the Mental Lexicon in Multilinguals *64*
   Summary *71*

5.	TRANSFER OF SKILLS IN THE LPD	73
	Development of Skills *74*	
	Linguistic Operations and Memory *81*	
	Summary *84*	
6.	LANGUAGE DISTANCE AND MULTICOMPETENCE	87
	Language Distance *88*	
	Organization of a Sentence *92*	
	Cultural Distance and Vocabulary *96*	
	Summary *104*	
7.	PRAGMATIC KNOWLEDGE OF MULTILINGUALS	106
	The Nature of Positive Transfer *106*	
	Thought and Discourse *110*	
	Summary *117*	
CONCLUSION		119
REFERENCES		124
AUTHOR INDEX		139
SUBJECT INDEX		145

Preface

FOREIGN LANGUAGE INFLUENCE

Multicompetence

The main argument of this book is that people with more than one language have different knowledge of their first language (L1) than do monolingual people, and this difference can mainly be due to the effect of subsequent languages on the development and use of L1 skills.[1] According to Grosjean (1985, 1989, 1992), Cook (1991a, 1992), and Kecskes (1998), research on bilingualism has been under the influence of a monolingual view for decades although several researchers, including Meara (1983), Grosjean (1985, 1989, 1992), and Cook (1991a, 1992, 1993), disagreed with this view because it treats both languages as if they were the first language. Meara (1983, p. iv) argued that "there is no reason why a person who speaks both English and Spanish should behave in the same way as a monolingual speaker of either language." Grosjean (1985, p. 467) suggested that the bilingual is a "specific speaker-hearer" and not two monolinguals in one body. Bilinguals and multilinguals have a unique competence that Cook (1991a, 1992) called *multicompetence*, which in some respects contains a state of L1 knowledge different from that of monolinguals. Having reviewed the evidence for these differences, Cook (1992) concluded that people who know more than one language have a distinctive state of mind, *multicompetence*, that is not the equivalent to two monolingual states. He argued that multicompetence is not a final state of mind as the native monolingual's competence is but covers all stages of second language acquisition (Cook, 1992, 1993).

Why is it that the multilingual view started to be strongly articulated as opposed to the monolingual view only at the beginning of the 1990s?

---

[1] In this book the terms "bilingual" and "multilingual," and "bilingualism" and "multilingualism" are used interchangeably for two reasons. On the one hand this is common practice in the literature about multicompetence. Basically bilingualism is considered as one possible version of multicompetence. On the other hand, the structure and function of the multilingual Language Processing Device (as described here) are supposed to be very similar when it has two or more languages. The difference is in the operation of the LPD.

Why has the monolingual view been so influential for several decades? When in 1953 Roman Jacobson (1953) said: "Bilingualism is for me the fundamental problem of linguistics" (p. 20), linguists did not listen. So there came Chomsky and with him a very strong monolingual view on language which was based on the ideal speaker-hearer assumption. Ever since, the main question for linguists has been "What constitutes knowledge of language?" (cf. Chomsky, 1986), and not "What constitutes knowledge of languages?" although it is a well-known fact that more than 50% of the world's population speak not only one language but more (Cook, 1992; Jessner, 1997). Recently, however, there have been important changes both in theoretical and applied linguistics which have resulted in attempts to move away from the monolingual, syntax-centered view and look at language from a multilingual, holistic, and meaning-centered perspective. This new trend has inspired researchers in SLA and bilingualism to investigate the dynamism of multilingual development with its ups and downs and focus on issues neglected for years such as, for instance, "multicompetence" (Cook, 1991a, 1992), effect of L2 on L1 development (Kecskes, 1998; Kecskes & Papp, 1991; Papp, 1991), dynamic model of multilingualism (Jessner, 1997), transfer of sociocultural norms and patterns of interaction from one language to another (Kasper & Blum-Kulka, 1993; Kecskes, 1999; Oksaar, 1990; Yoshida, 1990), development of conceptual fluency in L2 (Danesi, 1992; Kecskes, 1998; Kecskes & Papp, 2000), and others. This book adds a new entry to this list because it discusses foreign language learning from a multilingual perspective. It is argued here that not only bi- and multilingual development but also intensive foreign-language learning in a classroom setting, which we consider a special case of multilingual development, can enhance L1 development and result in multicompetence. This is not a new idea: Vygotsky (1962) wrote several decades ago:

> Success in learning a foreign language is contingent on a certain degree of maturity in the native language. The child can transfer to the new language the system of meanings he already possesses in his own. The reverse is also true—a foreign language facilitates mastering the higher forms of the native tongue. The child learns to see his language as one particular system among many, to view its phenomena under more general categories and this leads to awareness of his linguistic operations. (Vygotsky, 1962, p. 110)

Although most applied linguists acknowledge (e.g., Cummins, 1979, 1995; Gass, 1987; Selinker, 1972) that there must be a bidirectional interdependence between the first language and the foreign language (FL), only one side of this interaction has been emphasized in the relevant literature (e.g., Cook, 1991; Cummins, 1979, 1984; Ellis, 1985; Larsen-

Freeman & Long, 1991). Much is known about the influence of the L1 on the FL learning process but much less about the opposite direction: the effect FL learning has on the development of mother tongue skills. Cummins' (1986) interdependence hypothesis states that:

> To the extent that instruction in a certain language is effective in promoting proficiency in that language, transfer of this proficiency to another language will occur, provided there is adequate exposure to that other language (either in the school or environment) and adequate motivation to learn that language. (p. 20)

The hypothesis predicts transfer not only from Lx to Ly, but also from Ly to Lx, unless the exposure and motivation conditions are negative. Although in principle transfer can occur both ways, Cummins emphasized that we generally see only unidirectional transfer from the first language to the other language. He attributed the lack of transfer in the opposite direction to the absence of motivation and exposure in an L2 or FL environment. We intend to demonstrate in this book that the interdependence hypothesis may work both ways in a foreign language environment under certain conditions, and Cummins was right when he considered motivation and exposure as very important conditions for positive transfer from L2 to L1. Intensive and effective FL learning can result in a unique form of multicompetence that strongly resembles additive bilingualism and has developmental processes similar to those characterizing the emergence of multilingualism.

Nature and Content of FL Influence

When determining the subject matter of this book we have to discuss the nature and content of the effect of FL on the L1. A survey of bilingualism (cf. Odlin, 1989; Weinreich, 1953/1968) demonstrated that the effects of cross-linguistic influences are not monolithic but vary to a great extent depending on the social context of the language contact situation. According to the nature of the L2—>L1 effect we can distinguish the following cases:

1. L2 or FL serves as lingua franca,
2. pidgin and creole,
3. immigrants studying the language of their new community,
4. bilingual L1 acquisition (the child is exposed to two languages from birth; e.g., De Houwer, 1990),
5. both languages are present, but one of them is dominant (Swedish in Finland or English in Ireland),
6. instructed FL in a relatively homogeneous language community.

There is much literature on all but the last case. This is mainly due to the fact that the FL—>L1 influence is usually not considered as a bilingual situation. FL learners are not supposed to become bilinguals because the target language community is not present in any way in the FL environment, and the FL is rarely the medium of communication outside the classroom. In this book we focus mainly on this particular case, that is, when the target language is a foreign language in a relatively homogeneous language community. The FL is learned through instruction in a classroom setting, and students usually do not have direct access to the target language culture. As said before, Vygotsky, Grosjean, Cummins, Cook, and others did notice that L2 affects L1 in some way in the foreign language environment as well. Why is it then that, with a few exceptions, no particular research has yet been done in this direction? One can think of several explanations. First of all, the FL—>L1 effect is out of the main scope of all the research disciplines that could be expected to include this issue in their agenda (second language acquisition, foreign language pedagogy, bilingualism, child language acquisition) because it is almost taken for granted that the only or the most important effect the foreign language has in an instructional environment is on the development of metalinguistic awareness of students, and it usually serves as an educational enhancement. This is quite a simplistic view because the FL—>L1 influence is much more complex than is usually expected. Students have suggested that one of the best ways to understand one's own language is to study a foreign language. This is basically true, but metalinguistic awareness is not the only way in which FL can affect the L1. Takano (1985), for example, wrote about younger Japanese native speakers who have to some extent phonemicized former allophonic variants such as [c] and [j] under the influence of English. This could happen, according to Takano, because all of them studied English throughout their school years. Depending on the intensity of language learning and the form of language contact (if any), the FL can affect the L1 in different ways. Caskey-Sirmons and Hickson (1997) demonstrated that the meanings that words have in the L1 can be influenced by the L2. They examined color terms in five languages, and found, for instance, that a monolingual speaker of Korean uses the word *paran sekj* (in English: blue) to mean something greener and less purple than a Korean who speaks English as well. Dewaele (1999) found that the second language (English) influences the choice of interrogative structures in French L1 speakers who have been living in London for at least 2 years. Holmstrand (1979) investigated how early teaching of a foreign language affected the teaching of other school subjects and, above all, the mother tongue. His study focused on the first six grades in elementary school in

Sweden. Holmstrand's findings indicated that the study of English had a stimulating effect on achievement in Swedish. These studies demonstrate that a foreign language can affect L1 in different ways. We think that the simplistic view according to which the FL enhances only metalinguistic awareness can partly be explained by the directions and goals of the research on transfer also.

Transfer

At this point it is essential to clarify how the term *transfer* is used in this book. From a multicompetence perspective there are three problems with the concept of transfer as used in the relevant literature (cf. Andersen, 1983; Gass & Selinker, 1983; Odlin, 1989). First, as the concept of transfer has been used mainly in the direction of L1—>L2 rather than the opposite L2—>L1, little interest has been generated to show the effect (or the lack of effect) of the L2 on the L1 (Cook, 1992; Papp, 1991). The term *transfer* was linked to the behaviorist theory of learning that emphasizes the effects of the L1 on the L2, but hardly says anything about the opposite direction. This lopsided use of *transfer* continues to dominate even in the literature that has nothing to do with behaviorism: Transfer is considered to be the result of learners selectively using their L1 knowledge while struggling with the complexities of the L2 (cf. Andersen, 1983; Kellerman, 1995). One of the main questions researchers have kept asking is about the reason for transfer: Is it difference or similarity between the two language systems that triggers transfer? Supporters of the Contrastive Analysis Hypothesis (Lado, 1957; Stockwell, Bowen, & Martin, 1965) argued that the greater the difference between the two language systems, the greater the likelihood of interference. Research from the 1980s suggested that the opposite is true: Similarity between languages can result in transfer (cf. Andersen, 1983; Kellerman, 1995). Odlin (1989) gave the following definition to the term: "Transfer is the influence resulting from similarities and differences between the target language and any other language that has previously (and perhaps imperfectly) been acquired" (p. 37). After surveying of the relevant research Kellerman (1995) also came to the conclusion that the notion of similarity is one of the main driving forces behind transfer. In his framework, transferability depends on the perceived distance between the L1 and the L2 and the structural organization of the learner's L1. However, there is no reference in his studies to a possible bidirectional influence suggesting that the developing target language can also affect the L1 or any other previously acquired language.

Second, transfer can be either synchronic or diachronic, but the latter has almost been ignored in the SLA or bilingualism literature.[2] In the language development of a multicompetent person transfer can be understood as a historical source or as "part of the current knowledge state" (Cook, 1992, p. 581). The learner is an active participant in the learning process, and he or she makes decisions about what can and cannot be transferred (Kellerman, 1983, 1995). The L2 learning process has a history of its own with its own ups and downs. Language change is the result of the unique interplay and interdependence of the environment and the individual. Hyltenstam and Viberg (1993) said:

> Living languages are in a continuous motion, adapting to the social context in which they are used: they take form as different registers or lects, they appear in the written or spoken mode, and above all, they move with time, changing chronologically. A specific instance of chronological change occurs in the individual. (p. 3)

The language learner plays an important and active part in this dynamic process in which the monolingual L1 competence cannot be the goal; multilingual development differs from monolingual development in several aspects and results in a Common Underlying Conceptual Base which governs the functioning of all language channels. We think that multilingual development as understood in this book cannot be described in the terms of "interlanguage" (Selinker, 1972, 1992) because the latter refers to second language acquisition as a continuous and relatively straightforward developmental process on a continuum whose end-product is native-like competence. Consequently, the final goal of L2 acquisition is a speaker with two native competences. The problem with this approach is that there is nothing like an ideal bilingual who has native-like competence in two languages, because the two language systems are not autonomous in multilinguals (Cook, 1992, Kecskes, 1998; Papp, 1991), and the level of fluency in a language depends on the need for the language and is extremely domain specific (Grosjean, 1992). As a consequence of constant change in multilingual competence the nature and characteristics of transfer also keep changing all the time. Diachronic transfer is especially important when discussing how foreign language learning affects mother tongue development.

Third, transfer research has concentrated chiefly on the investigation of grammatical and structural phenomena and has had little to say about

---

[2]As exceptions Cook (1977, 1991) and Weinreich (1953) can be mentioned. Cook made a difference between "code-breaking" language (process of acquiring the knowledge of a language) and "decoding" language (the use of existing language for a purpose).

issues concerning language use and learners' sociopragmatic perceptions, although several findings demonstrated that "first language influence may be more complicated a matter than an account of structural relatedness or linguistic proficiency" (Kellerman, 1995, p. 130). There are studies that have directed attention to one or more of these problems. Odlin (1989) considered the overemphasis on morphology and syntax as one of the theoretical shortcomings of transfer research. Some scholars (e.g., Gass, 1987; Gass & Selinker, 1993) called for studies in bidirectionality of language transfer, saying that that type of research would lead to greater insight into what factors, other than purely structural ones, need to be taken into account when trying to understand the phenomenon of language transfer. Pavlenko (1998a, 1998b) and Jarvis (1997) argued for a unified cognitive account of many transfer phenomena under the umbrella of conceptual transfer, an elaboration of Kellerman's (1995) *transfer to nowhere:* "an unconscious assumption that the way we talk or write about experience is not something that is subject to between-language variation" (p. 141). Kellerman suggested that a distinction in levels of abstraction should be maintained: One level is about the acquisition of the means of linguistic expression whereas his *transfer to nowhere* is about the conceptualization that "fuels the drive towards discovering those means" (Kellerman, 1995, p. 142). As we understand it, Kellerman's approach implies that transfer can come about through both similarity and difference. There is a structural and a conceptual level of transfer: The former is dominated by similarity and the latter is affected mostly by difference. Conceptual transfer occurs at a level where cognition and language touch.

We consider multilingual development as a dynamic and cumulative process that is characterized by transfer of a different nature and results in a Common Underlying Conceptual Base (CUCB). Kecskes (1998) emphasized the evolving nature of transfer which usually leads to structural and lexical difficulties in the first phase of multilingual development and is dominated by unidirectional (L1—>L2) processes. This does not mean, of course, that there is no transfer at all in the opposite direction. There is some, but it is usually not significant. Transfer in this period is a matter of interaction of the language channels (what we later call Constantly Available Interacting Systems [CAIS]) rather than the conceptual system. That is why this linguistic transfer is usually considered as a negative phenomenon that generally signifies lack of some knowledge. The more proficient the learner becomes in the L2, and the more firmly multicompetence is established in the mind, the more positive the content of transfer becomes. This positive transfer is predominantly neither structural nor lexical but pragmatic, and knowledge transfer which is bidirectional and has a serious bearing on the language behavior and discourse organization of the multilingual speaker because it is a CUCB rather than a CAIS phenomenon. The changing nature of transfer requires a distinction between two types of transfer: (a) Transfer as a linguistic systems phenomenon: when the interaction of the two or more language systems results in the transfer of a sound pattern, lexical item, or structure from one language system to the other, and (b) transfer as a CUCB phenomenon: when knowledge or skills acquired through one language system become ready to be used through the other language channel(s). We, however, emphasize that transfer is a dynamic phenomenon, and because movement can happen in both directions on the multilingual development continuum, the occurrence of these two types of transfer is not necessarily sequential.

There are several examples in the literature that indirectly support the two-sided nature of transfer as described before. Within the context of Competition Model (MacWhinney, 1992), L2 learning is viewed as a process of cue acquisition that relies initially on transfer from L1 to L2. L2 learners tend to carry over the weightings from the L1: cues with the strongest strength have the strongest transfer. MacWhinney (1992) argued that "... emphasis should be placed on moving the learner through the period of transfer into a period of functional restructuring" (p. 386). Functional restructuring occurs at the conceptual level when multilingual development reaches a stage where the L2 language channel is strong enough to make modifications in the L1-based conceptual system. As MacWhinney (1992) said, "... there is good reason to believe that, after the earliest stages, L2 learners are spending a great deal of time creating a new set of conceptual categories" (p. 382). Interlanguage pragmatics (e.g., Kasper, 1996; Kasper & Blum-Kulka, 1993; Schmidt, 1993) also supports the claim about the changing nature of transfer by emphasizing that pragmatic transfer usually characterizes a later stage of L2 development, occurs at the conceptual level, and is bidirectional.

Corder (1983) suggested that we should not use *transfer* if we adopt a theoretical approach other than the behaviorists'. Kellerman and Sharwood-Smith (1986) suggested the term *cross-linguistic influence,* which is a broader term and can include not only transfer in the traditional sense but also several other aspects of language interaction such as avoidance and rate of learning. We, however, will continue to use the term *transfer* because it best describes the phenomenon used in this book. However, the definition of the term has to be tailored to our needs. For us, the word *transfer* denotes here any kind of movement or influence of concepts, knowledge, skills, or linguistic elements (structures, forms), in either direction between the L1 and the subsequent language(s). Our understanding of the term is not restricted to L1—>L2 influence but presupposes bidirectionality and includes not only structure and form transfer but knowledge and skill transfer. It is assumed that in the case of multicompetent speakers concepts, knowledge, and skills can flow between languages through the Common Underlying Conceptual Base, and this process can have either a neutral, negative, or positive influence depending on the concrete phenomenon in question. The theoretical basis for this relatively free flow and the different nature of transfer in the CAIS and CUCB is discussed in chapter 3.

The literature on language contact also emphasized the decisive role of social factors in determining the linguistic outcome of contact situations (cf. Odlin, 1989; Thomason & Kaufman, 1988). We agree with Thomason and Kaufman's assumption (1988, p. 35) according to which linguistic interference is conditioned in the first instance by social factors, not linguistic ones. This explains the changing nature of transfer as discussed previously. Thomason and Kaufman distinguished between *borrowing transfer* and *substratum transfer*. Borrowing transfer refers to the influence a second language has on a previously acquired language, usually the mother tongue. Substratum transfer involves the effect of a source language (usually L1) on the acquisition of the target language. We are interested in borrowing transfer here, but not exactly the type Thomason and Kaufman talked about. Borrowing transfer such as Thomason and Kaufman (1988) referred to has been documented in several studies (cf. Haugen, 1953; Schmidt, 1985; Weinreich, 1953/1968) describing a case where the L2 speech community has larger numbers, greater prestige, strong cultural influence, and political power. As a consequence, the mother tongue of speakers has undergone considerable attrition, which is especially well-documented in lexical semantics and syntax.[3] Transfer does not lead to any attrition in our case because the kind of transfer we are primarily interested in is neither lexical nor structural but pragmatic and knowledge transfer. It can have some negative effects but the usual outcome of the FL—>L1 effect is positive; that is, the L1 skills of the learners are enhanced under the influence of FL studies. The situation we focus on significantly differs from language contact situations described in the relevant literature because in the foreign language environment no direct contact whatsoever is established between the L1 of the students and the target language. This, of course, does not exclude the possibility of the phenomenon called borrowing transfer by Thomason and Kaufman (1988). They also claimed

---

[3]Some of the best known examples for borrowing transfer are as follows: Dyirbal, an Aboriginal language spoken in northeastern Australia exposed to English (Schmidt, 1985), Swiss Romansh influenced by German (Weinreich, 1968), and American varieties influenced by English (Haugen, 1953).

that minor structural influence from a prestigious literary language sometimes occurs through the written medium alone (1988, p. 78). This statement is important from the perspective of this book which focuses mainly on written language and aims to describe the nature and content of this particular type of transfer, as well as to examine in what circumstances it occurs.

THEORETICAL FRAMEWORK

Hypotheses

The content of this book has been developed on the basis of three main assumptions. Our first hypothesis is that competence in more than one language results in a kind of L1 knowledge that differs from the L1 knowledge of monocompetent people. This difference derives from the L2 influence. Because the L2 and the L1 are related in the mind, the L2 cannot be learned as a second L1. The two languages are represented in two different, but constantly available, interacting systems that have a CUCB.

One of the major issues of bilingualism waiting to be answered is: How do bilingual people build the mental representations for the two languages that they are acquiring? One extreme possibility is that the two languages form separate systems. Learners construct a system individually for each language (Genesee, 1989; Grosjean, 1989). The other extreme approach is that the two languages make up a single unified system (cf. Redlinger & Park, 1980; Swain, 1977). We accept neither of the extremist views and agree with those opinions according to which language requires a more complex representation, only some of which is shared across languages (Bialystok, 1994, 1995; Cook, 1991, 1992). The existence of a common underlying system is widely accepted by most researchers in the field of bilingual language representation (e.g., De Groot, 1992; Kroll, 1993; Kroll & Stewart, 1992). Although these researchers have divergent theories of bilingual language representation, all agree that languages have a shared underlying conceptual base which they refer to by using a great variety of different terms and descriptions. In chapter 3 we explain in what domains the two language systems overlap, and how the shared features affect the operation of each.

Hypothesis 2 is that the symbiosis of a subconscious, synthetic, top-down approach (L1) and a conscious, analytic, bottom-up approach (FL) to linguistic operations can have a positive effect on general language development. Vygotsky (1962) argued that mother tongue and FL develop in reverse directions. In the mother tongue, the primitive aspects of speech are acquired before more complex ones. FL shows the opposite development: The higher forms develop before spontaneous speech because FL learning is usually a conscious, task-oriented process based on controlled operations. Vygotsky (1962) said that "the child's strong points in a foreign language are his weak points in his native tongue, and vice versa" (p. 109). Based on this idea we assume that intensive FL learning can help the internalization of the L1 because consciousness developed in foreign language learning can be transferred to L1 activities. Consequently, when subconscious mother tongue skills are combined with conscious knowledge and skills developed in both the L1 and the FL in school, learners can be expected to reach a higher level of development in the L1 (Kecskes & Papp, 1995). Intensive FL learning can have a strong and beneficial effect on the development of the L1. However, this effect is only a possibility and does not necessarily occur. What is important is that a positive influence can be brought about.

Mention must be made here about the criticism concerning Vygotsky's approach to FL learning. Contemporary language teaching methodology emphasizes a less conscious and less grammar-driven approach to the target language in which task-based activities and spontaneously produced language play a very important role. This is especially true for young FL learners. Adults, however, are more dependent on a conscious approach to the target language where spontaneous production usually occurs only at a later stage of the acquisition process. We think that no matter what methodology is used in foreign language teaching, the acquisition process will always differ from L1 acquisition in what Vygotsky underlined in his book: Second and foreign language acquisition is always a more conscious, less spontaneous, and more controlled process than L1 acquisition no matter whether it occurs in a naturalistic or an instructional environment. The question is only to what extent consciousness and control are present in a particular case of L2 acquisition.

Hypothesis 3 is that because of the common underlying conceptual and knowledge base, new information, behavior patterns, language manipulating skills, speaking styles, and different ways of thinking learned and obtained through the FL can enhance the real-world knowledge of students, improve their general linguistic skills, and lead to a better understanding of not only the new culture but also their own cultural and linguistic identity. Communication in a language requires language proficiency and background knowledge. Background knowledge is a very complex entity that comprises several universal and language-specific components. Enhancement of background knowledge in any language leads to better understanding of the world and better communication. Studying a FL provides the learner with much more than just a command of the target language. It offers an insight into a different way of life and moves the learners as close as they are likely to get, in many cases, to a direct experience of the culture and values of the people of another country.

Cognitive-Pragmatic Perspective

This book does not fit into the mold of standard L2 texts. It concerns FL rather than L2 and examines language learning from a cognitive perspective rather than in terms of purely formal patterns. The direction, FL—>L1 is also unusual, and, as said before, is out of the scope of SLA research paradigms. Several issues raised in the book concern bilingualism, psycholinguistics, theoretical linguistics, language teaching pedagogy, education, and communication studies. The wide scope of the book, the interdisciplinary nature of issues, and the unique features mentioned previously require a theoretical framework that can amalgamate views from various research paradigms, as well as integrate and present concepts in a way that is clear to those outside the field. We think that a cognitive theory of language is the most suitable theoretical framework to bring together psychology, linguistics, and language pedagogy. The book examines all aspects of the influence of FL learning on the development of mother tongue skills from a cognitive-pragmatic perspective. Our disciplinary framework is based on the assumption that language research is basically cognitive research (Langacker, 1990; Nuyts, 1992). A significant amount of cognitive development results from the internalization of interpersonal communicative processes. In developing a model of the cognitive systems and processes responsible for linguistic behavior one obviously has to accept a knowledge-for-use, pragmatic perspective (Verschueren, 1987). This book aims at discussing the unique nature of language transfer in which not only concrete forms, elements, or structures are transferred but also functions, skills, and knowledge developed in another language. Consequently, the proper understanding of the relation between linguistic form and function becomes of utmost importance. Relations between linguistic form and function reflect human conceptual structure and general principles of cognitive organization (cf. Kövecses & Szabo, 1996; Nuyts, 1992; Sweetzer, 1990) and can best be accounted for in a theoretical framework that represents a knowledge-for- use conception.

Dichotomy of Proficiency

Mother tongue proficiency is a crucial question when FL influence is discussed. We acknowledge the relevance of distinguishing two types of one and the same language proficiency (Bernstein, 1962, 1964: restricted code and elaborated code; Cummins, 1979: basic interpersonal communicative skills and cognitive academic language proficiency; Cummins, 1991: conversational and academic language proficiency; D. Ellis, 1992: pragmatic code and syntactic code) when analyzing the quality of linguistic knowledge and skills. In fact, with its emphasis on background knowledge (experience with the world; "perception and understanding of the world") the cognitive approach allows us to set up two dichotomies. The first one distinguishes two sides of language development: one in which the sociocultural background is directly present ("second language") and another where this factor is missing, or is indirectly present ("foreign language"). The second dichotomy refers to the separation of two types of language proficiency: one is theoretically and linguistically linked to the oral style in which a broader (not only linguistic) context is present, and shared background knowledge is very important. This is called "pragmatic code," "restricted code," or "Basic Interpersonal Communicative Skills." For the other only (or mainly) the linguistic context is available, and therefore, it is more explicit, planned, and differentiated. It is usually referred to as "syntactic code," "elaborated code," or "Cognitive Academic Language Proficiency."

Bernstein and Cummins connected the development of the two codes with socialization and schooling. In relying on Bernstein's work one needs to address the perception that a "cognitive deficit view" is implied. We argue that the cognitive deficit view is partly the result of the misinterpretation of Bernstein's work and agree with Martin-Jones and Romaine (1987) who said that:

> as is often the case when research findings are popularized and spread outside the context in which they were originally defined, the ideas are circulated in watered-down versions. Take, for example, the terms "restricted and elaborated codes" first proposed by Bernstein (1962). These have been widely used in educational literature with little or no reference to the theoretical issues that Bernstein was addressing. This, in turn, led to the formulation of a deficit hypothesis that was directly linked to Bernstein's work. (p. 35)

Gumperz and Hymes (1972) also defended Bernstein: "It should . . . be stressed that it is orientation and use of communicative codes that is in question, not fundamental capacity for logical analysis and conceptual thought" (p. 468). Two Hungarian studies found similar results. Biró (1984) conducted an experiment with Hungarian student in Transylvania and compared the language of students attending schools in towns and the language of village school children. Papp and Pléh (1975) investigated the relationship of social environment and speech at the beginning of schooling through an experiment conducted in various living districts of

Budapest, the capital of Hungary. The final conclusion of the two studies was that there is a difference in the use of communicative codes and this difference is mainly defined by the social environment. However, this has nothing to do with what Labov said about Bernstein's work. Labov (1972) observed that in Bernstein's writing, "middle-class language is seen as superior to working class language in every aspect" (p. 204). This is not exactly what Bernstein said. He investigated use of language and happened to focus on working-class and middle-class children, and found significant differences in their language use. Therefore, his conclusion was that there is a significant difference between the codes required by these two different environments. Other researchers examined the language of town children and village children (Biró, 1984) and students living in different environments in a huge city (Papp & Pléh, 1975). The findings were similar: There exist two codes, and their use is determined by the environment (how language is required to be used by the environment and the immediate task). These codes, however, have nothing to do with fundamental capacity for logical analysis. Every human being has the ability to develop and use whichever code the actual environment requires. The line distinguishing two codes cannot be drawn explicitly because the nature of sign relations and meaning makes it impossible for any two codes to be completely independent (Ellis, 1992, p. 4). The main task of education is to give the chance to each student to develop both codes and be able to use them according to their immediate communicative needs.

In our opinion, the dichotomy refers to the dominance of one of the sides of language proficiency rather than to two different proficiencies. Bernstein's mistake is that he puts too much emphasis on culturally determined identity. His approach acknowledges the development of the social self, but neglects the individual self. According to Applegate and Delia (1980), Bernstein ignores the nature and role of a genuine cognitive process in communication. He fails to consider that a significant amount of cognitive development results from the internalization of interpersonal communication processes (Blumer, 1969; Ellis, 1992). The individual's experience varies according to the needs of the environment. Each individual is capable of developing whichever code is triggered or required by the immediate environment, and also remains to be able to develop the other code if need occurs. (This is where the importance of education comes in.) Codes are quite fluid and flexible, and people can move in and out of them as experience and need requires. Bernstein (1962, 1975) was right when he underlined that experience with the code is more important than anything else. Codes are cognitive models of social knowledge that emerge from practices and beliefs; therefore, as Ellis (1992) noted, the benefits of living a code rather than mere exposure to it are substantial.

Referring to Berlin (1971) and Swadesh (1971), Ellis (1992) argued that in recent years there has been a shift in the study of language and linguistic processes from a perspective according to which all languages are of equal complexity to an evolutionary perspective. The latter approach assumes that development proceeds from globality to increased differentiation and articulation. In linguistic evolution this means development from an unspecialized global language use dependent on shared knowledge of social relations to an autonomous system of specialized, explicit, and highly differentiated communication (Ellis, 1992, p. 5). The separation of these two sides of language proficiency, that is, the development of the two codes, becomes especially articulated in school where language begins to function as an executive or regulator of thinking (Luria, 1982; Vygotsky, 1962). Our findings (Kecskes & Papp, 1995; Papp, 1991) demonstrated that differences between the two codes become heightened in school with the ontogenesis of written speech whose development is connected with schooling. Learning how to organize one's thoughts in written form requires a high level of abstraction and careful verbal planning, which develops into special learning strategies based on conscious and controlled activities. Internalized natural speech that is unrehearsed and discontinuous is reshaped according to the norms of writing, which is planned and internally coherent.

From our perspective it is important to emphasize that both codes have several varieties. In the pragmatic code based on natural speech one really has to be an insider to follow the subtlety of new and assumed information. Outsiders to the code have to rely on common knowledge, or knowledge derived from codes of a similar nature (Ellis, 1992). Two persons speaking two different varieties of the pragmatic code experience difficulty understanding each other. Group-specific communication is characterized by the use of special pragmatic codes. The problem is that the syntactic code also has several group-specific variations (legal, administrative, academic, and so forth), but the directions of specification are entirely different in the two codes. It is true, however, that some versions of the pragmatic code are closer to the academic version of syntactic code used in school. This explains why Bernstein and others have found that middle-class children do better in academic tasks in school than children speaking another version of the pragmatic code. Adamson (1993) argued that:

> it is true that casual and academic varieties are somewhat different in their vocabulary and structures, that for social reasons proficiency in the academic variety is important for school success, and that middle-class children acquire this proficiency more easily than working-class children because their spoken variety is similar to the academic variety. Thus, the question of how academic language differs from everyday language is an important one, and a definition of academic language is needed. (p. 31)

We agree with Adamson that middle-class children acquire the academic variety with ease because it is closer to their vernacular.

In sum, what is important for us here is that the two codes exist, and they are equally learnable. The closeness of the vernacular to one or the other means only advantage or disadvantage at the start, but that can be overcome during the years in school. Furthermore, it is a mistake to identify pragmatic code with natural speech and syntactic code with written speech. Both codes can appear in oral production as well as written language production. We elaborate on this issue in chapter 2.

WHAT DOES THIS BOOK OFFER?

1. A multilingual perspective that emphasizes that knowledge of two or more languages results in a unique and complex competence that is not equal to the sum of knowledge of monolingual speakers of those languages.

2. An attempt to demonstrate that effective FL learning can lead to multicompetence even if the sociocultural background of the target language is not present. This development, however, is only a possibility and not a necessity, and can usually be brought about by intensive, effective FL learning or having the target language at least partly the medium of instruction.

3. A cognitive-pragmatic perspective on language representation and processing, which means a move away from the lexical-syntactic approach that has been dominant in bilingual research. This move, however, does not represent a denial of achievements of the lexical-syntactic approach. It tries to incorporate rather than deny those results and to discuss them from a different perspective.

4. A discussion of the effect of FL learning on the use and development of mother tongue skills that focuses not only on demonstrating that this influence exists but also explaining how this takes place by reexamining and discussing issues such as conceptualization in an L2, metalinguistic awareness, linguistic relativity, the relationship of thought and word, transfer of skills, and others.

5. An opportunity for educators to rethink and reevaluate the importance and impact of FL teaching and learning on the development of human personality, mother tongue use, and overall growth of the individual.

ACKNOWLEDGMENTS

Many people have assisted us in the preparation of this book, but, of course, only we are responsible for any shortcomings. We are particularly indebted to Judi Amsel, Executive Editor of Lawrence Erlbaum Associates, who found our book proposal intriguing and encouraged us to develop the manuscript. Without Dr. Amsel's continuous support and belief in the value of our ideas this book would not have been written.

In the process of writing this book we received extremely important advise, guidance, and insights from several colleagues. We are especially grateful to the following individuals: Aneta Pavlenko, Temple University, for her willingness to read the whole manuscript and for offering us very important feedback about the content and for sharing with us her ideas about conceptualization and transfer; Roger Shuy, Georgetown University, for insightful discussions about the interpretations of the Sapir–Whorf hypothesis and multilingual development; John Costello, New York University, for his valuable comments on some parts of the manuscript; Jehannes Ytsma, Fryske Akademy, for sharing his ideas with us about trilingualism; Jean-Marc Dewaele, Birkbeck College, University of London, for a very long and heated and inspiring conversation about concept formation in second language learners in a cafe in Innsbruck.

We wish to thank our former students at the University of Montana and the State University of New York at Albany for their comments and observations concerning early pieces of this book that we used in some classes as teaching materials or discussion topics.

We would like to acknowledge the extremely insightful, helpful, and stimulating review by an anonymous reader recruited by Lawrence Erlbaum. This reviewer's invaluable recommendations helped us finalize the manuscript. We also owe thanks to Sondra Guideman for her very important editorial work and patience.

Our work on the manuscript was strongly supported by Bertalan Papp, Tünde's father, whose love and knowledge of languages, sincere interest in the topic, and continuous concern with our progress was an inspiration, especially for Tünde.

Finally, a special word of thanks is due to Brady Harrison, our colleague at the University of Montana, for playing long games of tennis with Istvan when he needed a break.

Istvan Kecskes
Tünde Papp

Foreign Language
and
Mother Tongue

CHAPTER

1

Mother Tongue and Subsequent Languages

MOTHER TONGUE

This book is about the effect of foreign language (FL) learning on the development of mother tongue skills. Because the terms *mother tongue* and *foreign language* are given different senses in the relevant literature it is important to clarify how they are used here. According to Skutnabb-Kangas and Phillipson (1989) *mother tongue* can mean the following:

1. The language learned from the mother.
2. The first language (L1) learned, irrespective of "from whom."
3. The stronger language at any time of life.
4. The mother tongue of the area or country (e.g., Byelorussian in Byelorussia).
5. The language most used by a person.
6. The language to which a person has the more positive attitude and affection.

Kaplan (1990) makes a serious attack on *mother tongue* calling it an "awful term": "Before I address the kinds of problems that affect non-native speakers, let me try to deal with that awful term 'mother tongue' " (p 7). He goes on to explain why he does not like the term: ". . . I abjure the notion of so-called 'mother tongue' teaching in this country because the people being taught may be fluent in English without reference to what their mother tongue actually is/was" (p. 8). Ferguson (1982, p. vii) also suggested that ". . . the whole mystique of native speaker and mother tongue should probably be quietly dropped from the linguist's set of professional myths about language." We think that what they both opposed is not 'mother tongue' but what the term suggests to most linguists and educators: a monolingual approach to language development, description and education. Although we agree with some of the statements they make about *mother tongue* as used in the relevant literature we do not think that the term is as much discredited as Kaplan and Ferguson claimed. In fact, the term may have an emotive coloring for many of us, both authors and readers, meaning the language our mother first exposed us to, the language we try to maintain no matter how difficult it is when living in a country where that language is not valorized, and referring to the language that is closest to our heart no matter how many other languages we can speak. Luc Sante (1996) described how he felt about his mother tongue in the following way: "For me the French language long corresponded to the soul, while English was the world" (p. 127).

The use of the term *mother tongue* in this book can also be explained by practical reasons. Because we are mainly interested in homogeneous language communities in which the FL is studied in classroom circumstances we use mother tongue as a synonym to first language. The two terms *mother tongue* and *first language* are used interchangeably throughout the book. To define *foreign language* and distinguish it from second language (L2) is a much more difficult task.

FOREIGN LANGUAGE

We argue that FL differs from L2 because of the sociocultural environment of the acquisition process and the linguistic background of the learners. All the other differences derive from these two important factors. In the second language environment (SLE), language learners have full exposure to the target language (not only to the language system, but to its frame as well) because it is the dominant or the only language of the community. This is not the case in the foreign language environment (FLE) where students' experience and activities in the target language are almost always restricted to the time spent in the classroom. Whereas L2 students usually (but not always) come from several countries speaking a variety of native languages, FL students almost always have one native language in common (Hammerly, 1991). From our perspective this is a crucial difference because language learners target the FL from a common linguistic background. What we examine in this book is how (if in any way) this common linguistic background is affected by the development of another linguistic system. This kind of investigation would make less sense in the SLE for several reasons. First, the main issue here is whether FL learning can also result in the development of multicompetence. (Nobody questions that multicompetence can develop in a SLE.) The real issue is whether an extensive exposure to the target language system without the constant presence of the target language culture can result in something that is the essential consequence of L2 development. The SLE offers better conditions for students to develop multicompetence than the FLE, but that is just a potential because to benefit from those conditions is mostly the responsibility of the learner. Second, students in the SLE do not have a common linguistic background, which makes the investigation of L2 → L1 effect quite complicated (but not impossible). Third, because we want to examine the L2 → L1 effect it is important how strongly the L1 is established in the mind and what its role is in the language community. The conditions of L1 use are entirely different in the SLE and the FLE. In the FLE the L1 of learners usually functions as primary means of communication, but this is not the case in the SLE. L1 in the SLE is more vulnerable and subject to change than it is in the FLE, where L1 is usually the only means of communication.

The American tradition does not recognize the dichotomy of L2 and FL although the differences—linguistic background and environment—are usually acknowledged as important in the relevant literature. Hammerly (1991) said that ". . . it is hard to understand why most language educators mention 'ESL' and 'EFL' in the same breath or place them side by side in lectures, book titles, and so on" (p. 4). As an explanation Phillipson (1992) argued that

> in the USA the major professional thrust has been towards second language acquisition problems within the country, with more concentration on linguistics and psycholinguistics than pedagogy. In Britain there tends to be a focus on educational problems, even if the approach and methods reflect a narrow ELT focus rather than a general educational one. (p. 251)

This is the result of the fact that while Americans have been trying to solve the problem of English language teaching within their country, the British have been teaching English all over the world. The situation has changed by now because the United States wants to have a share in the EFL business, and this endeavor has had a serious impact on teacher training and research. Recently a need to describe and analyze both the theoretical and practical differences between a SL and a FL has emerged.

FL VERSUS L2

The Continuum Approach

Stern (1981) distinguished between learning a language through use in the environment (i.e., functionally) and through processes of language study and practice (i.e., formally). According to Stern, there is a psycholinguistic–

pedagogic continuum with a formal approach on one end of the continuum and a functional approach on the other end. A concrete language learning situation is always in between; that is, it contains both functional and formal elements. For instance, FL programs that incorporate a study-abroad element or immersion programs can exist in both environments. If we keep Stern's approach in mind, it is clear that in SLA we have more functional than formal elements because the target language community is present and language learners can interact with the environment in the target language. The SLE can also have several formal, instructional elements, for instance, in the case of bilingual K–12 programs, immersion programs, or target language tutoring. FL learning can be put at the other end of Stern's continuum. Although FL learning can have several functional elements (e.g., in dual language programs, intensive foreign language programs with a study abroad element, use of educational technology), formal instruction is dominant in most of the FL learning situations. Because the target language is usually not present (or is present only in a restricted way) in the community, FL students lack the background experience and knowledge they need to develop a nativelike command of the target language. Immersion programs in Finland (Bjorklund, 1995; Kaskela-Nortamo, 1995) have demonstrated that immersion students (i.e., Finnish students immersed in Swedish) cannot be compared to simultaneous bilingual students (who come from bilingual families). Bjorklund argued that

> it is of little use to compare immersion students to simultaneous bilingual students even if both student categories have the same goal of bilingual competence. A simultaneous bilingual student has a context domain of everyday life activities which automatically gives the same kind of lexical input as native speakers receive. This is not always the case with immersion students, whose context of everyday life activities in the target language is almost always restricted to the time spent in school. If this fact has not been recognized, and immersion students are treated like simultaneous bilingual students there is an obvious mismatch between the students' expected lexical knowledge in the foreign language and experienced contexts. (p. 159)

We accept the continuum approach to SLA and FL learning acknowledging that they have quite a lot in common, and it is almost impossible to find a sterile SLA or FL learning situation. It must be emphasized, however, that there are some crucial differences between the two ends of the continuum. These differences require expression in the methodology (both research and teaching) applied to the SLE and the FLE. If the intention is to develop the right methodology for each environment, we must examine the nature of these differences, looking first at the differences between the acquisition of the L1 and subsequent languages.

Completeness, Nativelike Proficiency

Several researchers have come to the conclusion that nativelike competence is only possible in one language. Schachter (1988) pointed out that even learners who appear to be nativelike in a second language have a linguistic knowledge that significantly differs from that of a typical native speaker. Gass (1990) argued that most non-native speakers (NNSs) never reach a point of being indistinguishable from native speakers (NSs) of a particular linguistic community. Investigating the grammatical intuitions of fluent non-native speakers of French, Coppetiers (1987) found that NNSs' intuitions about a set of French sentences significantly depart from the intuitions NSs of French have about the same utterances. Although these studies talk about completeness, nativelike competence, productive competence, and mastery of a second language, it is not the whole knowledge of language they focus on but grammatical intuition and knowledge only. The real question is whether just grammatical intuition counts when mastery of a language is discussed. Is it really just grammatical competence that cannot become nativelike, or something else? Answers to these questions must be sought in human cognition rather than just in grammatical development.

Cognitive development and linguistic development go hand in hand in the L1. They are inseparable especially after children enter school because language becomes the main regulator of thinking (Vygotsky, 1962). In subsequent language development the crucial question is the extent to which the target language is involved in the overall cognitive development of the learner. This is where the difference between SLA and FL learning has to be sought.

Luria (1982) said that human cognition is a product of the cultural–historical environment in which it evolves and can be examined in terms of the internalization of social interaction. If language learners miss (or partly miss) this cultural–historical environment and social interaction occurring in that environment their language use will always be different from that of NSs to a certain extent. How much of this cultural–historical environment and the chance for social interaction are objectively present for NNSs, and how much of this objectively given possibility are NNSs able or willing to utilize for the development of their target language skills and knowledge? We want to underline not only the importance of the objective circumstances in which language acquisition occurs but also the responsibility of the individual language learner. When living in the target language community L2 learners often create a FLE for themselves because they have minimal social interaction with native speakers and their environment (Kecskes & Papp, 1991). This fact supports Stern's argument about the psycholinguistic–pedagogic continuum that emphasizes the individual learner's responsibility in the acquisition process. Consequently, it is not just the environment that makes the difference between SLA and FL learning but learner attitude as well.

Investigating the use of situation-bound utterances (SBUs) by adult NNSs of English, Kecskes (1999) found that individual learner differences play a decisive role in students' selection of SBUs in various speech situations. Linguistic behavior of adult NNSs with a high command of L2 appears to be dominated by their individual choice. This coincides with Beebe's (1988) opinion that

> second language learners may never attain nativelike proficiency to the best of their ability because they may find that the reward of being fluent in the target language is not worth the cost in lost identification and solidarity with their own native language group. (p. 63)

It should not be forgotten, however, that individual learner endeavors are constrained differently in the two environments. Learners in the SLE have the option to either immerse in the sociocultural environment or ignore it to a certain extent. FL learners rarely have this choice. They can use every opportunity to spend some time in the target language country and look for target language sources (e.g., TV, journals, newspapers, contact with NSs of the target language, etc.) in the FLE, which can enhance their experience with the target language culture.

Content of Context

Several attempts have been made to explain the difference between SLA and FL learning (e.g., Berns, 1990; Chaudron, 1988; Gass, 1990; Hammerly, 1991; VanPatten & Lee, 1990; VanPatten, Dvorak, & Lee, 1987). All these studies refer to the context of acquisition as a decisive factor in making a difference (if any) between SLA and FL learning. The problem is that the studies focused only on the surface, that is, the physical environment, and the presence or absence of the target language community. None targets the content of the context. Berns (1990) said that India is clearly a L2 learning context for English and referred to Germany as close to a SLE because learners can have the exposure to English via several sources such as media or tourism. However, the gist of this issue should be sought elsewhere.

Sociolinguistic research (e.g. B. Kachru, 1983) has identified salient functional characteristics of non-native English contexts that distinguish non-native varieties of English from one another and from native varieties (e.g., British English or American English). Y. Kachru (1986) argued that institutionalized non-native varieties of English have their own unique linguistic features, which deserve to be accepted as legitimate variations because they are the results of communicative needs of the users of these localized forms of English. The differences that these varieties exhibit serve specific sociocultural needs such as satisfying certain conventions of linguistic interactions and specific strategies of communication, and they are the reflections of a particular sociocultural environment.

Y. Kachru (1986) suggested that these unique features of localized varieties of English must be treated as evidence for bilingual creativity rather than as evidence of fossilization. In India, English is a lingua franca because it is used for national purposes and is also the medium of instruction in educational institutions, but the social-cultural-historical background that is mapped on the English system of signs does not even resemble the British English or the American English social-cultural-historical background. This results in a unique use of the English language system where the Indian conceptual base is mapped on the English system of signs.[1] Both input and output significantly differ from what they are like in the British English or the American English environment. We now examine three aspects of the acquisition process (i.e., tasks, input, output) to establish differences (if any) between SLA and FL learning.

Tasks and Processes

Gass (1990) argued that the fundamental processes involved in learning a nonprimary language do not depend on the context in which the language is learned. She said that the psycholinguistic tasks learners have to face do not depend on the learning situation because what learners have to do in both contexts is the same: come up with a grammar of the target language (i.e., grammatical competence) and develop the ability to put that knowledge to use.

Not everything seems to be clear about these tasks if we examine them from a cognitive-pragmatic perspective. The first problem is acknowledged by Gass herself in the notes: She is aware that grammatical competence is not the only knowledge that has to be learned because there are also pragmatic knowledge and sociolinguistic knowledge, among others. That's right, and they are inseparable from grammatical knowledge, which basically means syntactic knowledge in the traditional sense. Cognitive linguistics rejects this interpretation, suggesting that grammar is not arbitrary because syntax is motivated by semantics. For Langacker (1987), "grammar is simply the structuring and symbolization of semantic content" (p. 12), and Lakoff (1987) argued that one objective of the cognitive approach is to "show how aspects of form can follow from aspects of meaning" (p. 491). In the cognitive approach semantic representations that constitute the semantic pole of a linguistic sign are equated with "conventionalized conceptualizations" (Langacker 1987, p. 94). Taylor (1993) argued that if the meanings of linguis-

---

[1] It is, of course, a two-way street—the particular variety of English used in that environment also affects the Indian conceptual base.

tic forms are equated with conceptualizations and these conceptualizations are conventionalized in a language, then the conceptualizations are made available to speakers of a language by the language system that they have learned. This fact has a very important consequence for the L2 versus FL debate. Formal differences among languages are reflections of differences in conceptualization. When acquiring a nonprimary language, learners have to learn not only the forms of that particular language but also the conceptual structures that are associated with those forms. Here is the main difference between SLA and FL learning. Whereas in the SLE, learning forms and conceptual structures represented by those forms simultaneously is possible, in the FLE learners are usually expected to focus on the forms while learning little or nothing about the conceptual structures those forms represent. This fact seriously affects what Gass called fundamental processes of acquisition and often results in a production that is good and understandable but lacks the idiomaticity of native speaker speech. However, the lack of knowledge of underlying conceptual structures in the target language does not mean that FL learners use target language forms without conceptual structures. Not having full access to the conventionalized conceptualizations of the target language, FL learners usually rely on the conceptual base of the mother tongue. They map target language forms on L1 conceptualizations (cf. Potter, So, Von Eckardt, & Feldman, 1984; Kroll & Stewart, 1994). Consequently, their problem is primarily not grammatical but conceptual. Grammatical and lexical problems usually derive from conceptual failures. Acquiring a L2 or FL requires reconceptualization (i.e., changing at least a part of the existing L1-based conceptual base), which involves not only lexical and cultural concepts but also grammatical categories.[2]

There is also some problem with what Gass (1990) called "the ability to put grammatical knowledge to use" (p. 35). It is not clear why learners have to develop this ability because they already know how to communicate in one language so they know how to put an existing grammatical knowledge into use. They will not start to learn from scratch how to communicate in the target language but will attempt to modify their existing communicative skills according to the requirements of the target language. When learners set out to learn a new language, they automatically assume (until they have evidence to the contrary) that meanings and structures will be somewhat similar to those in their own language (Swan, 1985a, 1985b). This kind of equivalence assumption puts them ahead of the game; that is, it makes it possible for them to learn another language without at the same time returning to childhood and learning to categorize the world all over again. The more learners are exposed to the target language environment the more they understand that the equivalence assumption is wrong, and the

---

[2]Issues of reconceptualization are discussed in Chapters 4 and 5.

faster they begin to adjust to the specific communication requirements of the target language.

As pointed out previously, the problem of language acquisition and the difference between SLA and FL learning are not necessarily caused by grammatical knowledge and communicative skills. The grammar of a nonprimary language is completely learnable, and the communicative skills are acquirable. We have hundreds of years of experience of how to learn and teach them. The real problem is in conceptualization. This is why there is nothing like full mastery of an L2 or FL, and this is where multicompetence should be distinguished from monocompetence. FL learners have not only to master the grammatical structures and communicative peculiarities of the new language but also, in order to be nativelike, they have to learn to think as native speakers do, perceive the world the way native speakers do, and use the language metaphorically as native speakers do. Because this conceptual fluency is the basis of all linguistic acts in a language (Danesi, 1992), problems occurring in grammar and in the use of communicative skills are also, quite frequently, the result of inadequate conceptual fluency.

Danesi argued that students typically use target language words and structures as *carriers* of their own native language concepts. In this respect our children A. and T. are very good examples to explain the differences between SLA and FLL. A. was 16 years old and T. was 10 years old when they came to the United States. A. studied English quite intensively from age 11 in a typical foreign language environment and had excellent teachers with very good target language proficiency. T. did not know a word of English before she arrived in the United States. Now when NSs communicate with T. they do not have the slightest idea that they are talking with a NNS. Most of her teachers in high school never knew that she is not a native-speaker. T. (presently 19 years old) can speak like an American, behaves like an American, and can think like an American, and she can do the same in her other language as well. She has been trained and educated to be a complete bilingual and bicultural person who acts according to the proverb: "When in Rome, do as the Romans do." Her socialization processes were tied to the American culture rather than to the Hungarian. She has not only had the opportunity to live in an American English milieu but also used this opportunity to her benefit. The point here is that her cognitive–conceptual development was regulated mainly by the English language and American sociocultural environment because she has received her education in English since age 10. Her conceptual base is governed by American English rather than Hungarian, so her conceptual fluency is close to that of native speakers. When she speaks Hungarian reconceptualization occurs from English to Hungarian. This is not the case with A., who was 16 when he came to the United States with a firm conceptual base developed in his native Hungarian. He spoke good English, which helped him through school because it was good enough to transfer the knowledge developed in Hungarian into English. The difference between the two children is that A. received his basic education in Hungarian with English as a FLE in Hungary and his socialization tied to Hungarian culture rather than to the American. At the same time T. was schooled mainly in English with English as a SLE in the United States and her socialization tied to American culture. As a result she developed a firm conceptual base in English. A. (now 25 years old) can *consciously function* like an American but his conceptual base, value system and natural reactions are Hungarian-based. In his case reconceptualization occurs from Hungarian to English. T. is the other way round. For her modifications occur in the other direction: from English to Hungarian. Her underlying conceptual system is English-based, which is not the case with A. The example of these children also demonstrates that the major difference between SLA and FL learning boils down to what Danesi calls "conceptual fluency," which is more accessible for students in a SLE than in a FLE.

Conceptual Fluency

Among FL learners there is an assumption that no real fluency is possible in the foreign language unless the learner spends some time in the target language country. Every language learner traveling in the target language country has experienced a certain kind of frustration that is the result of not conveying meaning the same way as native speakers do, that is, using wrong or unnative-like expressions, phrases, and words. What these learners lack most is *conceptual fluency*, which means knowing how the target language reflects or encodes its concepts on the basis of metaphorical structuring (Danesi, 1992) and other cognitive mechanisms (Kövecses & Szabo, 1996). This kind of knowledge is as important as grammatical and communicative knowledge. In fact, we think that it is even more important than the other two because conceptual knowledge serves as a basis for grammatical and communicative knowledge. For example, in order to be able to use conditional sentences in English properly, one must understand how the conditional is conceptualized in English. Or when a NS says, "I don't get your *point*," he or she scans the conceptual domain in the mind that has the form "ideas are geometrical objects" (Danesi, 1992). In the FLE learners acquire grammatical knowledge and communicative knowledge without firm conceptual knowledge in the target language. That makes their language use significantly different from that of NSs.

One would think conceptual fluency is important only for advanced language proficiency. That is only partly true. Language learners can achieve fairly good fluency in the target language without conceptual fluency in the L2 mainly because several aspects of language learning are not conceptual. For instance, these aspects may be perceptual, indexical, iconic, or denotative, and they can be obtained by the FL learners without much difficulty. The important thing for us here is that language acquisition takes place in a different way in the SLE and the FLE. In the SLE there is an intensive interplay between language development and conceptual development, which can usually result in close-to-native proficiency. In the FLE, however, grammatical knowledge and communicative knowledge are obtained without the target language conceptual base, with reliance on the existing L1 conceptual base, which rarely results in nativelike proficiency and usually leads to fossilization of several incorrect forms. These fossilized forms are very difficult to get rid of, even if the learner has the chance to spend a long period of time in the target language country.

Metaphorical Competence

Research suggests that at least a certain portion of the human mind is programmed to think metaphorically (cf. Danesi, 1992; Johnson, 1987; Lakoff, 1987; Lakoff & Johnson, 1980). Metaphor probably underlies the representation of a considerable part of our common concepts. Coining an analogous term to grammatical competence and communicative competence, Danesi (1992) suggested that *metaphorical competence* (MC) is as important as the other two because it is closely linked to the ways in which a culture organizes its world conceptually. Not only are thinking and acting based on this conceptual system but in large part communication is as well. Therefore, language is an important source of evidence of what that system is like.

MC is a basic feature of NS speech production because NSs usually program discourse in metaphorical ways. According to Winner (1982), the recent experimental literature has made it clear that if "people were limited to strictly literal language, communication would be severely curtailed, if not terminated" (p. 253). One reason that FL learners' speech does not sound nativelike is that they use literal rather than metaphorical or figurative language.

At this point, however, Valeva's (1996) criticism of Danesi's approach appears to be correct. She argued against the reduction of conceptual fluency to MC. There are many literal concepts, in the sense of being directly understood, without any metaphorical processes. This is absolutely true: MC is a very important part of conceptual fluency, but it would be a mistake to equate MC with conceptual fluency.

Our definition of conceptual fluency relies on the graded salience hypothesis described by Giora (1997). According to this hypothesis "understanding metaphor does not involve a special process, and that it is essentially identical to understanding literal language" (Giora, 1997, p. 183). Figurative language does not involve processing the surface literal meaning first (Gibbs, 1984; Giora, 1997). After reviewing and reinterpreting the relevant literature Giora (1997) argued that figurative and literal language use are governed by a general principle of salience according to which salient meanings (e.g., conventional, frequent, familiar, enhanced by prior context) are processed first. Thus, for instance, when the most salient meaning is intended (e.g., the figurative meaning of a fixed expression such as "Get out of here"), it is accessed directly, without having to process the literal (less salient) meaning first. However, when the opposite occurs, and a less rather than a more salient meaning is intended (e.g., the literal meaning of a conventional expression such as, for instance, "Help yourself") comprehension usually involves a sequential process, upon which the more salient meaning is processed first, before the intended meaning is derived (cf. Gibbs, 1990; Gregory & Mergler, 1990). When more than one meaning is salient, a parallel processing is induced. So salient meaning can be either figurative or literal depending on the context. In our understanding conceptual fluency means the ability to process salient meaning first. Consequently, the real question from our perspective is to what extent conceptual fluency (and not metaphorical competence!) can be developed in a foreign language environment? Can FL learners be expected to develop native-like conceptual fluency? To answer these questions we will have to review research on MC as well as other constituents of conceptual fluency.

Based on the results of a pilot study Danesi (1992, p. 495) suggested that metaphorical competence, even at the level of comprehension, is inadequate in typical classroom learners. In his opinion the reason is not that students are incapable of learning metaphors, but most likely that they have never been exposed in formal ways to the conceptual system of the target language. Another study by Danesi (1992) that focused on *metaphorical density* in non-native speakers' essays found that student compositions showed a high degree of literalness and contained conceptual metaphors that were alike in both Spanish and English. Danesi concluded that after 3 or 4 years of study in a classroom the students learned virtually no new way of thinking conceptually but relied mainly on their L1 conceptual base. There are no studies yet that compare the metaphorical competence of L2 learners and FL learners. But there is little doubt that L2 learners would do better.

Danesi argued that grammatical, communicative, and metaphorical competence constitute overlapping layers in discourse programming, and MC is teachable in classroom situations just like grammatical and communicative competence. He urged educators to develop instructional techniques and materials to acquire MC. In fact, as mentioned earlier, the focus of attention should be on conceptual fluency rather than on MC. The importance of developing conceptual fluency has been emphasized in other contexts in a number of research reports. Discussing the production of idioms Irujo (1993) suggested that students should be taught strategies to deal with figurative language, and those strategies would help them take advantage of the semantic transparency of some idioms. Kövecses and Szabó (1996) argued that teaching about orientational metaphors underlying phrasal verbs results in better acquisition of this difficult type of idiom. Bouton (1994) reported that formal instruction designed to develop pragmatic skills seemed to be highly effective when it was focused on formulaic implicatures. These studies suggest that conceptual fluency (including MC) can be developed in the classroom if students are taught about the underlying cognitive mechanisms.

All this sounds reasonable, but there is one thing for sure. Conceptualization and language development go hand in hand in first language acquisition; consequently, concepts grow and evolve rather than are learned. In a second or foreign language the development of conceptual fluency differs from that in the L1. The closer a learner is to the left on the SLA → FL learning continuum, the more the reverse is true of what happens in the L1: Concepts are learned rather than evolve. This is a significant difference between the two processes.

SUMMARY

In this chapter we argued that L2 development and FL development should be considered as two different entities because the underlying mechanisms responsible for the two types of development have more differences than similarities and result in two different types of language productions. The first (i.e., FL development) is characterized by formalistic rather than functional features, emphasizes knowledge over skill, and uses literal rather than metaphorical language due to underdeveloped conceptual fluency. The second (i.e., L2 development) is characterized by functionalist rather than formalistic features, emphasizes skill over knowledge, and is expected to demonstrate close to native conceptual fluency. This dichotomy is the result of the accessibility of sociocultural background of the target language that is responsible for the underlying cognitive mechanisms of language production.

There are important quantitative and qualitative differences in both the input and output. Whereas the quantitative side of L2 input is controlled by both the L2 learner and the environment, a FL learner has very little choice in determining the amount of input, which is usually restricted to the hours spent in the classroom controlled and structured by the teacher. The quality of input in the SLE is supposed to be better than that in the FLE because L2 input represents a greater variety of language use and is usually produced by NSs. Differences in input result in differences in output. There are two types of language use: stereotyped and creative. SLE encourages conventional responses to familiar situations, whereas FLE focuses on sentence-level creativity (i.e., how to generate correct sentences in the target language).

Although the differences between the SLE and FLE are quite obvious it has to be underlined that multilingual experience of individual learners is generally connected with both environments. For instance, FL learners usually have access to study-abroad programs, and L2 learners may study a third language in school or college. However, the differences between the SLE and FLE are important for us to emphasize because they seriously influence the development of multicompetence, which develops only if the L1-based conceptual system begins to change to accommodate the requirements of the new language. Gass (1990) argued that the effect of the environment is dependent on a number of factors, including the language learned, how concrete the information is, and how accessible the information is to the learner. This means that there are certain aspects of learning that are not or are just partly available through minimal exposure and explicit instruction. Conceptual fluency seems to be one of the main factors that is available primarily implicitly in natural settings. It is very likely that instruction can support the development of conceptual fluency in the target language only indirectly through the conscious process of learning, which is usually expected to result in cognitive enrichment rather than fundamental changes in the L1-based conceptual structures. However, the methods that are effective in the development of conceptual fluency still remain to be investigated.

CHAPTER

2

Foreign Language Influence on Written L1

THE L2 → L1 EFFECT

The idea of investigating the effect of foreign language (FL) learning on the development of mother tongue skills originates from a longitudinal experiment that was conducted in Hungary with native speakers of Hungarian learning either English, French, or Russian in different types of secondary schools (T. Papp, 1991).[1] A summary of some of the main findings of that experiment is given in this chapter chiefly because most of the issues discussed in the following chapters were raised while the results of the experiment were being evaluated. Also, several parts of the same data were reanalyzed from different perspectives as new research questions were being generated. The aim of the Hungarian experiment was to find out how FL learning influences mother tongue in a decisive period (age 14–16 years) when first language (L1) development and use enter into a stage where individual writing, learning, and problem-solving strategies and styles are being developed (T. Papp, 1991).

There are several different views on cognitive development, but

> the major proponents of each would agree that preadolescent and adolescent cognition is characterized by growth in the following areas: (1) hypothetical reasoning that involves inductive and deductive processes; (2) the coordina-

---

[1]The experiment was first detailed in the dissertation of Tunde Papp for the candidate degree, defended at the Hungarian Academy of Sciences, Budapest, Hungary, on September 10, 1991 (T. Papp, 1991).

tion of abstract ideas, rules, and systems; and (3) the use of various abstract symbol systems, such as those that characterize mathematics, physics, formal logic, and language. (Kamhi & Lee, 1988, p. 154).

Most researchers consider L1 fully acquired before the age of 14, and this assumption is not questioned here as far as the basic language skills are concerned. However, we agree with Berko Gleason (1993) and Collier (1992), who claimed that L1 acquisition is an unending process throughout our lifetimes with different tasks at different developmental levels. For instance, a student entering high school must acquire a huge amount of vocabulary in every discipline of study and continue the acquisition of complex writing skills, processes that continue through our adult lives as we add new contexts of language use to our life experiences. At the age of 14 students enter a cognitively more demanding environment, high school, where the requirements and school activities significantly differ from those in the elementary and middle school. We return to this issue at a later point.

The most important question waiting to be answered before the experiment was how to measure the influence of FL on the mother tongue skills. We hypothesized earlier that this influence (if it exists) must be cognitive and pragmatic in nature rather than syntactic or lexical. Consequently, we had to find some procedures that could help us measure the indirect effect of the second language (L2) on the L1 production. Because we wanted to focus on the broadest possible scope of the L2→L1 influence we developed three procedures, of which two were used when the results of the longitudinal experiment were evaluated. The third was applied later. The first two procedures focused on structural well-formedness and the use of linguistic memory versus visual memory in written production (Kecskes & Papp, 1995; Papp, 1991). The third procedure measured the metaphorical density of texts produced by the participants of the experiment (Kecskes & Papp, in press). In this chapter only questions concerning structural well-formedness are discussed. The other two procedures are analyzed where the findings are appropriate to support and enhance the content of arguments and suggestions about multicompetence and the effect of FL learning on the L1. It has to be emphasized that the experiment focused only on FL learning that takes place in classroom circumstances and involves some kind of instruction. Second language acquisition (SLA) in a natural setting was outside the scope of that work. During the experiment only written speech was examined. Consequently, all our findings refer to the use of written speech.

WRITTEN SPEECH

Vygotsky (1962) argued that written speech is the most elaborate form of speech because it requires a high level of abstraction. Written speech is a separate linguistic function that differs from oral speech in both structure and mode of functioning. It demands conscious work and deliberate analytical action. In written speech, learners have to create the situation in order to represent it to themselves. Planning is of utmost importance because, lacking situational and expressive supports, communication must be achieved only through words and their combinations. Vygotsky suggested that the study of grammar of the native tongue and writing are crucial for the mental development of children because these two topics help children rise to a higher level of speech development by making them aware of what they are doing with language and teaching them to use their skills consciously. FL learning shows a great deal of similarity to that process. Vygotsky (n.d., cited in John-Steiner, 1985) argued that

> if the development of native language begins with free, spontaneous use of speech and is culminated in the conscious realization of linguistic forms and their mastery, then development of a foreign language begins with conscious realization of language, and arbitrary command of it and culminates in spontaneous, free speech. But, between those opposing paths of development, there exists a mutual dependency just as between the development of scientific and spontaneous concepts. This kind of conscious and deliberate acquisition of a foreign language obviously depends on a known level of development of the native tongue . . .[2] (p. 48)

For our experiment it is very important that the mutual dependency between the FL and mother tongue presupposes that conscious mastery of forms, planning, and analytic skills developed in FL learning are likely to support mother tongue development.

Written speech is developed by instruction in elementary education.[3] Cummins (1984) claimed that "a major aim of schooling is to develop students' ability to manipulate and interpret cognitively-demanding context-reduced texts" (p. 141). Before 1990 in the state-run Hungarian elementary school system the teaching of composition was usually based on rather rigid patterns, and the primary goal was not creativity itself but practicing and acquiring skills for organizing and constructing written compositions. Creativity was important only within the required schemata. Students' productions were not characterized by individual approaches, style, and particular handling of the linguistic material but by the use of learned patterns, which required activities that were carefully guided by the schemata themselves. Investigating the language use of village children and city children in Transylvania, Biró (1984) came to the conclusion that the rigid schemata for composition taught in school are alien to the natural language use of those children, who produce the texts not naturally but under the force of school requirements and as a result of regular practice. The appli-

---

[2]When Vygotsky wrote about FL learning he intended to refer to instructed FL learning in school.
[3]*Elementary education* refers to the first eight grades of schooling. *Secondary education* refers to Grades 9 through 12.

cation of this writing style does not become a natural part of their language production. Individual differences are not visible at this stage yet, because all students use the same schemata.

Entrance to high school represents a dividing line. Because high school encourages creativity and the use of individual approaches and styles, the change in the school requirements is a real challenge for students. Since they had no required schemata and guidelines to work from, students had to learn how to handle linguistic material independently. In the experiment we wanted to examine this period of change in cognitive and language development. Elementary education aimed to make the use of language a conscious process by highlighting and practicing basic text-producing skills. The question is how language use changes under the new requirements in high school. How much of the basic text-producing skills becomes internalized? What external factors affect internalization? Will students develop a writing style of their own that keeps the well-contructedness of sentence structures and text (as was required by the patterns they learned and practiced) and moves in the direction of higher level language use, or without particular guidance will they more or less fall back on a writing style that is closer to the spontaneous structure of oral speech?

At the beginning of the experiment our assumption was that FL learning would play an important role in determining in which direction the students' written speech develops. We hypothesized that the difference between the two codes can be explained mainly by the development of learning, and the emergence of task-solving strategies based on controlled and conscious activities that are connected to schooling. In order to support this claim, we had to measure the qualitative level of the use of the mother tongue. Mother tongue development is a very complex process including, among other factors, the development of the vocabulary, use of different syntactic structures, and application of communication strategies (Kecskes & T. Papp, 1991; T. Papp, 1991). In this experiment we concentrated mainly on the use of syntactic structures for two reasons. First, well-structured sentences and the adequate use of more complex sentence structures are the best signs of the developmental level of mother tongue use. Second, because one of our starting points was Bernstein's theory, we tried to adapt the methods he and his followers as well as their critics used so that the results of our work could be legitimately compared to their results (Bernstein, 1962, 1973; Lawton, 1970, 1986; Loban, 1963; Loban, Ryan & Squire, 1963).[4]

---

[4]Other methods, such as the Botel, Dawkins, and Granowsky (1973) index of syntactic complexity, also focus on the use of complex sentences. Their index takes into account language development and performance studies as well as experimental data on children's processing of syntactic structures. These structures, as they are in the Lawton–Loban method, are assigned weighted scores ranging from 0 for simple sentences like *It is interesting* to 3 for complex, embedded sentences.

How does measuring structural well-formedness fit into our theoretical framework? Is there not a contradiction between what was claimed earlier about the nature of transfer and the method selected to measure L1 development? How can findings based on structural well-formedness support the claim that the L2→L1 transfer is primarily cognitive and pragmatic in nature? These are all legitimate questions. In order to give adequate response to them we need to direct attention to some very important issues concerning transfer and change in language use. First, we cannot expect the L2→L1 transfer to be the same as the L1→L2 transfer. As demonstrated later, a relatively weak L2 will not affect L1 in any visible way. A constantly strengthening L2 competence, however, can have an impact on how L1 is used, but this effect cannot be expected to occur in the form of some sort of structure or vocabulary transfer (although there may be such examples). Rather, it will influence the way in which L1 is used; for example, it will result in a more sophisticated use of the L1, which may occur in the form of better text-developing skills, more complex and well-constructed sentences, or a more selective use of the vocabulary. We did not look for direct effect of the L2 on the L1 because there hardly seems to be anything like this. What we looked for was a quantifiable positive qualitative change in the use of the mother tongue. The main issue was how this positive change (if any) could be demonstrated quantitatively.

If quantitative proof is needed, it is essential to turn to concrete linguistic elements that are used in language production: structures and words. That is why we focused on structural well-formedness and metaphorical density of texts when we attempted to demonstrate a change in the use of mother tongue under the influence of the L2. Therefore our research question was not whether there are any structures or lexical items that are transferred from the L2 to the L1, but in what direction the L1 use develops if learners have FL training or use a foreign language as the medium of instruction. Is there any difference in the L1 use of those students who are taught content area through a FL, those who study a FL intensively, and those who take FL classes just as an educational enhancement?

Our hypothesis was that if there is a demonstrateable difference in the L1 use of various types of FL learners, then that difference is likely to have been brought about as a result of a less or more intensive use of the FL. It should be underlined however, that we focused on FL learning and not on individual FLs. Each class was different: Students studied different FLs with different intensity. Our primary goal was to investigate if the study of any FL influences the use of L1 in any way. This does not mean, of course, that we ignore the importance of typological or cultural differences and the interplay of the two language channels in the development of multicompetence. (One of our three hypotheses deals with this issue, and we return to it in some of the following chapters.) We hypothesized that after a certain threshold is reached in FL proficiency the use of the other language (or languages) will be affected considerably.

HYPOTHESES

1. Intensive and successful FL learning can have a strong and beneficial influence on the use of L1 skills.
2. Intensive FL learning helps the internalization of L1 because linguistic operations based on conscious ways of thinking used in FL learning can be transferred to L1 activities.
3. Transfer from a FL to L1 is especially intense and beneficial if L1 and the FL differ from each other in configuration, because languages with different sentence-organizing forces (i.e., *grammatical word-order languages* and *pragmatic word-order languages*) develop different learning strategies (Kecskes & Papp, 1991). Combining these strategies can support and even speed up cognitive developmental processes.

THE EXPERIMENT

The longitudinal experiment was conducted in three different types of classes with 14- through 16-year-old Hungarian students studying English, French, or Russian as a FL. The locations of the experiment were three Hungarian high schools. All the students had the chance to study Russian for at least 4 years before entering high school because Russian was compulsory from the 4th grade of elementary school at that time in Hungary. Consequently, English or French was already the third language for some participants.[5] Many had already studied some English as well, but French was entirely new to the immersion class.[6]

In the *immersion class*,[7] some school subjects, such as for instance math, biology, and chemistry, were taught in the FL. Thirty-six students were involved in the immersion class whose language was French. In the *specialized class*, students studied English or Russian. They had seven or eight FL classes a week, but the target language was not the medium of instruction in any content class. All school subjects were taught in Hungarian. A total of 35 stu-

---

[5]Not all participants had a third language; the second section of the intensive class studied Russian only.

[6]Russian was compulsory from Grade 4 in Hungarian elementary schools until 1990.

[7]*Immersion* in this experiment refers to FL-medium programs designed for majority-language students, for instance, Hungarian students learning content through English in Hungary (Duff, 1995).

dents took part in that class. In the *control classes*, students had 2 or 3 hours of FL instruction a week in either English or Russian. All school subjects were taught in Hungarian. 33 students were involved in the control classes.

The students' social background and education were approximately the same in each of the three classes.[8] Most students came from middle-class families, and all had good grades (equivalent to 3.5–4.0 GPA in the U.S. system) in elementary school. The selected high schools were renowned and prestigious institutions. The level of L1 use was tested at the beginning of the experiment. No significant differences were recorded in any of the three different types of classes, mainly because all students used the same syllabus and books, practiced the same composition format, and had the same number of classes a week in Hungarian language and literature in the elementary school.

Methods of Testing

L1 and FL development and use were tested in writing three times during the 2-year period. Each time the method of testing was different. We wanted to find testing methods that suited the purpose of the experiment and the developmental level of students in the best possible way.

The first test aimed at establishing the level of mother tongue use among students who studied Hungarian language and literature using the same curriculum and learned how to write a composition in a given format. Therefore, students were asked to write a composition entitled "My home," which is a fairly easy topic to write about. We wanted to give students the chance to be as creative as possible within the confines of a format that they knew very well. Because that was the entry test we wanted to record every possible difference in the use of L1 that existed among the three groups of students.

The second test was given 9 moths after the first test was administered. It has to be emphasized that there was no composition teaching whatsoever in high schools at that time in Hungary.[9] Students were often expected to write compositions in different subjects, but they were completely on their own in determining the format and content of their written speech. Topics also varied and did not resemble the ones students had to work on in elementary school. Therefore the second test aimed at identifying the changes in the language use of students after a 9-month period.

This test consisted of three parts. First, because we wanted to find out how much of the traditional composition format students still remembered,

---

[8]At the time of the experiment all Hungarian schools were run by the state and had the same curriculum.

[9]At least to our knowledge.

we asked them to write a composition entitled "My life in 20 years." The format was well known, but the topic was unusual and nothing like the ones students had to write about in elementary school. This topic required imagination and a somewhat personal writing style. Second, students were asked to develop a text in their FL based on a series of pictures that formed a story. Third, students had to repeat the second task in their native tongue. The series of pictures was basically the same with a slight change in the content of a picture and a couple of pictures missing from this version. That was something students were not prepared for in elementary school. Not only the task and topic were unusual, but also unusual was the fact that they were expected to write the story first in the FL. For the proper outcome of the whole experiment it was important that students were expected to do basically the same task in the FL and L1, but they had to perform the task first in the FL. Research and teaching practice demonstrate a strong influence from the L1 on production in the FL. We wanted to find out if this effect could be brought about the other way, and how strong the influence of FL is on production in the mother tongue (Kecskes & T. Papp, 1995). The results of the picture series task, however, are not discussed here; they are accounted for in Chapter 5.

The third test was administered at the end of the experiment, one year after the second test. Students had already been in high school for 2 years when the third test was given to them. By that time they were supposed to have developed writing styles of their own and be able to handle any kind of writing exercise in their own way, so the task was chosen accordingly. Students received several classified advertisements from newspapers in Hungarian and the FLs. They had to respond to one advertisement in the L1 and to respond to a different one in the FL they studied. There was no more support; students were completely on their own and had to activate all the creativity they were supposed to have developed. The task was unusual, and students had to create the format of the response on their own; there were no schemata to apply. In responding to an advertisement students were expected to introduce themselves or take the role of someone else. They could use conventional formulas or ad hoc sentences generated by their imagination. This task was expected to be a real dividing line among students.

Methods of Evaluation

We used a modified version of the Bernstein–Lawton–Loban method to measure the qualitative level of mother tongue use (Bernstein, 1962, 1973; Lawton, 1970, 1986; Loban, 1963; Loban et al., 1963). This is based mainly on the use of complex sentences with particular emphasis on the frequency and types of subordinations therein. Linguists investigating child language acquisition have demonstrated that clauses of time, clauses of place, and noun clauses functioning as objects are acquired earlier than other types of subordinations (Clark & Clark, 1977; Limber, 1973; Slobin, 1973). These constructions appear in both oral and written speech more frequently than any other clauses. In our survey, we distinguished these three types of clauses from the others.

We used four indexes that are interrelated, interdependent, and connected with the use of subordinations to measure the level of conscious activities in the L1. These indexes demonstrated to us what different kinds of strategies learners used when a task had to be solved, how they constructed sentences, and how confident they were in using linguistic structures.

The frequency index was calculated as

$$FI = \frac{\text{total of subordinations}}{\text{total of finite verbs}}$$

This index tells us how frequently subordinate clauses are used in a text. As Lawton (1970) suggested, it is essential in an English text to use the total number of finite verbs instead of the total number of sentences. This type of analysis, however, is not as simple in Hungarian because there is a frequent sentence type in which the finite form of *lenni* ("to be") is omitted in the present tense. This omission occurs when the subject of the main clause or the subordinate clause is in third person (either singular or plural) and the predicate consists of a zero copula and an NP. For instance:

A lány, akivel beszélgettél még nagyon fiatal.[10]
The girl, whom-with you-talked still very young.
(The girl you talked with is still very young.)

Azt hiszem, hogy Péter katona.[11]
That believe-I, that Peter soldier.
(I believe that Peter is a soldier.)

Because this sentence type appears quite frequently in Hungarian, the first two tests (i.e., frequency and unusual subordination) could be inaccurate with Hungarian data; however, we decided to keep it so that our findings could be compared with other works based on Hungarian data and using Lawton's method of analysis, which includes both the frequency index and the unusual subordination index (see, for example, Biró 1984). In addition, all the students who took part in the experiments were native speakers of Hungarian, and therefore they used the sentence type in question accord-

---

[10]The underlined part is the main clause.
[11]The subordinate clause is underlined.

ing to their individual needs and competence. No significant conclusions can be made using only this index because the frequent use of the simplest subordinations (e.g., time, place, object) can produce very good results.

The second index was the *unusual subordinations* index:

$$US = \frac{\text{total of unusual subordinations}}{\text{total of finite verbs}}$$

The simplest subordinate clauses (e.g., time, place, object) are acquired and used almost automatically (Kecskes & Papp, 1991; Lengyel, 1981). They function like formulaic chunks whose use does not require special kinds of conscious activity (Kecskes, 1995). The other types of subordinations are connected with a later stage of development as they require special mental planning (Lengyel, 1981). That is why this index tells us the most about the development of the student' creativity.

Loban's *weighted index of subordination* which was the third index is based on four categories of subordinate clauses and is represented as

$$LI = \frac{\text{total number of B, C, D}}{\text{total number of A, B, C, D}}$$

A (1 point): A subordinate clause that is directly dependent upon a main clause.

B (2 points): A dependent clause modifying or placed within another dependent clause.

C (2 points): A dependent clause containing a verbal construction (i.e., infinitive, gerund, participle).

D (3 points): A dependent clause modifying or placed within another dependent clause which, in turn, is within or modifying another dependent clause.

This index demonstrates how students use the potential of the language. If this value is high and the frequency index is low, it means that well-constructed sentences can be found in the text.

The *Loban number*, the fourth index, refers to the complexity of sentences.

$$LN = \text{total point value of A, B, C, D}$$

If this value is high, the text contains a number of more complex, embedded sentences.

Because any of the four indexes can be misleading if used separately, evaluation was always based on an analysis of the numerical data of all four indexes. This complex evaluation ensured that the test results were interpreted objectively. In the Appendix we demonstrate how the different kinds of indexes were used during the analysis of a text. The example is based on an English text, which makes it easier for the reader to understand the procedure. Exactly the same procedures were used when Hungarian texts were analyzed.

DISCUSSION

Space does not permit us to demonstrate and discuss all findings of the experiment. We focus only on those issues that are especially worth taking a close look at from the perspective of this book. Table 2.1 gives a summary of

TABLE 2.1
Summary of Surveys

		Survey 1			
INDEXES		FI	US	LI	LN
IMMERSION	BOYS	0.45	0.21	0.25	7.09
CLASS	GIRLS	0.51	0.25	0.23	11.96
INTENSIVE	BOYS	0.33	0.11	0.22	7.62
CLASS	GIRLS	0.43	0.27	0.23	8.12
CONTROL	BOYS	0.42	0.21	0.29	4.14
CLASS	GIRLS	0.55	0.34	0.21	5.35
		Survey 2			
INDEXES		FI	US	LI	LN
IMMERSION	BOYS	0.53	0.285	0.268	10.66
CLASS	GIRLS	0.481	0.276	0.233	14.58
INTENSIVE	BOYS	0.308	0.115	0.28	5.33
CLASS	GIRLS	0.384	0.213	0.252	11.86
CONTROL	BOYS	0.412	0.197	0.138	5.25
CLASS	GIRLS	0.386	0.199	0.195	7.00
		Survey 3			
INDEXES		FI	US	LI	LN
IMMERSION	BOYS	0.349	0.132	0.2	5.4
CLASS	GIRLS	0.410	0.177	0.246	7.875
INTENSIVE	BOYS	0.291	0.163	0.219	5.1
CLASS	GIRLS	0.257	0.121	0.234	5.95
CONTROL	BOYS	0.206	0.039	0.181	2.88
CLASS	GIRLS	0.225	0.053	0.158	4.00

Note. **FI** = FREQUENCY INDEX; **US** = UNUSUAL SUBORDINATIONS; **LI** = LOBAN INDEX; **LN** = LOBAN NUMBER.

the results of all three surveys detailing numbers by the four indexes and gender. The first thing one notices in the table is that most of the numbers show a decreasing tendency; that is, results seem to be best in the first test and worst in the last test. This reading of numbers is very misleading. As explained at the beginning of this chapter, the aim of the experiment was not to demonstrate some kind of increase but rather to relate to each other the results of three groups of students who studied a FL with different intensity and to demonstrate how the use of mother tongue changed under the influence of FL learning. The results cannot be understood properly without taking into consideration two variables: type of test and relation of the four indexes in each test. If we just compare the results of the three tests without careful analysis of these variables, no objective answer can be given to the research questions. What is important for us here is the change in the relation of test results among the participating groups. How do the results of each group change in relation to the results of the other two groups within each test?

As a reminder, here is a summary of developmental levels and tasks. Test one is a composition on a well-known topic. The expected developmental level (EDL) is firm composition skills, adequate use of schemata, and moderate creativities within the confines of format. Test two is a composition on an unusual topic. The EDL is developing individual writing skills, the ability to step out of well-known format, and increasing creativity. Test three involves a response to advertisements. The EDL is established writing style, the ability to choose the format appropriate for the task, and creative use of language.

Baseline Measures—Test I

The results of the first test demonstrate that there was no basic difference among the three group of students when they started high school. All four indexes were quite close in each group with few differences. As discussed earlier, the rather homogeneous production of the three groups can be explained by the common syllabi and textbooks, the same pattern of practice, and common educational goals in Hungarian language and literature in the elementary school. When the experiment started, the mother tongue skills of students were not significantly different. It is important, however, to note that the control class was slightly ahead of the other two classes in the FI, US, and LI in the first survey. The only exception was the LN, which refers to the complexity of sentence structures. Higher numbers refer to more complex, embedded sentences used by the students. Consequently, it is not the number of subordinate clauses that counts but their complexity. A text can have numerous simple subordinations but still have a relatively low LN. This is basically the difference between the control group and the other two groups: The control group students (especially girls) have relatively high FIs and USs, but their LNs are low. This means that these students used numerous subordinate clauses, which were mainly type A. The results of the immersion group and intensive group show a different picture. Students in those two groups used fewer subordinate clauses with more complex structures.

Where does this difference come from? We can only guess. The immersion class students were not expected to have any previous experience with their FL—French was new to each student who was accepted into that class. They, however, had to pass a written logical test for acceptance in Hungarian (Duff, 1995). Students in the intensive class were selected based on their results in English or Russian. All control class students studied Russian because it was mandatory in the elementary school, and some of them had limited experience with English.

The immersion class and intensive class students had somewhat more intensive FL experience and supposingly stronger logical skills than the students in the control class. Although this difference exists from the very beginning it can be demonstrated only in one of the indexes in the first survey. Why? The task was something these students were supposed to be equally good at (because of composition pattern practice and their excellent grades in the Hungarian language): composition on a familiar topic. To do something unique and outstanding would have been very difficult because they were expected to recite what they had learned. In addition, their FL experience was not intensive enough to have a serious impact on the mother tongue skills. The question is: will this slight difference (which is not necessarily the result of previous FL learning) develop into a significant difference during the 2-year period of the experiment even though immersion and intensive classes are not exposed to Hungarian in school as much as the control class?

Type of Task

If we look at the three tasks theoretically without any student population in mind we can hypothesize that a composition (Test 1 and Test 2) will give students the chance to use subordinations more often than a response to an advertisement does. The numbers in Table 2.1 seem to support this hypothesis. In comparison to the results of the first test there is an increase in most numbers in the second test, with the exception of the control group, who had decreasing numbers in most categories. The results of the second test and the third test show a decrease in all the numbers. Consequently, the type of task was quite decisive in the use of subordinations and complex sentence structures. This demonstrates that we cannot use an external approach that compares values to each other test by test but need an internal approach that compares values to each other within each test.

Comparing Achievements of Classes

In the first test the control class slightly exceeded the immersion class and the intensive class in each category with the exception of the LN. In the third test the scores of control class were lower than those of the other two classes in each category. The distance between the control class and the immersion and intensive classes seems to have increased by each test. In addition, the immersion class is a clear leader in all categories but two,[12] both in the second and third test. However, the FI index shows that the control group still kept something of its advance (gained in the first test) over the intensive group in the second test, but in the third test the intensive group is clearly ahead of the control group.

Examining the US index shows that the decrease in the number of subordinations may result in the decrease of unusual subordinations. From this respect it is important to examine the FI index and the US index in the first test and the third test. The numbers show a decreasing tendency but not necessarily in the rate of US and FI. In the first test, for the immersion class, US (0.21) constituted 46% (0.45) (boys) and 49% (0.51) (girls) of the total FI values. For the intensive class, the US constituted 33% and 62%, of the FI values, and for the control class, US constituted 50% and 60% of the FI values. These rates changed in the third test: For the Immersion class, 39% and 43% of the subordinations were unusual; for the intensive class, percentages were 56% and 48%, and for the control class they were 19% and 24%. These numbers demonstrate that in spite of the different exercise types the students were required to do in the first and third tests, the proportion of unusual subordinations to the total number of subordinations did not change much in the immersion class and the intensive class, but it significantly decreased in the control class.

If the LI is high, well-constructed sentences can be found in the text; this index shows the proportion of complex subordinations to the total number of subordinations. This proportion changed only to a small extent in the immersion group and the intensive group, whereas it significantly decreased in the control group.

Finally, the LN index increased with one exception in the second test and significantly decreased in each group in the third test. This is mainly due to the tasks (i.e., response to an advertisement in the third test and a composition in the second). However, despite the LN decreasing, the LI remained basically the same in the first two groups. This means that these two classes

---

[12]Boys in the intensive class are better in US and LI in the third test.

maintained the quite frequent use of B, C, and D sentences. The drastic decrease of LN in the control group confirms that this class couldn't compete with the other two any more.

PRINCIPAL FINDINGS OF THE EXPERIMENT

First, intensive and successful FL learning can facilitate L1 development significantly. The experiment demonstrated two different kinds of tendencies in the use of L1. Whereas the immersion and specialized classes developed in the direction of creative use of their mother tongue, the control class could hardly maintain the previous level. Although the immersion group (because their curriculum focused mainly on the FL) had fewer classes in the L1 and less exposure to the L1 in school than the specialized and control classes, their production in L1 exceeded that of the two other types of classes. The specialized and control classes had the same kind of instruction in the L1, but by the end of the survey period the L1 level of the specialized class exceeded that of the control class. The results of the experiment demonstrate very clearly the reason for the two kinds of development.

Additionally, the immersion and specialized classes developed the previously learned patterns further and handled them not as schemata any more but as essential parts of their linguistic means and communicative competence, amalgamating them with the conscious knowledge conditioned by linguistic operations used in both L1 and FL activities. In the control class an opposite process was recorded. Although these students had more instruction in the L1 than the immersion class and as much instruction as the specialized class, the instruction in the L1 itself was not enough for the students to adjust to the new requirement (i.e., the creative use of the language). Their written production became similar to their speech. It was more casual and spontaneous and resembles the dialog format (see a sample text in the Appendix). The use of B, C, and D sentences becomes sporadic in the written speech of these students. Their production is characterized by simplification on the one hand and by hypercorrection (Marcellesi & Gardin, 1974) on the other—a typical sign of the use of restricted rather than elaborated code. When these students tried to use an unusual, not acquired, and not sufficiently practiced sentence construction, they often failed to convey the meaning they wanted, and their production seemed to be out of place or linguistically complicated in an unnatural way.

The findings of the experiment suggest that the significant difference in the L1 development in the three different class types is mainly conditioned by the intensive and successful FL learning because no other external factor was present to facilitate this change.

Second, the differences between the restricted code and the elaborated code can be explained by the ontogenesis and development of written speech. The experiment indicated that the differences between the restricted code and the elaborated code can be explained not by the different processes of socialization, as Bernstein (1962) claimed, but by the ontogenesis of written speech, whose development is basically connected with schooling. This process requires a high level of abstraction and careful verbal planning and develops into special learning strategies based on conscious and controlled activities. By combining subconscious mother tongue skills with conscious knowledge developed both in L1 and FL in school, learners can be expected to reach a higher level of development in the written L1.

The intensive FL learning in the immersion and specialized classes gave strong impulse to the development of some L1 skills. The knowledge of the students in the L1 was activated, and writing skills in the L1 developed in the direction of creative language use. The intensive and resultant FL learning may help mother tongue education to a significant extent by activating passive knowledge and making the use of L1 more conscious.

Third, written planning in L1 becomes sophisticated and develops more intensively under the influence of FL learning. By the end of the experiment, the students in the immersion and specialized classes became quite confident in their use of complex sentences of different types. The use of L1 in the immersion and specialized classes showed a strong developmental tendency in the direction of more sophisticated use of the mother tongue. Subordinate clauses were better constructed than at the beginning of the experiment, and embedded sentences were more frequently used and were more complex. The semantics of subordinations was characterized by the use of more unusual types. This tendency got stronger no matter what kind of style the students' tasks required. Written planning developed and became more elaborated.

The control class did not show this kind of development; 3 hours of instruction in a FL a week is not enough to bring about this positive change. The beneficial effect of FL learning on the development of mother tongue skills is just a potentiality, not a necessity. Not all kinds of FL learning lead to the development of multicompetence. FL studies can bring about changes in the monolingual system only if the language learning process is intensive enough and can rely on significant learner motivation.

How do we know what FL proficiency the students in the three classes had? How can the better FL skills of the immersion and intensive classes be documented? As mentioned at the beginning of the chapter, Test 2 and Test 3 contained a FL element as well. In Test 2 students were expected to write a story about a picture series, first in their FL and then in their L1. In Test 3 they were expected to respond to an advertisement in their mother tongue and then to another ad in their FL. As T. Papp (1991) demonstrated, the FL production was clearly dependent upon the intensiveness of study: The immersion class (i.e., *dual-language class*) where the FL was the medium of instruction had the highest level of proficiency, followed by the intensive class and the control class. There was a significant difference between the intensive class and the control class as well. The success of the dual-language and intensive FL education in Hungary was discussed in several other research papers (Duff, 1991, 1995; Horvath, 1990).

Fourth, the typological difference of L1 and FL may have a positive effect on the linguistic development of the student. The influence of the FL on the development of mother tongue skills depends not only on paralinguistic factors like intensiveness, effectiveness of the learning process, and motivation of the students but on linguistic factors as well. One of these factors is connected with language typology (Kecskes & T. Papp, 1991). The results of the experiment tend to demonstrate that the positive effect on the L1 was almost equally strong if the FL was English or French but less strong when it was Russian. Student motivation accounts for little here because all three languages, including Russian, had been voluntarily chosen by the students in the high school. The fact that the smaller part of the intensive class studied Russian was due to the students' choice. This was the case in the control class also. It is hypothesized that the effect of FL is especially beneficial if the L1 and FL differ in *configurationality*.[13] Configurational languages and nonconfigurational languages develop different kinds of learning and problem-solving strategies, and the ability to use both types in linguistic operations can have a positive effect on the linguistic development of students.[14] This statement sound rather speculative at this point, however, because the experiment did not generate enough data to support this claim, and further research is needed to investigate the issue. We return to it when language distance, language typology, and configurationality are discussed in Chapter 6.

SUMMARY

The principle findings of the experiment have some important points for education. There is no doubt about the fact that students coming to school at the age of 6 or 7 years have different social backgrounds, which have a serious impact on their language development. School, however, is supposed

---

[13]Configurational languages (e.g., English or French) have bound word order governed by grammatical rules. Nonconfigurational languages (such as Russian and Hungarian) have a relatively free word order governed by pragmatic rules (White, 1989).

[14]Canadian studies on immersion programs (Rehorick, 1991; Richard-Amato, 1988) have demonstrated the beneficial interaction of the two languages, but in those programs English and French (both configurational languages) are used.

to do two things: It should provide a relatively similar environment for each student, and an equal educational opportunity for learning no matter what environment they come from.[15] National standards attempt to balance differences deriving from the social backgrounds of students. In Hungarian schools, all students were drilled according to the same standards. This standardization has advantages and disadvantages. Students have less freedom and flexibility but have equal opportunity to acquire the basics of the use of their mother tongue. Each student has the chance to develop an elaborated code no matter what his or her social and linguistic background is. There is no doubt that when starting school students whose vernacular is closer to the elaborated code than to the restricted code will have an advantage over students who come to school with a less elaborated language code, but this is a difference created by previous opportunity rather than by ability or potential, and consequently it can be eliminated. In the elimination process two variables play a crucial role: individual effort and quality of instruction. The results of the experiment demonstrated that elementary school instruction in the L1 was not enough for students to learn how to handle the potentials of their mother tongue creatively and independently. They needed further reinforcement to support the internalization of the L1. However, this reinforcement is not provided by high school instruction, which requires an individual and creative use of language. As a result, students who get some additional reinforcement directly (through further instruction or individual effort) or indirectly (via intensive FL studies) do better than the ones who lack this impetus, no matter what their original social and linguistic background is. These findings coincide with what Biró (1984) discovered while investigating the language use of village students and city students in elementary schools in Transylvania. He argued that village students can meet the requirements of the elaborated code in their written speech, but this remains just a school language for them and not a natural way of communication. Basically, this is what happened to the students in our experiment. The first test demonstrated that all students could acquire the use of the elaborated code within the confines of learned and practiced schemata, but the use of the elaborated code was not properly internalized yet, and it did not become an essential part of language use of all the participating students. Many did not feel that the code was something of their own: It was just a school language for them. Consequently, when students were not required to use the acquired patterns and schemata any more, their language use went in the direction of a loosely structured, more casual, restricted code.

---

[15]This is, of course, an ideal situation. Inequalities in facilities, financial support, educational environment, and quality teachers make schools very different. However, taking into account these variables would lead the discussion away from the main point.

The experiment demonstrated that FL learning has the potential to affect the state of L1 knowledge and skills. This effect is dependent upon several variables, such as language proficiency, motivation, and the way of exposure to the target language. This claim concurs with the results of some earlier studies (Hancock, 1977; Masciantonio, 1977), which suggest that "foreign language learning offers a facilitating experience through which learners use language as a medium for expressing perceptions, concepts and inferences" (Hancock, 1977, p. 79). FL study may provide a vehicle for arriving at an ultimate goal of all education, rendering the learner more capable of coping creatively with the environment. The analysis of experimental results was, however, restricted to structural well-formedness only. This raises two important groups of questions, the discussion of which dominates the later chapters in this volume. The first focuses on more general issues that are important to discuss because the FL effect cannot be understood without a description of the mechanisms and processes characterizing functioning in two or more languages. The second group of questions is more specific to our subject matter and deals directly with the foreign language effect. This group includes questions such as: How is it that structural well-formedness in the L1 can be affected by L2? What goes on in the minds of multilingual speakers? How do the two (or more) language channels interact? How does the language processing device of multilingual speakers differ from that of monolingual speakers? How is thought developed in the multilingual mind, and how is it mapped onto words? How do thoughts appear on the surface? How does the language use of multilinguals differ from that of the monolinguals? Is there anything like interculture style (cf. Kasper & Blum-Kulka, 1993; Yoshida, 1990)?

We raise additonal issues as well, including: Are there areas other than structural well-formedness where the effect of FL learning on the development of multicompetence can be quantitatively and qualitatively demonstrated? Will any kind of FL learning affect the use of L1? Is there any way to establish and describe a threshold beyond which the FL effect on the mother tongue can be clearly demonstrated? What are the main characteristics of the FL effect?

APPENDIX

Pattern

Task: 1. Describe what is happening in the series of pictures in the foreign language you are studying.

34 CHAPTER 2

2.1. Describe what you see in the series of pictures.

2.2. Try to recall and describe the picture that was included in the previous series (that you had to describe in the foreign language) and is missing now.

Class type: Specialized (7 English classes a week).

Time: Second Test at the end of the first year.

The following text is a copy of the original production of one of the students. It contains each mistake the student made.

    1
Once upon a time a man was walking in a street and
                           2
suddenly he saw a very very pretty girl. She's got fair
                   3
hair and wonderful eyes. The man immediately falled in
              4   **5**   **6**
love with the girl. And he decided to know her, so he
                  7
began to shout. The girl falled in love with the man,
    8
too, because he looks like as her previous boyfriend.
  9   **10**
They decided to have a dinner in a restaurant. But
  11   **12**   **13**
there was a difficult problem! The man's wife. Their
                                14
marriage wasn't very succesful relationship, because
the wife was a little fat, and she was really very
       15
ugly. So, (to tell the truth) I can understand the man,
16
why he wanted to get marriage with the young, nice
    17   **18**
girl. Because I've forgotten to say, that they diceded
      19   **20**
to get marriage. I hope, it will be more succesful,
21
than the privious one.

Total of main and subordinate clauses: 21

FL INFLUENCE ON L1   **35**

Number of finite verbs: 20
Number of subordinate clauses, infinitive phrases, gerunds, and participles: 10
Frequent clauses (clauses of time and place, noun clause functioning as object): 5, 10, 18, 20
Unusual clauses (all the rest): 6, 8, 14, 16, 17, 21

Sentence types:

- A (1 point): a subordinate clause that is directly dependent upon main clause
- B (2 points): a dependent clause modifying or placed within another dependent clause
- C (2 points): a dependent clause containing a verbal construction (i.e., infinitive, gerund, participle)
- D (3 points): a dependent clause modifying or placed within another dependent clause that, in turn, is within or modifying another dependent clause.

Indexes

$$\text{FI (subordination index):} \quad \frac{\text{total of subordinations}}{\text{total of verbs}} \quad \frac{10}{20}$$

$$\text{US (unusual subordination):} \quad \frac{\text{total of un. subs.}}{\text{total of verbs}} \quad \frac{6}{20}$$

$$\text{Loban Index:} \quad \frac{\text{B, C, D}}{\text{A, B, C, D}} \quad \frac{1}{10}$$

Loban Number (total value of A, B, C, D): 22

Values: FI = 0.5
         US = 0.3
         LI = 0.1
         LN = 22

Example for the restricted code

The following text was produced by one of the participants of the experiment:

The man saw the girl, and thought: "She is very pritty."

He decided: I want to meet with the girl.
- Let's spend any time in a restaurant.
- Oh no, let's go home.
- Is there somebody?
- Just my mum.
The mum is cooking. They arrived.
- Hello mum, he's my new boy-friend.

The student is not confident enough to produce a description of events; dialog is used instead.

CHAPTER

3

Language Processing Device of Multilinguals

LANGUAGE PROCESSING IN BILINGUALS

As mentioned previously, one of the main issues in bilingual research concerns the relation of the two language systems: *To what extent are the two languages functionally independent, and to what extent do they constitute a single functional system?* Although there have been several attempts to investigate this problem with different types of bilinguals, we do not seem to know enough yet to describe what really goes on in a multilingual's mind. Durgunoglu and Roediger (1987) argued that this question is indeterminable because "the varying retrieval demands of different tasks produce different patterns of results and lead to opposite conclusions" (p. 377). In this book the focus of attention is on adult speakers of two or more languages. We find it important to emphasize this because approaches to bilingual development differ to a great extent depending on which period of development researchers are interested in. As mentioned earlier the extremist positions (Cook, 1992; Grosjean, 1989) state either that the two languages form separate systems (De Houwer, 1990; Genesee, 1989; Lambert, 1990; Neufeld, 1976) or that they make up a single unified system (Redliger & Park, 1980; Swain, 1977). There are also opinions that the truth lies somewhere in between. Bilinguals have two separate systems that interact constantly and overlap at certain points (Cook, 1992; Paradis, 1985; Perecman, 1989; Sridhar & Sridhar, 1980).

Here we would like to underline that this issue is more than just about the language systems: It also involves what the language systems stand for, what they represent, denote, and symbolize. In other words, this is about how language and cognition are connected in the mind. In our understanding the *bilingual or multilingual Language Processing Device (LPD) consists of two (or more) Constantly Available Interacting Systems (CAIS) and has a Common Underlying Conceptual Base (CUCB)*. This LPD is similar to the model proposed by Paradis (1979, 1985, 1995) and Paivo and Desrochers (1980). Our interest is in the FL→L1 effect, which results in a unique form of multicompetence. Therefore, our primary goal is to explain how this LPD is structured and how it operates, with a secondary goal to examine whether there is any way for a foreign language (FL) to fit into this system. First, we examine how language processing in bilinguals differs from language processing in monolinguals.

Using the framework of the universal grammar theory, Cook (1991) developed the idea of *multicompetence* as opposed to *monocompetence* to describe the compound state of a mind with two grammars (p. 112). He argued that this dichotomy has serious consequences in the field of second language (L2) research because the grammar of a L2 in a multicompetent speaker cannot be the same as the apparently equivalent grammar in a monolingual. Based on this argument it does not make much sense to expect L2 or FL learners to develop the same kind of competence that adult native speakers have because the bidirectional influence will result in a unique competence that shows both similarities and differences to the native monolingual competence. As was discussed in Chapter 1, not only Cook but also several other researchers came to the conclusion that L2 or FL learners cannot be expected to develop native-like (i.e., monolingual) competence (Coppetiers, 1987; Gass, 1990; Schachter, 1988). Cook (1992) suggested that the concept of multicompetence gives a new perspective to L2 learning because it allows us to treat L2 learners not as deficient monolinguals but as people in their own right. If we accept Cook's argument there is nothing for those SL and FL learners to be ashamed of, if they reach only near-native competence, because even at a very high level of proficiency, multicompetence is not the sum of two or more well-developed systems but is a system on its own right. Therefore, it is essential that multicompetence differs from the competence of a person who has that language system as the only language. Cook (1991, 1992) suggested that linguists can take up as a starting point either a monolingual view—"What constitutes knowledge of language?" (Chomsky, 1986, p. 3)—or a multilingual view—"What constitutes knowledge of languages?" There is no doubt that, as discussed in the Preface, both theoretical linguistics and second language acquisition (SLA) research have been biased by the monolingual view for decades. As a result, even bilinguals are quite skeptical about their language competence (Grosjean, 1989) because they expect themselves to have two equally developed, native-like language systems. This is simply impossible if the concept of multicompetence proves to be acceptable.

In this book we take the multilingual view as a starting point to explain from a cognitive–pragmatic perspective what constitutes the knowledge of two languages. Before we make an attempt to describe the language system of bilinguals, a critical note about the concept of multicompetence seems to be essential. Cook (1992) and other researchers speaking about the unique competence of bilinguals focus only on grammatical competence and are less interested in how this unique competence affects the development of cognitive and pragmatic skills and knowledge. We argue that the primary difference between the monolingual and multilingual LPD is conceptual rather than grammatical, and the unique multilingual system is not the exact equivalent of either monolingual system but is the essential consequence of the conceptual development of multilinguals.

SPEECH PRODUCTION MODELS

Levelt's Speech Production Model

Levelt (1989) described a speech production model for monolinguals consisting of four stages: message generation, grammatical encoding, phonological encoding, and articulation. Each stage contains several procedures, which constitute the speaker's procedural knowledge and make it possible for the speaker to operate on the declarative knowledge that becomes available at each stage during encoding. Levelt clearly separated the containers of declarative knowledge (i.e., knowledge base and the mental lexicon) and the processors[1] that operate on that knowledge. According to Levelt's theory the *conceptualizer*, that is, the message generator, is responsible for three things: communicative intention, planning the content (i.e., macroplanning), and planning the form of the message (i.e., microplanning). Macroplanning means "selecting the information whose expression may realize the communicative goals" (p. 5). Microplanning includes marking referents as given or new, assigning topic and focus, and deciding on a proper speech act (Poulisse, 1993). Message generation is affected by the speaker's knowledge base—consisting of encyclopedic knowledge, situational knowledge, and actual knowledge (i.e., what has been said before in the interaction). The output of the conceptualizer is a preverbal message that is fed into the next component called the *formulator*. The formulator is responsible for grammatical and phonological encoding, which takes place through extensive interaction with the lexicon. In Levelt's theory the mental lexicon contains not only word meanings but also syntactic, morphological, and phonological information about the lexical items. Semantic and

---

[1]*Container* and *processor* is our terminology.

syntactic information make up the *lemma* of the word, and morphological and phonological information constitute its *form*. In the course of production the conceptual information in the preverbal message activates the appropriate lexical items, which trigger the syntactic information attached to them. This is how grammatical encoding starts. As a result of that process, a surface structure emerges, which goes through phonological encoding based on the information in the form components of words. In the last step, the *articulator* transforms the phonetic plan produced by the phonological encoder into overt speech.

There are some features of this system that are worth special attention. First, the speaker also has a speech comprehension system that is used to parse both internal and overt speech (Levelt, 1989). Second, the conceptualizer has a monitoring device that receives the parsed message from the speech comprehension system. This gives the speaker a chance to evaluate the message and make repairs if needed. Third, in Levelt's model are two sources of declarative knowledge. One is the knowledge base with actual, situational, and encyclopedical information; the other is the mental lexicon. They stand like independent entities: The first interacts with the conceptualizer, and the second with the formulator. Finally, the speech production process is very fast because it is mostly automatic. Only message generation and monitoring require the speaker's control—all the other processes are executed automatically.

Adaptation of Levelt's Model to Multilinguals

Although Levelt's model was designed for the L1 it has been very popular among researchers investigating bilingual speech production. Several attempts have been made to incorporate L2 knowledge into the model (cf. De Bot, 1992; De Bot & Schreuder, 1993; Green, 1993; Poulisse, 1993). It is not our goal here to evaluate those attempts. We want instead to offer some modifications to Levelt's model while highlighting the main differences between a monolingual and bilingual or multilingual model.

The Sapir-Whorf Theory Revisited. The most controversial issue of modeling a bilingual LPD is the nature of the CUCB where declarative knowledge, images, and concepts are situated and preverbal thought is shaped. The main questions at the stage of conceptualization are whether preverbal thought is language independent and where and how language assignment takes place. The latter question is irrelevant when the monolingual LPD is discussed because the monolingual conceptual base is homogeneous, that is, contains knowledge and concepts based on the L1 only, as well as received or developed through the L1. No wonder that researchers focusing on L1 development have been convinced that in the conceptual base everything is language independent and that the conceptual base contains mainly universal concepts that are lexicalized in different ways in different languages.

The most extreme view on this issue is that of Chomsky (1987), who saw the lexicon of a language as a set of labels to be attached to concepts that are language independent and are determined biologically rather than culturally. He maintained that "acquisition of vocabulary is guided by a rich and invariant conceptual system which is prior to any experience" (p. 33). This has been the ruling monolingual view for several decades, although this approach has not taken into consideration any bilingual experience. The symbiosis of two language systems, however, articulates conceptual differences and culture dependency, and the monolingual view can hardly be maintained for multilinguals. In spite of this, a considerable part of the bilingual literature argues for a language-independent prelinguistic conceptual level (cf. Caramazza, Gordon, Zurif, & DeLuca, 1976; De Bot & Schreuder, 1993; Paradis, 1985; Perecman, 1989; Zurif & Blumstein, 1978).

Recently some attempts have been made to change this view and to seek room for language and culture specificity in the process of conceptualization. The starting point of these approaches is Levelt's system in which information about which register to use is present in the preverbal message and lexical items must be selected accordingly. Green (1986, 1993) and Poulisse (1993) assumed that language choice is represented as intention in the conceptualized message. Using Levelt's dichotomy between macroplanning (i.e., intentions) and microplanning (i.e., further information to realize intention), De Bot (1992) suggested that macroplanning is language independent and microplanning is language specific. He argued that although the generated message is preverbal, it is constructed bearing in mind the concrete linguistic expression. Green (1993) also came to the conclusion that language specification is needed both at the level of concepts and at the level of word forms in the case of a bilingual LPD. He referred to cases where the L2 does not provide a lexical concept but the L1 does, and the speaker wants to produce an utterance in the L2 that expresses the intended meaning. He thought that in such cases it is unavoidable to specify the language of expression at the conceptual level.

We argue that language and especially culture specificity is already present at the conceptual level, not only in the process of conceptualization (i.e., message generation) but also in the blueprints of most concepts. The CUCB is a container of mental representations that comprise knowledge and concepts that are either language and culture neutral (i.e., universal or useable through both channels) or language and culture specific.[2] This suggestion concurs with the new wave compound model proposed by Paradis

---

[2] Images are language independent.

(1995, 1997). He claimed that multilinguals have a compound system consisting of two parts: two or more lexicons that store word forms, phonological and morphosyntactic properties, lexicosemantic specifications, and constraints; and a single store for multimodal mental representations that are acquired through experience in discourse. Consequently, these representations are linguistically and culturally grounded. Monti-Belkaoui and Belkaoui (1983) also noted that when concepts involve different or unique cultural, social, or environmental processes or phenomena the underlying dimensional structures differ in ways that reflect these processes.

Pavlenko (1996, 1998a) emphasized the importance of direct experience with the concept in its own cultural environment. She investigated the nature of concepts in the mental lexicon of Russian–English adult bilinguals and FL learners in comparison with the concepts of monolingual Russians and Americans. The participants of the experiment watched and recalled a 3-minute silent film. Their narratives were recorded and analyzed. Based on her findings Pavlenko concluded that "bilingual cognition is not code-dependent but rather concept-dependent, with the language of origin of the bilingual's concepts related to the learner's history" (p. 68). She suggested that cultural exposure is crucial in the development of concepts.

The full acquisition and proper use of a concept requires the learner to know not only its lexical–semantic counterpart and the associated declarative knowledge but also the multimodal mental representation and culturally based behavioral scripts and schemas that are acquired through genuine communication. Learners need direct experience with concepts in the target language because the conceptual system of each language operates differently. Lakoff and Johnson (1980) argued that "our ordinary conceptual system in terms of which we both think and act is fundamentally metaphorical in nature" (p. 3). Metaphor is not just a matter of language, that is, of mere words. Human thought processes are largely metaphorical because a considerable part of the human conceptual system is metaphorically structured and defined. There is psychological evidence to support the cognitive reality of metaphorical structuring (e.g., Gentner & Gentner, 1982; Hunt & Agnoli, 1991; Sweetser, 1990).

The language and culture dependency of the CUCP leads us to the issue of *linguistic relativism*, which is the rejection of the monolingual view and goes back to great philosophers such as Locke and Leibniz as well as great linguists including von Humboldt and Sapir. Locke (1690/1959), for instance, was convinced that lexical variation reflects cultural differences among different speech communities. He argued that

> if we look a little more nearly into this matter, and exactly compare different languages, we shall find that, though they have words which in translations and dictionaries are supposed to answer one another, yet there is scarce one

of ten amongst the names of complex ideas, especially of mixed modes, that stands for the same precise idea which the word does that in dictionaries it is rendered by. (p. 49)

Wilhelm von Humboldt (1903–1936) expressed similar ideas, saying that "thinking is not merely dependent on language in general but, up to a certain degree, on each specific language" (p. 2). He considered different languages as bearers of different cognitive perspectives and different world views. These ideas were further developed by Sapir and Whorf. Linguistic relativism, known as the Sapir–Whorf theory (Sapir, 1921; Whorf, 1956a, 1956b) emphasized the bidirectional relation between language and cultural or cognitive structure and has been rejected from a monolingual, universalist perspective that made the *intertranslatability postulate* one of the basic maxims of modern linguistics. This maxim claims that anything can be expressed in any language (cf. Lenneberg, 1953; Searle, 1969). A multilingual approach requires that the theory be reexamined from the perspective of a possible CUCB.

The acknowledgment of a bidirectional influence between the L1 and L2 in multilinguals as well as the claim of cognitive–linguistic interdependency through thought and word by Vygotsky must lead us to rethink the Sapir–Whorf theory. Sweetser (1990) argued that "few linguists or anthropologists would be upset by the hypothesis that learning a word for a culturally important category could linguistically reinforce the learning of the category itself" (p. 7). Her conclusion is that there seem to be areas of interdependence between cognition and language. This is basically what we emphasized earlier about the CUCB. The main criticism against the Sapir–Whorf theory is true: A considerable part of the basic cognitive apparatus is not dependent on language and culture. That makes it possible for human beings to share a lot of prelinguistic and extralinguistic experience that is likely to shape language rather than to be shaped by it (Sweetser, 1990). Consequently, the strong version of linguistic relativism has to be rejected, but the weak version of the theory seems to be supported by the multicompetence approach. It can hardly be denied that language has some kind of a limited role in shaping cognition. We return to Humboldt's argument, which postulated that thinking depends on a specific language up to a certain degree. The real issue here is not dependency, but the degree of dependency. This concurs with Wierzbicka's (1993) view that the real question is "to what extent languages are shaped by 'human nature' and to what extent they are shaped by culture" (p. 7). The multilingual CUCB contains concepts that are language specific because they represent a unique part of the culture associated with that language (Kecskes, 1998).

A cross-linguistic study (Osgood, May, & Miron, 1975) of universals and language-specific elements in the lexicon also supported a limited form of linguistic relativism. Osgood et al. found that connotations associated with certain words are quite similar across languages but a number of words have special emotional significance that varies in different languages. One difficulty of multilingual development is that each language has its own metaphorical and figurative system that are not compatible with the metaphorical system of another language: Americans "make money," Russians "work for money" ("зарабатывать"), Hungarians "look for money" ("pénzt keres").

Slobin (1991, 1996) claimed that language does not shape our thought; it acts as a filter on the way we talk about it. This weak version of linguistic relativity is acceptable for even nativists such as Pinker, who said that ". . . one's language does determine how one must conceptualize reality when one has to talk about it" (Pinker, 1989, p. 360). This approach matches Levelt's theory of speech production as well. As discussed earlier, in Levelt's theory thoughts are coded in language by matching conceptual structure with appropriate lexical items. For this encoding process to start, the speaker must organize the conceptual structure so that it matches semantic specifications in the lexicon. If no appropriate lexical representations can be found, the thoughts cannot be coded. This process of regimenting conceptual structure and finding lexical representations for the thought structures is called *thinking for speaking* by Slobin (1991, 1996).

Features of the Bilingual or Multilingual LPD. The degree of conceptual dependency on one specific language is determined by several variables, including the nature of multilingual development, age, environment, distance of languages, and the way in which the languages were acquired. Discussing the proportions between the universal and the culture-specific aspects of languages in general, Humboldt (1903–1936) emphasized that

> there is a number of things which can be determined completely a priori, and which can be separated from the conditions of a particular language. On the other hand, there is a far greater number of concepts, and also grammatical peculiarities, which are so inextricably woven into the individuality of their language that they can neither be kept suspended between all languages on the mere thread of inner perception nor can they be carried over into another language without alternation. (pp. 21–23).

This line of thinking is based on the ideas of 17th-century philosophers (e.g., Descartes, Leibniz, Pascal) who maintained that there is a limited innate stock of human concepts. Wierzbicka (1993), their most dedicated follower, suggested that we should look for these universal human concepts not in the world around us but in our own minds. In her opinion "only very few and very simple concepts have any chance of belonging to the shared lexical core of all languages" (p. 16). It is not our goal here to discuss which concepts belong to the universal category (on this issue, see Wierzbicka's publications). What is important from a multilingual perspective is the existence of a limited number of universal concepts (e.g., "I," "this," "say," "want," etc.).

The majority of concepts, however, are not universal. When knowledge and concepts get into the CUCB they are not language independent because they come through one of the channels only. A part of these concepts, *one-language concepts*, are more or less culture specific: they can be used only through one channel, or if used through both channels they either keep the word form denoting them in the language of origin or need special explanation or description in the other language because there is no appropriate label (i.e., word) for them in the other language. For instance, in the conceptual base of a Hungarian–English bilingual the concepts denoted by the terms *sweepstakes*, *baseball*, and *doggy bag* exist as English-based concepts, whereas *ballagás* (i.e., senior high-schoolers saying good-bye to their school, teachers, and fellow students) and *kóstoló* (i.e., a tray full of meat that people present to their friends after a pig killing) are Hungarian-based concepts. They are available through the other language with special explanation only. The Russian concepts "perestrojka" and "glasnost," the French "détente," or the English "software" are so strongly language specific that speakers of other languages have to develop those concepts as new ones in their own languages to use them through other language channels. This is known as *borrowing*.[3] The language specificity (or better to say, culture specificity) of certain parts of the knowledge base is also supported by the fact that academic skills are usually tied to one of the languages, and the aim of bilingual education is to neutralize these skills, that is, make them available through both channels.

The numbers of universal concepts and one-language concepts are not very significant. The rest of the concepts, the overwhelming majority, can be placed on a continuum that represents the distance or closeness of concepts coming into the CUCB through the two or more language channels. Using the term created by Bierwisch and Schreuder (1992) and applied systematically by De Groot (1992, 1993) we denote these concepts as *decompositional*. Decompositional concepts have both common and different conceptual nodes such as, for example, Russian "obed" and English "lunch." On our imaginary continuum decompositional concepts having much in common are placed on the left. The remaining concepts are placed to the right, indicating that they share fewer conceptual nodes. Position of concepts on the continuum depends on the distance of closeness of cultures and languages. For a Hungarian–Russian bilingual there is more in common in the concept denoted by the Hungarian word *ebéd* and the Rus-

---

[3]Sometimes there are attempts to create a word in the target language to denote the new concept. Very often this kind of endeavor is unsuccessful, as in the case of French *logiciel*, which is supposed to substitute for the English word *software*.

sian word *obed* than for an English–Russian bilingual in the same concept. We speculate that a considerable part of knowledge and concepts can become neutralized in the conceptual base, especially if they are situated at the left edge of the continuum sharing several conceptual nodes. Neutralization means making knowledge or concepts obtained through one language channel available through the other language channel with little or no reconceptualization (i.e., with little addition or subtraction). The process of neutralization is similar to what Slobin (1991, 1996) called "thinking for speaking." An adaptation of Slobin's theory to the multilingual situation requires that the bilingual or multilingual speaker construct the necessary target language filters for organizing any experience into a verbal account of that experience, in accordance with both the communicative goals and the collection of formal options available in the given language.

The adult monolingual LPD is a relatively steady mechanism with more up than down movements, whereas the bilingual–multilingual LPD is a constantly changing system (Cook, 1992; Green, 1993). The levels of proficiency in the dual-language system are not constant but keep changing. Moreover, the two languages are usually not equally used or valorized. There seems to be nothing like balanced bilingual because the bilingual LPD is generally dominated by one of the languages at a certain point of development and use or in a certain period of time. As a result of dynamic movements, the state of CUCB always depends on several variables including the multilingual's learning history, environment, communicative needs, and language valorization. This is also true for the concepts constituting the CUCB: They are highly dynamic and flexible (cf. Keil, 1986, 1989; Pavlenko, 1998a). Keil (1989) provided evidence in the knowledge-based concepts framework that a restructuring of a concept may also involve a reorganization of the whole conceptual domain. This explains how multilinguals can neutralize culture-specific concepts and make them useable through both language channels.

The use of the monolingual LPD is largely automatic, and only message generation and monitoring require special attention and more consciousness (Levelt, 1989). The conceptual system of the monolingual LPD feeds into only one language channel; therefore, "the processing routines from conceptual to phonological forms have become automatized. Each level of representation emerges from the next in a continuous, uninterrupted fashion, and the distinction between pairs of representatives is likely to be poorly defined" (Perecman, 1989, p. 237). Bilingual language production, however, needs more conscious attention at each level and is less automatic because bilinguals have to make a choice at each level. The process is far from continuous and uninterrupted as it is for monolinguals. Consequently, the distinctions between levels of representation are more articulated than in monolinguals. Some researchers have found longer reaction times in bilinguals than in monolinguals using the same language (Flege, 1987; Nathan, 1987; Perecman, 1989). Magiste (1979) also reported that bilingual children took longer to name an object than monolinguals did.

It is important to emphasize that in the bilingual–multilingual LPD both language channels are constantly available no matter in which language the actual production occurs (Kroll, 1993; Perecman, 1989; Preston & Lambert, 1969). The two language channels constantly interact during production, which may result in mixing, switching, modifications, and a temporary dominance of either language. Levels differ from each other in the degree of interaction because interaction between levels is progressively weaker as processing moves upwards from the lexical semantic level to the articulatory level. Evidence suggests that "language mixes are more common at the lexical than at the phonological level of processing, both in aphasia and in normals" (Perecman, 1989, p. 233). The interaction is the weakest at the phonological level. Flege (1987) argued that young children establish distinct phonetic categories for each language.

Importantly, Levelt's model is for speech production, and our focus in this book is mainly on written speech. Is this model adaptable to written speech? As far as the structure of the model is concerned, we think it is. There are differences, however, in the operation of the model for written speech, and they involve three interrelated factors: speed, message generation, and monitoring. When written speech is produced message generation and monitoring may require more consciousness and time.

THE COMMON UNDERLYING CONCEPTUAL BASE

There is little doubt about the existence of a CUCB in bilinguals.[4] This idea is accepted by most researchers. Because the main focus of this book is on the effect of FL on the development of mother tongue we must examine whether FL learners can also develop a CUCB.

One of the strongest arguments for a CUCB is Cummins' (1979, 1984, 1991) interdependence hypothesis, which proposed that the development of literacy-related skills in L2 is partly a function of prior development of literacy-related skills in L1. This hypothesis implies that a common underlying proficiency characterizes bilingual proficiency, especially as regards academic and cognitive aptitude, and there is one integrated source of thought for both languages. As mentioned in the Preface, Cummins emphasized that in principle, transfer can occur both ways between L1 and L2, but in prac-

---

[4]A counterexample can be provided by Penfield and Roberts (1959), who discussed two functionally distinct systems that operate through a mental switch that serves to switch one system on and the other system off.

tice we generally see only unidirectional transfer from the minority to the majority language. The interdependence hypothesis sets up two conditions for transfer to occur: adequate exposure to L*y* (either in school or environment) and adequate motivation to learn L*y* (Cummins & Swain, 1986).

Cummins explained unidirectionality giving the lower status to the minority language, which is basically correct for the situations he investigated. In the Hungarian experiment described in Chapter 2, however, the linguistic environment differed to a great extent from the Canadian and U.S. environments. In Hungary all three FLs involved in the experiment were highly respected by the students. It was their choice to study a particular language.[5] Consequently, the motivation condition set up for the transfer to occur was met in each of the three classes during the experiment. The adequate exposure condition, however, was present only in the immersion class and the intensive class. The experiment has shown that exposure to the FL for 2 to 4 hours per week is not adequate exposure. That much time was not enough for any significant transfer to occur and a CUCB to develop.

Occasionally Cummins referred to the content of common underlying proficiency as *conceptual knowledge* (cf. Cummins, 1989, 1991). He emphasized that conceptual knowledge rather than specific linguistic elements is transferred from one language to the other (Cummins, 1991). His iceberg model represents bilingual proficiency. The two icebergs (L1 and L2) are separate above the surface: The two languages are significantly different in outward conversation. Beneath the surface, the two icebergs are fused, and the two languages have the same central processing system. Both operate through this common system. Baker (1996) used a similar approach, but he called the unitary part the central operating system.

Our understanding of this common system is broader than that of either Cummins' or Baker's. Cummins developed his theory to explain the acquisition and use of academic language by bilinguals. In contrast, we conceptualized the CUCB as the basis of all bilingual linguistic actions, a container that includes everything but the language system itself (i.e., rules plus lexicon). It is in the CUCB where the sociocultural heritage and previous knowledge of the learner are confronted with the new information entering into the CUCB through both language channels, and real-world knowledge mixes with academic knowledge, developing into something that is frequently referred to as *sociocultural background knowledge* (cf. Adamson, 1993; Kecskes, 1994). It is the conceptual base where thoughts originate and are then mapped onto linguistic signs that get to the surface through either language channel. Due to the CUCB, information-processing skills and educational at-

---

[5]This was true even in the case of Russian, which was not highly respected at all by the public, but the students who selected that language in our experiment liked it and respected it. They were motivated to study it.

tainment may be developed through two languages as well as through one language. Cognitive functioning and school achievement may be fed either through one language or through two languages if both are well developed. Both channels feed the same central operating system (Baker, 1996).

At this point we can answer the question, "What constitutes multicompetence (i.e., knowledge of languages)?", and we can address how this competence differs from the competence of a monolingual speaker. In contrast to a one-language-based conceptual base and one language channel of the monolinguals, bilinguals and multilinguals have a CUCB that is a common knowledge base for both languages and two language channels that are usually operational in both directions. The existence of the CUCB as well as the constant interaction of the two language channels make bilingual and multilingual competence unique, and neither of the participating languages can be compared to the monolingual system. CUCB represents the level that Bialystok (1991) called conceptual representation in contrast to formal representation and symbolic representation. Bialystok argued that at this level language is organized only around the meanings it represents. These representations of meanings are based on semantic and conceptual information that is carried through the language. The CUCB contains only concepts, not the words that represent them.

As discussed earlier, the problem with CUCB is that although it is an underlying conceptual system for both languages, a considerable part of concepts and knowledge is language and culture specific because concepts are learned and acquired through either language channel (Kecskes, 1998). Therefore, the blueprints will contain the culture-specific information that refers to their origin. This is the other point where our understanding of CUCB differs from the "common underlying proficiency" of Cummins (1989) and the "central operating system" of Baker (1996). In our view the CUCB consists of mainly culture-specific rather than universal and neutral concepts.

Dodson and Thomas (1988) conducted a 3-year longitudinal experiment with monolinguals (Welsh or English), developing bilinguals (Welsh–English) and competent bilinguals (Welsh–English) with Welsh–English bilinguals who attended six different types of schools: English- and Welsh-medium schools, mixed language schools unstreamed for language, mixed language schools streamed for language (Welsh or English), and bilingual education schools. The students were tested over a period of 3 years at ages 5, 6, and 7. A great variety of tests were used to measure the level of concept development of each child: Piagetian tests of Conversation and Classification, tests of addition, subtraction, and seriation, the Goodenough–Harris Draw-a-Man/Woman test, the Wechsler I.Q. subtests (Animal House and Block Design), and the Wechsler Coding-A test (Dodson & Thomas, 1988, p. 467). On the basis of information obtained by means of questionnaires sent to parents children were categorized as "preferred-language Welsh or preferred/only-language English" (there being no monoglot Welsh; Dodson & Thomas, 1988, p. 469). The preferred language represents the individual children's general preferred language, which is an aggregate of their language use in all major areas of their life. Dodson and Thomas noted that there was one exception: interactions with teachers in school; for a number of children the general preferred language was not the same as the language of education and classroom interactions. Comparing the results of the Welsh preferred-language children with that of the English preferred/English only-language children they found that the latter group performed significantly better on the Piagetian conservation tests at ages 5 and 6. But the Welsh preferred-language children caught up in this group of tests in the third year. Dodson and Thomas (1988) suggested that

> One possible explanation for the superiority of the English preferred-language or monolingual group over the Welsh preferred-language group lies in the nature of the languages themselves; it might be argued that Welsh is not as efficient an instrument as English for general communication, and therefore of less help for Welsh preferred-language children in their development towards the formation of stable concepts than English is for English preferred-language or monolingual children. (p. 479)

Dodson and Thomas acknowledged that there is no concrete evidence for this so it would be a mistake to emphasize the superiority of one language over the other in any respect. Their results, however, can be used to argue for the language-specificity of the CUCB. The language in which concept development occurs can significantly influence the nature, content and structure of the CUCB. Consequently, only a part of the CUCB is language and culture-neutral, that is universal. The CUCB contains mainly language/culture-specific elements, many of which can be made available through both channels.

It is important to note that knowledge and skills are usually relatively easy to neutralize. A skill or knowledge acquired through one language channel may be almost immediately ready to be used through the other language channel as well, especially if there are appropriate lexical items to express them. We assume that neutralization depends mainly on two variables: nature of the knowledge or concept and the pressure of the environment. The first can be illustrated by any concrete concept or piece of knowledge about the world. The second, however, is more complicated. The CUCB is not a static system but a container whose content constantly changes under the influence of the outside world. The more often concepts need to be embodied in words the stronger their blueprints are carved into the mind, and vice versa—the less frequently they are used the more opaque they become. This phenomenon is connected with code mixing and code switching and is explained by the peculiar relation of word and thought, discussed in the next chapter. Here an example will do. Let us take, for instance, a balanced bilingual (if there is anything like that)[6] family whose L1 is Hungarian and whose L2 is American English. They live in the United States and although they communicate in Hungarian at home, they use American English concepts in their Hungarian speech production. These concepts do not have Hungarian labels, and their use in Hungarian speech does not bother anyone because each member of the family experiences the same environment where the use of these concepts is essential. Word mixing seems to be a natural phenomenon in this environment, which does not force the speakers to neutralize those concepts or knowledge. The situation changes when the family members spend some time in Hungary. There they can choose from several options. They can avoid using American English-based concepts and knowledge in their Hungarian speech, but that might be rather painful sometimes when speaking about their American experience because those concepts and knowledge are badly needed. They must make an attempt to neutralize those concepts and knowledge, that is, make them available through the other language channel. They can try to find a close Hungarian equivalent, or they can explain and describe using the Hungarian language.

As noted earlier, Cummins' interdependence hypothesis claims that literacy skills gained in Lx will support the development of literacy skills in Ly. The Hungarian experiment (Kecskes & Papp, 1995; Papp, 1991) demonstrated that certain writing skills and language-manipulating skills are also transferable between the FL and the mother tongue. In contrast to knowledge and skills, as discussed previously, concepts cause trouble. When a new concept gets into the CUCB, it is generally not neutralized but is kept intact. It is not deprived of the language- and culture-specific information that goes with it. Balanced bilinguals and advanced L2 learners do not have a problem with this because the clearer the attached information is, the firmer the concept becomes in the mind. When they need to use a concept, they know exactly what word to look for as a possible representation for the concept in the lexicon of the appropriate language channel. What about foreign language learners? Do they also have a CUCB? According to Cook's (1992) multicompetence theory, they do. It seems to be appropriate, however, to look at what Cummins and others say about this issue before a firm answer is given to the question.

---

[6]Although we argued earlier that a balanced bilingual may not exist because one of the languages is always dominant, we keep the term for practical reasons and use it as applied in the bilingual literature: to refer to bilinguals who have achieved advanced proficiency in both languages.

The theory of common underlying proficiency of Cummins (1984) was developed to explain bilingual educational attainment and school achievement. The LPD with two or more channels and a CUCB, however, serves to explain multilingual competence and language processing (Kecskes, 1998). At first glance neither the CUP nor the CUCB have much to do with FL learning because the conceptual base of a FL learner is dominated by the L1. The FL is usually not developed enough to function as a channel through which knowledge and skills may be fed into the conceptual base. Moreover, words learned in the FL do not have their direct representation in the conceptual base but are connected to L1 concepts through their L1 equivalents. This is what Weinreich (1953/1968) called a *subordinative* type of relation between word and concept. The L2 word is just a simple code that is linked to a conceptual representation through the corresponding L2 word.

The thresholds theory postulated first by Toukomaa and Skutnabb-Kangas (1977) and by Cummins (1976, 1979, 1984) to explain research findings on cognition and bilingualism can help us decide the question whether FL learning has any effect on the conceptual base or not. The theory distinguishes two thresholds, each representing a level of language competence that has consequences for the learner. The first threshold must be reached so as to avoid the negative consequences of bilingualism. Beyond the second threshold children have age-appropriate competence in both languages and are expected to have cognitive benefits from bilingualism. Although research basically supports the thresholds theory (cf. Bialystok, 1988; Clarkson, 1992; Clarkson & Galbraith, 1992; Swain & Lapkin, 1982; Swain, Lapkin, Rowen, & Hart 1991), it has been widely criticized because it is not clear how to define the level of language proficiency, for example, what the threshold might be in linguistic terms. However, empirical data in the studies suggested transfer of knowledge and learning processes across languages and that well-developed L1 literacy entails cognitive benefits for the acquisition of subsequent languages. The threshold hypothesis was supported by the Hungarian experiment as well, but in the opposite direction. In the immersion and intensive classes, knowledge developed in the L2 was transferred to L1 activities, but this transfer did not occur in the control class where students could not reach the second threshold in the FL. Although the threshold levels are only hypothetical, our findings also tend to demonstrate that it is relevant to talk about thresholds even if these levels cannot be determined linguistically.

The existence of thresholds slightly modifies the multicompetence theory because multicompetence seems to begin to develop only after a certain threshold in the subsequent language is reached. Before that, FL learning is likely to be no more than just a kind of educational enhancement that hardly affects cognitive development and does not result in the development of a multilingual LPD with a CUCB. Our findings (Kecskes, 1998;

Kecskes & T. Papp, 1995; T. Papp, 1991) demonstrated that multicompetence develops when the bidirectional interaction and interdependence between the L1 and Lx results in a CUCB as well as an integrated language system with two channels, neither of which is exactly the same as the monolingual system.

SUMMARY

In this chapter we argued that multilinguals have a unique language processing device that consists of a common underlying conceptual base and two or more constantly available interacting systems, none of which is the same as the language system of a monolingual. A German-English bilingual, for instance, has a German language system that is different from the language system of a monolingual German native speaker and an English language system that differs from that of an English native speaker. This difference can be explained by the existence of the CUCB and the constant interaction of the two language channels. The CUCB is the result of the multilingual conceptual development and consequently is not language independent. Concepts, knowledge, and skills get into the CUCB through both channels and very often keep their language- and culture-specific features. Beyond-threshold-level competence in both languages ensures a relatively free use of the content of the CUCB through both channels.

To explain what happens in the multicompetent mind and what the nature and content of CUCB are, we have to accept a limited form of linguistic relativism. This, however, does not mean that language- and culture-specificity of concepts is lost in the CUCB. Sante (1997) wrote about his experience as follows:

> The first thing you have to understand about my childhood is that it mostly took place in another language. I was raised speaking French, and did not begin learning English until I was nearly seven years old. Even after that, French continued to be the language I spoke at home with my parents. [I still speak only French with them to this day.] This fact inevitably affects my recall and evocation of my childhood, since I am writing and primarily thinking in English. There are states of mind, even people and events, that seem inaccessible in English, since they are defined by the character of the language through which I perceived them. My second language has turned out to be my principal tool, my means for making a living, and it lies close to the core of my self-definition. My first language, however, is coiled underneath, governing a more primal realm. (p. 123)

Santa explained how and why the word "coffee" is English and "sirup" is French in his mind. Investigating conceptual representation in the bilingual memory van Hell and de Groot (1998) also came to the conclusion that ". . . verbs may often be represented in language-specific conceptual stores, whereas nouns more often share a conceptual representation in the memory of bilinguals"(p. 7).

Psychologists tend to accept that the role of language in a child's gradual development toward the formation of stable concepts is more decisive than Piaget and his followers thought. Even Piaget (1968), who claimed that logical operations were "coordinations among actions before they are transposed into verbal form so that language cannot account for their formation," goes on to underline that "language indefinitely extends the power of these operations and confers on them a mobility and a universality which they would not have otherwise . . ." (p. 93). The real question, however, is not whether a particular thought can be expressed in another language or not. The supporters of the intertranslatability maxim were right when they argued that basically anything that can be said in one language can also be said in any other one. The question is to what extent, and with what precision, this can be accomplished. Cognitive research demonstrated that there is a certain dominance of the language in which cognitive development was completed. If so, the fluent use of the L2 in the multilingual LPD is possible only if speakers make adjustments in order that the partly language-specific knowledge can be used through the L2 channel too. Consequently, the real issue is how this can be done. How can thoughts generated in one language be transferred to another language, and what particular efforts do speakers need to make to create a new concept in the target language, reconceptualize, or simply relabel? These issues are discussed in the next chapter.

CHAPTER

4

Thought and Word

THE CONCEPTUAL-LINGUISTIC INTERFACE

The bilingual–multilingual language processing device (LPD) is a unique symbiosis of two or more languages with a common underlying conceptual base (CUCB) and two or more separate linguistic channels, each of which has less independence than a monolingual system because there is constant interaction among the channels at each level. Although bilinguals may seem functionally monolingual in most aspects of their language processing, the constant interaction of the channels of their LPD may result in a language behavior (either overt or covert) distinct from that of the monolingual (Kasper & Blum-Kulka, 1993; Kecskes, 1998; Yoshida, 1990). In the following chapters we discuss the relation of preverbal thought generated in the multilingual mind to lower and higher level linguistic units such as word, sentence, and discourse. To put it another way, we attempt to explain the processes preverbal thought goes through while it is embodied in words, sentences, and discourse units. Why is an explanation such as this needed in a book about multilingualism, especially about the effect of foreign language (FL) learning on the mother tongue skills? The answer is simple: We want to discuss not only the already existing findings but further perspectives for research as well. This endeavor requires to describe how thought and word are interrelated in the multilingual mind.

The distinction between conceptualization (i.e., intended message) and verbal formulation implies that there must be a mapping between the conceptual representation and the selection of word meanings. Green (1993) suggested that such a mapping might differ between languages because languages differ in terms of how concepts are lexicalized. Russian, for instance, has only one word жена for the concept "wife," whereas Japanese has two words to denote that concept depending on whether the reference to the speaker's wife comes from the speaker himself—*kanai*—or from his interlocutor—*okusan*.

How does preverbal thought (i.e., message) become lexicalized in the bilingual–multilingual LPD? What is the relation between thought and word in multilinguals? Do people knowing two or more languages think differently from those who know only one? Seeking answers to these questions, most researchers have attempted to use a monolingual perspective developed by specialists interested only in monocompetence, with nothing or very little to do with multicompetence (cf. Jackendoff, 1990, 1991; Levelt, 1989; Levin & Pinker, 1991; Talmy, 1985). Monolingual theories postulate conceptual primitives such as MOTION, FIGURE, PATH, MANNER, GROUND, and CAUSE. There is no one-to-one match between the conceptual primitives and surface elements in a language. A single conceptual primitive can be expressed by a combination of elements on the surface, and a particular combination of conceptual primitives can be expressed by a single surface element (De Bot & Schreuder, 1993). According to monolingual theories, as discussed earlier, conceptual structure and preverbal message are not language and culture specific. When describing multicompetence most researchers keep this assumption in mind, and it is unavoidable for them to try to solve the problem of how language is assigned to the language-independent preverbal message. They must find something that supports lexicalization. For Bierwisch and Schreuder (1992), this something is the *VBL* (i.e., *verbalizer*). It is the VBL's function to find out what can be expressed in a given language. However, even with the VBL, supporters of a language-independent CUCB get into difficulties when trying to explain lexicalization. They must acknowledge some kind of language assignment in the CUCB, and the preverbal message has to contain information about which language is to be used. As De Bot and Schreuder (1993) explained, "the VBL extracts language choice information from the preverbal message and divides the message into chunks that can be lexicalized" (p. 205).

We assume that in order to solve the problem of mapping thoughts onto words we must do two things. First, we must develop a multilingual approach to replace the monolingual perspective. Second, we assume that the CUCB is not language and culture independent. As discussed previously, concepts and images in the mind are the results of the sociocultural development of the individual. Because most concepts evolve in communication with the environment, language and culture play a decisive role in their formulation (cf. Pavlenko, 1996). As discussed earlier, languages predispose their speakers to conceptualize experience. In order to understand the roles of the sociocultural environment and language in concept formation one needs to adapt Vygotsky's (1962) approach, which insisted that thought and word are inseparable because they are two sides of one thing and when taken separately neither of them possesses the properties of the whole. From this perspective it is crucial to describe how the conceptualizer connects to the formulator. According to Levelt (1989), the conceptualizer has two levels, the macrolevel and the microlevel. Neither level is language specific in the monolingual theory, but this approach can be used to accommodate language assignment in the multilingual speaker. De Bot (1993) argued that the macrolevel, where intention originates, is language independent, whereas the microlevel, where thought is shaped, is language specific.

Bringing together Vygotsky's, Levelt's, and De Bot's ideas we have come to the conclusion that it is the microlevel of the conceptualizer where the interaction of thought and words takes place. When thought is being formed there must already be an interaction between the chunks of message and the words it will be embodied in. This interaction finalizes the shape of the verbal message. Vygotsky quotes O. Mandelstam: "I have forgotten the word I intended to say, and my thought, unembodied, returns to the realm of shadows" (cited by Vygotsky, 1962, p. 119). Conceptualization and verbal formulation are united through thought and word, which are amalgamated through word meaning. The relation between thought and word is a process, "a continual movement back and forth from thought to word and from word to thought. Thought is not merely expressed in words; it comes into existence through them" (Vygotsky, 1962, p. 125). Because thought and word are not cut from one pattern, there are more differences than likenesses between them. Speakers cannot put thoughts on words directly like ready-made units because, as Vygotsky said, "the structure of speech does not simply mirror the structure of thought" (p. 126).

As a result of the thought–word interaction, thought usually undergoes several changes as it turns into speech. The same can be said about the word. Word meaning changes depending on the neighboring words in the utterance and as required by the context in which it appears. The result of this process is the sense of the word that is gained from the context.[1] Let us take an example:

A. While driving home Mr. Brown hit a cat on the road.
B. We must hit the road soon if we don't want to be late for the wedding.

The knowledge of the English language supplies the word meaning, and the knowledge of the world supplies the sense of the word in the given context. The word meaning of *hit* in the dictionary is as follows: "1. to come in con-

---

[1]We often ask, "In what sense is this word used in the sentence?"

tact with forcefully; to strike; 2. To cause to make sudden and forceful contact; to knock; to bump" (Morris, 1976, p. 625). The sense of the word in sentence A is "to kill something by car," and in sentence B, "set out." Vygotsky (1962) said that a word in context means both more and less than the same word without context. It means more because the word acquires new content from its environment. It means less because the context limits and narrows its potential word meaning. The relation between sense and word is much looser than between word meaning and word. Sense keeps changing synchronically because it is shaped by the actual thought. Word meaning changes diachronically. Sometimes it takes words decades to change their meaning. For example, the words *gay* or *cool* had different primary word meanings in the 1950s than they have now. Before discussing the thought–word relation in the bilingual–multilingual LPD we have to look at what contemporary semantic theory says about this relation.

CONCEPT AND WORD IN LINGUISTIC THEORY

In theoretical linguistics there has been an important change since the beginning of the 1980s because a number of linguists have come around to the view that the lexicon is the central component of a person's internal grammar, with the syntax as subsidiary (Hudson, 1984). Chomsky claimed that parametric variation takes place in the lexicon (Chomsky, 1986, 1989). With the appearance of corpus linguistics (Sinclair, 1987, 1991), cognitive linguistics (Langacker, 1990; Nuyts, 1992), several monographs on the acquisition of the lexicon in psycholinguistics (Lehrer & Kittay, 1992; Aitchison, 1994; Gleitman & Landau, 1994) and the revival of functional linguistics (Dik, 1980; Dressler & Barbaresi, 1994) the lexicon has taken its deserved place in linguistic analysis. Following linguistic theory current L1 acquisition theory has been focusing on a lexically based framework. The lexical learning hypothesis proposes that lexical items, along with their properties, trigger the reconstruction of a child's grammar; that is, grammars are lexically driven (see, e.g., Clahsen, 1992; Klein, 1995; Weisenborn, Goodluck & Roeper, 1992). According to the new approach the conceptual system that emerges from everyday human experience is the basis for natural-language semantics, and word meanings may not apply at all outside the relevant background assumptions since meaning and its frame are inseparable from one another (Sweetser, 1990). Meaning is rooted in human cognitive experience: experience of cultural, social, mental, and physical worlds. Consequently, background knowledge that constitutes frames for meaning is as important as language structure in shaping meaning of linguistic signs. This approach confirms what Vygotsky suggested: there is a unique symbiosis between thought and word. They are united through meaning, which is the result of their interaction.

Conceptualization in the L1

Because L1 vocabulary researchers have made impressive progress in learning about conceptualization, it makes sense to consider what this research has to say about concept formation (Cruse, 1990, 1992; Gleitman & Landau, 1994; Grimshaw, 1994; Lakoff, 1987; Lakoff, G. & Johnson, 1980; Lehrer & Kittay, 1992; Pinker, 1994; Ross, 1992; Sweetser, 1991).

Concept and Word. The nature of the human conceptual system is currently a matter of conjecture and controversy. Our conceptual competence in various respects, subsists in our linguistic competence and is not separate from it (Ross, 1992). The conceptual system and linguistic system are related through the interdependence of concepts and words.

Most of the controversy centers on the question of how concepts and words are related to one another. A natural language possesses an inventory of lexical forms, and these are mapped onto the concept network (Cruse, 1992). However, lexical items cannot be simply equated with concepts. Concepts are represented by words, but this representation is rather contradictory. The contradiction is caused by three issues. First, the human mind has a central meaning for a concept and relates variations to this central meaning. Certain concepts are treated as archetypes, and others are seen in relation to these central concepts (Cook, 1997). Rosch (1977) postulated a prototype theory, claiming that the mind puts objects into three levels. The *basic level* contains those objects that people notice immediately when they look at the world around them, such as chair, tree, and house. These central prototypes are the ones already encountered. When we look at a street, for instance, we tend to see things as cars, houses, and shops, not just sheer shapes and forms. This is how our world is organized in our minds. Above the basic level we have a *superordinate level*, and below it there is a *subordinate level*. The superordinate level is labeled by more general terms, which are abstractions and are not directly available to our eyes. The subordinate level is labeled by more specialized categories. Cook (1997) argued that "the mind sees the world in three levels of abstraction going from the most general to the most specific, with the basic level coming in the middle as the most useful everyday term" (p. 91). For instance:

Superordinate:	vehicle	furniture
Basic:	car	chair
Subordinate:	four-wheel drive	armchair

Second, the overall concept usually extends beyond the sections labeled with a word. (Basically, this was claimed by Vygotsky also.) The conceptual content comprises background knowledge that is part of the native speaker's sociocultural heritage. This makes many concepts language specific. The Hungarian word *ebéd*, for instance, is usually given as an equivalent of English *lunch*. This is definitely correct, if we ignore the sociocultural differences, but the Hungarian concept denoted by the word *ebéd* comprises the main meal of the day that is functionally more comparable to American *dinner* than to *lunch*.

Third, word meaning also contains specific properties that are not present in the concept. These word-specific semantic properties make it possible for speakers to have alternative lexical access routes to a single concept. Cruse (1992) argued that cognitive synonyms map onto identical concepts. The meaning properties that differentiate cognitive synonyms like *give up; capitulate, surrender,* and *chicken out* [2] can be viewed as properties of the individual lexical units, distinct from properties of the common concept. Word-specific semantic properties include such things as emotive coloring and various kinds of contextual affinities (see Cruse, 1990, for a more detailed discussion of word-specific semantic properties). According to the view developed by Cruse (1990, 1992), lexical semantic relations (i.e., word-specific semantic properties) are opposed to conceptual semantic relations. For instance, if the word *surrender* serves to activate the concept "surrender" directly, without modulatory effect, whereas the words *chicken out* (i.e., "to act in a cowardly manner") activate the same concept but with a modulatory effect, then the words *chicken out* stand in a meaning relation to the word *surrender*. Each member of the synonymy group underlines a different side of the same concept "surrender": *Give up* implies the activity of the agent, whereas *capitulate* involves surrender under prearranged conditions. Consequently, the whole meaning of a word comprises the associated concept (together with its pattern of connections within the concept network) plus any word-specific properties. Thought and word are united through meaning.

Words differ from one another in terms of word-specific semantic properties. Cruse talks about the *plain word*, which does not have any word-specific semantic properties, and the *charged word*, which has semantic distinguishing features.[3] The problem with Cruse's approach is that in unbound discourse very often the situation itself charges a word (Kecskes, 1997, in press).

A. Please bring that parcel here.
   Sorry, it's too heavy. I cannot *move it*. (plain word)
B. We need that book ASAP. Go and get it.
   OK, I am on my way.
   Move it. (situationally charged word)

---

[2]These are our examples and not Cruse's.

[3]In an earlier work (Kecskes, 1994), I referred to words with specific semantic properties as *loaded words*. This is exactly the same concept that Cruse referred to as *charged words*. When I wrote that article I did not know about Cruse's paper yet.

Words can get charged in two ways: They either have word-specific semantic properties in their word meanings (e.g., *chicken out*) or get charged in the situation where they are used (see example B). Because this difference is significant we suggest the two word types be distinguished by different labels: When a word has word-specific semantic properties in its word meaning it should be called a *loaded word* (e.g., *pass away*–"die"; *chicken out*–"surrender"), and when a word's basic semantic function is extended pragmatically to cover other referents or meanings (as in example B) the word should be labeled as a charged word.

Concept Formation. Brooks (1978) argued that the L1

> learner is likely initially to acquire a concept representation based upon a particular instance. This may be the first instance encountered by the learner, and thus it may not necessarily be a "best" instance. Subsequent encounters with other instances bring about changes that may alter the stored representation of the concept toward the direction of typicality. However, such changes will continue to depend upon the particular instances and situations encountered by the learner. (p. 68)

Because the learner does not acquire the concept at the first encounter, several other encounters of the same concept in various contexts should follow until the concept is firmly established in the learner's mind. Gagné (1977) claimed that "concrete concepts that are learned by young children are often given fuller meaning and greater precision when they are later brought to the formal level (as defined concepts) by learning in school" (p. 99). Thus, concepts in the L1 are not learned; rather, they grow. Conceptual content constantly changes under the influence of input and the environment. The more frequently the learner is exposed to a certain word in the input, the more firmly the concept becomes established in the mind. However, the development of meaning relations between words and concepts is more than a simple clustering of meaning aspects. As Vygotsky (1962) pointed out,

> . . . word meanings evolve. When a new word has been learned by the child, its development is barely starting: the word at first is a generalization of the most primitive type; as the child's intellect develops, it is replaced by generalizations of a higher and higher type—a process that leads in the end to the formation of true concepts. (p. 83)

The development of concepts and word meanings occurs simultaneously in the first language. Conceptualization is supported by the sociocultural environment, which is responsible for the background knowledge that is as important as linguistic input for the proper development of concepts. As explained previously, conceptual content is usually broader than word meaning content, but this broad conceptual domain is not represented as a whole in every occurrence of the word denoting the concept. A word in an utterance represents only one possible occurrence of the concept and, in most cases, highlights only one particular part of the conceptual domain. For example:

A. Please hear me out.
   OK, but hurry up because I don't have much time.
B. I didn't hear any noise last night because I was sleeping.
C. If I were you I wouldn't go there.
   Okay, I hear you.

These examples represent one concept, but each occurrence highlights different aspects of that concept.

Linguistic General Relativity (LGR). Lakoff (1972) argued that "natural language concepts have vague boundaries and fuzzy edges" (p. 183), which makes it extremely difficult to characterize entries in the mental lexicon. True definitions are rare occurrences in word meanings. Putnam (1975) estimated a few hundred in English, and even these are under contention (Lakoff, 1987). LGR means that every meaning element depends synchronically on every other (Ross, 1992), and the value or sense of a meaning element (i.e., its particular meaning) depends on what it is combined with and in what perlocutionary role. Ross suggested that widely accepted views of the componentiality of utterance meaning be rejected because

> we are not combining fixed meaning-values (like fixed quantities) under a single structural syntax, but are combining varying values in a syntax-affecting way. Instead of the notion of units of meaning combined by insertion into syntactical slots to make sentential wholes, we have meaning units whose identity depends reciprocally on which meaning-units they combine with, so as to determine a semantic whole that has a definite syntactic structure as a result of the semantic adjustment. Thus, the explanatory order is exactly the reverse of what is usually supposed. (p. 145)

If we accept this approach we have to completely reorganize language teaching by focusing on meaning units rather than syntactic structures. Meaning units, in a particular combination, require a certain syntactic structure, and, in another combination, they require a different syntactic structure (cf. Sinclair, 1991). Language teaching methodology usually works with fixed meaning values. That is why students frequently say, "I can understand each word in this sentence but don't know what the sentence means." This declaration is the result of a sentence-centered, fixed meaning unit-based approach (Kecskes, 1997). Criticizing the modern view on semantics Leibniz (1903, as cited in Wierzbicka, 1993, p. 9), who said that "if nothing can be understood by itself nothing at all can ever be understood." Other languages and cultures can be understood to the extent to which we can rely on shared concepts. Wierzbicka argued that we need a natural semantic metalanguage that can help us define other concepts and explain the difference between concepts belonging to different cultures. FL learning needs to rely on word definitions because the L1 experience in which concepts usually go through a long evolving process cannot be repeated. Concepts do not evolve in the FL but are usually learned. There is not enough input and context for FL learners to form an experimental multimodal representation that goes beyond word definition and forms a concept (Kecskes, 1995; Pavlenko, 1998a).

Lexical Representation. One of the crucial questions of FL learning is how a learner arrives at the lexical representation for the verb in a sentence. Two ideas form the focus of a large amount of current research on the question. Pinker (1989) proposed that the analysis of the situation can make it possible to determine the meaning of a word and that the meaning of a word in turn makes it possible to determine its lexical syntax. According to the second idea (Fischer Gleitman, & Gleitman, 1991; Gleitman, 1990; Gleitman & Landau, 1997) the analysis of the sentence makes it possible to determine (parts of) its semantics. Grimshaw (1994) argued that neither the situation nor the argument structure is enough to determine the meaning of a word in a sentence—usually both are needed. The argument structure is not enough because of the existence of large numbers of many-to-one semantics-to-syntax mappings. For example, the set of verbs that subcategorize for noun phrases is both enormous and extremely disparate semantically (Grimshaw, 1994):

A. Jim weighed the peaches.
   Jim weighed 186 pounds.
B. Mary asked me the time.
   Mary asked me a question.

Pinker (1994) argued that if someone were to hear, "I glipped the paper to shreds," presumably he or she could figure out that *glip* means something like "tear" because of the semantics of *paper* and *shreds*. In other words, inferring that *glip* means "glip" from hearing *paper* and *shreds* is a kind of cognitive inference using knowledge of real-world contingencies, the same that could be used to infer that *glip* means "glip" when seeing paper as being glipped to shreds. What Pinker talks about usually works, but not always. There are many verbs that collocate with the same words but have different meanings depending on their argument structure. For example:

A. When the boys noticed me they stopped talking.
   When the boys noticed me they stopped to talk.
B. Please remember to close the windows before you leave.
   Don't worry. I remember closing the windows before I left.

These examples support Grishaw, who argues that both situation and argument structure are needed to determine the meaning of a word in the sentence.

Having discussed the nature of the CUCB and how concepts and words are interrelated, we next go further in the direction of the surface production and examine how the mental lexicon is organized in multilinguals.

DEVELOPMENT OF THE MENTAL LEXICON IN MULTILINGUALS

How Do FL Learners Acquire New Words?

Vocabulary development in the multicompetent speaker shows considerable differences in comparison with the monolingual speaker. Ushakova (1994) argued that the L2 is incorporated into the classification system already available in the L1 and relies on the previously developed semantic system. What happens when adult FL learners start to learn new words in the target language? It is conceivable that they will relate a word in the FL to its translation equivalent in the L1 and will do so by constructing a lexical link between the two words. Encountering a new word in the FL, the learner tries to reach into the conceptual base to find the concept the foreign word denotes. Because the conceptual system of the learner is L1 based, the right concept can be reached only through a word that denotes the concept in the L1. Consequently, there can hardly be any direct route between the foreign word and the concept at that phase of development. The only way for the FL learner to reach the concept is through the L1 translation equivalent:

FL word → L1 translation equivalent → L1 concept

cukor (Hungarian)   *sugar* (English)   "sugar"

Weinreich (1953) discussed this type of organization of word knowledge referring to it as *subordinative*. His approach is similar to that of the word association model suggested by Potter et al. (1984). Both Weinreich and Potter et al. acknowledged that this model is transitional only. Whereas Weinreich assumed that the subordinative type develops eventually into a coordinate type, Potter et al. suggested that the developmental shift takes place to the compound type or, as it is called, to the concept mediation model. The difference between the compound and coordinate systems was first described by Ervin and Osgood (1954), who claimed that the development of either system is facilitated by the environment in which the bilingual development takes place. They assumed that compound bilinguals have one concept denoted by different words in the L1 and the FL. This type of bilingualism develops in a FL environment or in a L2 environment where both languages are spoken more or less interchangeably. The coordinate system where both the L1 word and the FL word have their own conceptual representations develops when a person uses L1 at home and L2 at work or acquires L2 in a different cultural setting. It seems to be quite difficult to justify the coordinate system because the representational space is not wasted by storing the same or similar concept twice, once in each language (De Groot, 1993). Earlier we also refuted the existence of a coordinate system by arguing that multilinguals have an LPD with a CUCB.

From the perspective of FL learning we accept the dichotomy of the word association model and the concept mediation model (Potter et al., 1984) and agree with Kroll (1993), who argued that in adult FL learners there is a development shift from the word association model to the concept mediation model. The existence of the word association model and the concept mediation model and the developmental relation between them seem to justify the findings of the Hungarian experiment, described in Chapter 2, which led to the conclusion that only after reaching a certain threshold in the FL can we speak about the development of multicompetence. The threshold in this development is represented by the developmental shift from word association to concept mediation. Consequently, multicompetence, as understood here, is connected to concept mediation. When words from the FL develop direct links to the concepts in the CUCB, we can claim that the speaker possesses multicompetence.

Some other studies (cf. Chen & Leung, 1989; Kroll & Curley, 1988) based on picture naming and word translation also demonstrated that the lexical representations are dominant when adult FL learners are in an early phase of FL learning. This means that FL words are mediated through the L1. As their fluency in the FL increases, learners rely more on concept mediation between the two languages than they do at an earlier stage of their language development and can integrate meaning across languages. However, the transition from word association to concept mediation is a long process, and word association remains active as a parallel form of vocabulary development.[4] Several studies experimenting with bilingual translation (Kroll, 1993; Kroll & Stewart, 1990, 1992) came to the conclusion that transla-

---

[4] Our own experience as trilinguals seems to support this unique feature of multicompetence. Whenever we encounter a completely new word in English, French, or Russian we often access the concept by trying to find the Hungarian translation equivalent first.

tion from L2 to L1 is reliably faster than translation from L1 to L2. Kroll (1993) explained this asymmetry by suggesting that translation from L2 into L1 can be done on a lexical basis, whereas translation from L1 into L2 requires concept mediation. As mentioned previously, Kroll (1993, p. 69) developed a model of the bilingual hierarchical memory (i.e., revised hierarchical model) that takes into account both the asymmetry in translation and the developmental shift from word association to concept mediation.

We adapted the model for FL learners. The model suggests that in adult FL learners the L1 lexicon is substantially larger than the FL lexicon. Another important feature of the model is that it emphasizes that the strength of connections between the L1 and FL lexicons and between each lexicon and the conceptual system varies as a function of relative fluency in the FL and relative language dominance (Kroll, 1993). The higher the fluency is in the FL, the stronger the connection is between the FL word and the appropriate concept in the CUCB and the less the learner has to rely on L1 word association. Lexical connections from the FL to the L1 are stronger than from the L1 to the FL. Kroll explained this asymmetry by noting that FL words are usually taught by associating them to L1 words but not vice versa. This seems to support our hypothesis that the CUCB is not language independent and is usually dominated by the stronger language of the multilingual speaker. The asymmetry in lexical mappings means that each FL word is likely to have a mapping to the L1, whereas only a few L1 entries are likely to have mappings to the L2. Conceptual links for the L1 are stronger than for the FL. At a higher level of fluency conceptual mappings are possible for the FL, but these links are usually weaker than those for the L1. This is a clear consequence of the fact that the conceptual system is metaphorically structured as a result of L1 development. The growth of FL proficiency brings about changes in the CUCB. Better fluency in the FL requires reconceptualization, neutralization, and modification in the metaphorical structure of the system to accommodate new information.

Kroll's model suggests that in the LPD of a bilingual there are both lexical and conceptual connections between the two languages but the strength of these links differs. With the increase of fluency in the FL, the reliance on conceptual mediation between the two languages grows, although lexical connections remain active all the time. In L1 acquisition conceptual development and lexical development progress simultaneously, but this is not the case in multilingual development, especially if the L2 acquisition occurs after early childhood. The more L1-based the conceptual system is, the more difficult it is for the FL learner to reach the state of concept mediation in the FL. In the first language the word serves to activate the concept either directly without modulatory effect, such as *die* → "die," or with a modulatory effect like *pass away* → "die." This process is the same in the FL only if there is a one-to-one mapping between the L1 concept and the target language concept (which occurs very rarely), and the target language word is not charged. For example:

Bring me a chair, please.
Hozz nekem egy széket kérlek. (Hungarian)

When there is no one-to-one mapping, the FL word activates the L1 concept with its language-specific semantic and pragmatic properties. This usually leads to mistakes and misunderstandings. American students, for instance, usually have a very difficult time figuring out the meaning of the Russian utterance, "Где ты пропадал?" The target language word пропадать activates the L1 concept "disappear," which can be represented by several words: *disappear, be missing, be lost, vanish*, none of which has the same word-specific semantic and pragmatic properties as the Russian word does. пропадать in that context expresses a certain kind of resentment of the speaker, so the best translation seems to be the following: "Where on earth have you been?" Differences in the concept network and word-specific semantic properties between the two languages lead to a number of difficulties, discussed in the following sections.

Conceptual Level

Difficulties at the conceptual level are connected with the type of concept representations in the CUCB. Three concept representation types can be distinguished: one-language concepts, decompositional concepts, and universal concepts. A one-language concept requires the development of a new concept in the CUCB, whereas decompositional concepts require reconceptualization. Universal concepts and closely related decompositional concepts call for relabeling only, which is a lexical rather than a conceptual process.

Forming a New Concept. As said before, there are concepts that exist in the target language but cannot be found in the mother tongue of the language learners. It is hard to find equivalents in Hungarian, Japanese, Russian, or other languages to English concepts like, for example, "sweepstakes," "potluck," and others. Yet language learners have few problems because new concepts are easy to develop if there is a clear explanation of their content with the necessary background information.

Reconceptualization. The real challenge for bilingual or multilingual development occurs when an existing concept has to be modified to accommodate a similar concept from another language. Reconceptualization takes place with decompositional concepts: A modified conceptual domain has two labels, one in the L1 and another in the L2. Sometimes there is an equivalent, but it is slightly different in the second language, such as "morning"—*Reggel* (Hungarian): Утро (Russian). This phenomenon is usually based on sociocultural differences or divergences in conceptual semantic relations.

Divergences in conceptual semantic relations can be demonstrated by the semantic relations between English words describing parts of the day and Hungarian words describing the same phenomena:

"morning"   *hajnal, reggel, délelőtt*
"afternoon" *délután*
"evening"   *este*
"night"   *este, éjszaka*

The difference between Hungarian and English is especially articulated in the conceptualization of "morning." In English this concept can refer to a period from 12:00 am to 12:00 noon, whereas Hungarian divides this long period into three phases. *Hajnal*[5] refers to the time until the sun rises, *reggel* denotes the time between sunrise and around 9:00, and *délelőtt* is the period from around 9:00 to 12:00.

Kecskes (1995) conducted an experiment with Japanese learners of English to investigate the acquisition of verbs of speech (e.g., *talk, speak, tell, say, discuss*) and verbs of perception (e.g., *see, watch, notice, observe, perceive*). The semantic domain of perception and speech is less dissected in Japanese than in English. In Japanese in both groups there is a lexicopragmatic dichotomy. The speech verbs *iu* and *hanasu* have distinctive pragmatic domains. *Iu* is used for reported speech and speech acts not associated with a recipient. *Hanasu*, on the other hand, requires a recipient of the speech act and is used primarily to describe the speech interaction between two or more participants. In the verbs of perception group there is a lexicopragmatic dichotomy of *miru* and *kizuku*. *Miru* can stand for "look at," "see," and "watch." *Kizuku* can be equivalent to *notice*, but it is closer to *take notice of*. The difference between *miru* and *kizuku* is not only lexical but pragmatic as well. *Miru* describes intentional actions, whereas *kizuku* denotes unintentional, accidental actions. The experiment demonstrated that transfer from the native tongue concepts is very strong and little or no reconceptualization occurs. Japanese students look for English words that can describe best the concepts they have in their own language. If they do not find any, they usually make an intelligent guess or rely on syntactic clues to find an appropriate verb. They understand very little of the English intralingual differences. These findings concur with those of Ushakova

---

[5]To make things even more complicated, Hungarian *hajnal* has another possible English equivalent, *dawn*. The difference is that the English word refers to the process of the rising sun whereas the Hungarian word denotes the period between midnight and sunrise.

(1994), who argued that acquisition of L2 primarily consists of incorporating and plugging the newly established structures and lexical items into the ones worked out earlier, as well as employing already existing verbal skills.

Differences in the Metaphorical Structure. If the invariant of lexical semantic representations of a concept in the L1 has an equivalent in the target language, such as English *hit* equal to Russian бить, the language learners' task is not necessarily made easier because the metaphorical use of invariants differs to a great extent in each language. The equivalency of invariants is disturbing rather than supporting the acquisition process because, based on their L1 conceptual system, language learners want to give the same metaphorical functions to the target language invariant as the L1 invariant has. In the following situation both English *hit* and its Russian equivalent бить are used in their invariant function, representing the concept "hit."

A. Why did Bob want to hit you?
I have no idea. He was probably mad at me when I told the truth.
B. Почему Боб хотел побить тебя?
Я не знаю. наверно он рассердился, когда я сказал правду.

There is a kind of equivalency between the two words in their invariant function. If we look at the metaphorical domain they cover we will see great differences:

Hurry up. We must hit the road soon if we don't want to be late.
OK, I am coming.

In order to express this sense Russian needs another word:

Давай, спеши. Мы должны поехать скоро, если мы не хотим опоздать.
Ландо, иду.

This is true the other way around as well. Russian бить has a metaphorical domain that differs from that of English *hit*.

Его бьет лухорадка.   He is shivering with fever.

Lexical Level

Problems for L2 or FL learners occur not only at the conceptual level but also at the lexical level because lexical semantic representations of a concept can differ to a great extent in languages.

Relabeling. Relabeling occurs in the case of universal or closely related decompositional concepts that are usually the same or very similar in both languages. These concepts are at the basic level in Rosch's (1977) prototype theory. Concrete concepts usually have an equivalent in the target language so students have to acquire only the new label:

"Weather"

Weather (English)—*tenki* (Japanese)—*pogoda* (Russian)—*időjárás* (Hungarian).

Polysemy and Lexical Plurality. Polysemy in one language is lexical plurality (i.e., many distinct words) in another and vice versa. The English word *see* in Italian can be *vedere* or *osservare* or *scopire* or *comprendere* or *connoscere*. English *see, notice, observe,* and *perceive* can all be equivalent to the Italian *vedere*. The explanation of this phenomenon lies in the differences between the conceptual systems of the L1 and the target language. Words do not randomly acquire new senses in a language. New senses are acquired by cognitive structuring, and the multiple synchronic senses of a given word are normally related to each other in a motivated fashion (Sweetser, 1990). A great deal of polysemy is due to metaphorical usage, and the lack of systematic correlation between lexical items in the L1 and in the target language can be accounted for by differences in the metaphorical use of lexical items in the two languages.

Lexical Semantic Representations. As mentioned earlier, a concept can have several lexical semantic representations (e.g., "die" can be *die, pass away,* or *expire*) that differ from one another in word specific semantic and pragmatic properties. Even if we find a concept that exists in both languages we cannot be sure that the words denoting that particular concept have the same word-specific semantic or pragmatic properties. In fact, we can almost be sure that they do not have the same word-specific semantic properties. They are likely to be loaded in an entirely different way (Kecskes, 1994). From this perspective it is interesting to compare how English and Russian denote the concept "eat."

English words denoting the concept "eat" include *eat, consume, devour,* and *gorge.*
Russian words denoting the concept include есть, кушать, питаться, and жрать.

The closest equivalency is between the two relatively neutral words *eat* and Russian есть. It is much more difficult to find such close equivalency between the other lexical items because each has its own modulatory effect.

Pragmatic Ambiguity. Sweetser (1990) discussed pragmatic ambiguity, when a word's basic semantic function is extended pragmatically to cover other referents or word meanings.Pragmatic ambiguity may occur in the case of situationally charged words: The situation itself provides the word with some semantic or pragmatic property that, originally, is not a part of the semantic content of the word.

A. Sorry, I don't think I can agree with you at this point.
   OK, shoot.
B. Jim, I think you really did a wonderful job.
   Oh, get out of here.

In the conversations above the words *shoot* and *get out* are charged by the situations. This is where languages really differ from one another—in their figurative use. Each language has its own system of charging, and the systems are usually not compatible.

SUMMARY

Conceptualization and verbal formulation are connected through the unique symbiosis of thought and word, the interaction of which results in the meaning of the linguistic unit in question. The CUCB of multilinguals contains culture-specific elements and is dominated by one of the languages, usually by the one that is or was the carrier of cognitive development. Although concepts gradually grow in the L1, they are usually learned in the L2 because the new language is incorporated into the existing conceptual system. Depending on the circumstances of the acquisition of subsequent languages, new words learned in the L2 have access to the CUCB through word association and later through concept mediation as well. These two processes do not exclude each other; rather, they interact and coexist during multilingual development. Concept mediation, as we understand it, needs a certain modification of the existing L1-based concept for the new L2 concept to be accommodated in the CUCB properly. We called this process neutralization, and it may result in a concept that is neither exactly the L1 concept nor the L2 concept but may be something in between. Concepts developed in this way constitute the basis for the unique conceptual field of multilinguals that Yoshida (1990) called intercultural, and that can result in the development of a discourse style termed intercultural style by Kasper and Blum-Kulka (1993). We return to this issue in a later chapter.

The characteristics of the new L2 concept depend on how firmly the original L1-based concept was established in the CUCB. The fuzzier and the less developed the L1-based concept is, the easier it is to modify under the influence of the incoming L2 concept. When, for instance, a 9-year-old native speaker of Chinese comes to the United States as an immigrant, her L1-based CUCB is full of weakly established concepts because her basic cognitive and language development have not been completed yet. Those concepts are subject to change. It is thus crucial at what age and in what environment the acquisition of the L2 begins, what the content of acquisition is, and how intensive the acquisition process is. From our perspective it is important that the Hungarian experiment demonstrated that intensive FL learning and programs in which the FL is the medium of instruction can partly change word association for concept mediation. If such change happens, the FL may have a serious impact on the conceptual base of the learner.

CHAPTER

5

Transfer of Skills in the LPD

People using two or more languages have a common underlying conceptual base (CUCB) that functions like a warehouse for the knowledge obtained through the two language channels. The CUCB makes it possible for multicompetent speakers to transfer concepts, knowledge, and skills gained in one language to the other language channel. We assume that a differentiated approach is needed for each type of transfer. In the previous chapters an attempt was made to explain what facilitates concept and knowledge transfer. Now the focus is on skill transfer.

The experiment discussed in Chapter 2 demonstrated that students with intensive foreign language (FL) learning background (i.e., immersion class and intensive class) tend to be better at manipulating language for composing a text than their counterparts who were not exposed to a FL so intensively. Where does this better manipulation skill come from? What is the role of FL learning in the development of that skill? Can a skill gained through the FL channel be used in the first language (L1)? According to several studies (e.g., Ben-Zeev, 1997; Lauren, 1991; Peal & Lambert, 1962; Ricciardelli, 1992; Thomas, 1992), bilinguals are superior to monolinguals in manipulating language for their oral and written communicative purposes. Bilinguals differ from monolinguals in a very important way: For bilinguals linguistic experience is spread over two languages. The experience is encoded in either of the two languages and can be expressed in both languages, and the information representation can be transferred between the two languages (Malakoff, 1992). However, this transfer is possible only if the two language processing systems have a common underlying representation. The findings of the Hungarian experiment suggest that students who studied a FL intensively or were in a class where FL was used as a medium of instruction developed a language manipulation skill similar to that of bilinguals. Does this mean that intensive FL learning can result in a competence similar to that of bilinguals? To find an answer to this and discuss some other aspects of knowledge transfer, this chapter attends to cognitive theory and attempts to describe the skill the participants acquired when studying how to develop text types in L1, the access route to that skill, the common underlying system that facilitated the transfer of L2 skills to L1 and made it possible for L2 to support the internalization of a skill in L1, and the characteristics of skills transferred from L2 to L1.

Cognitive theory distinguishes between static information and dynamic information in the memory. The former is called *declarative knowledge* and the later is referred to as *procedural knowledge* (Anderson, 1983, 1985). Whereas declarative knowledge or factual information may be acquired quite fast, procedural knowledge, such as, for instance, developing a language or learning how to write a composition, are acquired gradually and only with extensive opportunities for practice. The participants of the Hungarian experiment studied in the elementary schools how to develop several different text types. Developing a text requires a complex cognitive skill. Texts take several different conventionalized formats such as official documents, curriculum vitae, applications, newspapers advertisements, essays, school compositions, and the like. Some formats such as compositions or essays are more important for academic purposes than others; therefore, they are taught and practiced systematically in school. This happened in the case of the Hungarian students who were the participants in our experiment. They studied not only the format of composition writing but also how to tie sentences together, how to make a complex sentence out of two or more single sentences and other related knowledge. This procedural knowledge was systematically developed into skills, which resulted in a more or less similar handling of written speech by most students. There were no significant differences in the written production of the three classes at the beginning of the experiment. Although in the high school no more procedural knowledge was systematically developed, after 2 years the immersion class and the intensive class were ahead of the control class in the use of mother tongue skills. In order to have some understanding of what happened in the minds of those students we have to examine the stages of skill acquisition, discuss how knowledge acquired in one language can be used in another language, and describe how metalinguistic awareness works across languages.

DEVELOPMENT OF SKILLS

Stages of Skill Acquisition

Anderson (1983, 1985) distinguished three stages of skill acquisition: the cognitive, associative, and autonomous stages. During the cognitive stage students are instructed how to do the task. In our experiment Hungarian students were instructed how to develop a particular type of text in their L1. They were given representative samples of the format to be acquired, an explanation of how thoughts are represented and connected in a text, a demonstration of how to organize different thoughts into a coherent text, and information about the linguistic means that can be used to express a particular idea. This stage requires conscious activity on the part of the students, and the acquired knowledge is declarative. During the associative stage declarative knowledge is turned into its procedural form. At this stage students focus on the task as a whole and are expected to produce on their own with detailed feedback to follow. The autonomous stage requires fine-tuned performance of the acquired skill. There is much less demand on working memory or consciousness because the execution of the skill becomes basically automatic (O'Malley & Chamot, 1990). Students at this stage are supposed to be able to manipulate language according to their own needs and not as the instructor requires them to. This is the period when students are expected to develop their individual writing styles.

Anderson's approach has been criticized from various perspectives. The main argument against it is that students learn by doing and acting rather than by acquiring the rule first and then doing the task. According to Gagné (1985), students prefer to perform the skill as early as possible, no matter whether they are familiar with the rule or not. He suggested that cued performance is an efficient procedure to learn a complex cognitive skill because it gives students repeated opportunities for practicing the complete skill. Gagne claimed that instruction is effective when it provides cues for the students at critical points and includes modeling the desired performance. This approach comes close to Vygotsky's (1978) *zone of proximal development* theory, which emphasizes the importance of interaction between the learner and other people supporting the developmental process and claims that developmental processes do not coincide with learning processes; rather, the developmental process lags behind the learning process. According to Vygotsky, good learning is that which is in advance of development. He distinguished between the *actual developmental level* (ADL) and the *potential developmental level* (PDL). The former refers to the level of development of a child's mental functions that has been established as a result of certain already-completed developmental cycles. The ADL defines functions that have already matured, and the child can do them independently. The zone of proximal development refers to functions that have not yet matured but are in the process of maturation. There is distance between ADL and PDL when the child cannot yet master certain functions independently and does problem solving under the guidance of adults or in collaboration with more capable peers. Learning awakens a number of internal developmental processes that can operate only when the child is interacting or collaborating with people in the environment. Properly organized learning results in mental development, but the two are never accomplished in equal measure or in parallel because there are very complex dynamic relations between learning and developmental processes. Lantolf and Appel (1994) emphasized that "it is not the carrying out of a particular task that is the main feature of interpersonal activity, but the higher cognitive process that emerges as a result" (p. 10). In the case of the participants, in our experiment in Hungary, this higher cognitive process means the automatic application of conventionalized formats of text development to meet personal communicative goals, such as writing a personal essay or answering a newspaper advertisement.

Before the 1989–1990 political changes, Hungarian students were usually educated in a rather rigid, teacher-centered, Prussian type of school system (Duff, 1991, 1995). This was especially true in the elementary schools. After the political changes of 1989–1990 a more flexible system that approximates Western type of school education has seemed to be emerging. What Anderson (1983, 1985) called the cognitive stage still plays an important a role in the learning process: When the surveyed students studied how to develop different types of texts in the elementary school, first they learned the basic rules through demonstration and patterns, and only after that did they focus on the task as a whole. At least that must have been the standard approach. When the students were tested first, they were at the associative stage because the development of their individual writing style was not completed yet. This function was in the process of maturation and internalization. The students were in the zone of proximal development, interacting with their teachers, but the activity was not yet internalized. The findings of the experiment suggested that intensive FL learning supported the process of internalization of the L1 skill through transfer of certain knowledge or skills obtained in the FL. What has made that transfer possible? How does the CUCB of FL learners function? What is the state of L1 knowledge in the CUCB?

Nature of Transferable Knowledge and Skills

Foreign Language Environment and Age as Variables. The literature on bilingualism is full of studies reporting metalinguistic advantages for bilingual children over monolingual children (e.g., Ben-Zeev, 1977; Bialystok, 1986; Bild & Swain, 1989; Ricciardelli, 1992; Slobin, 1978). However, these findings can hardly be valid for a FL environment because there is a significant difference between the mastery of the FL attained at school and the standard colloquially described as bilingualism. Researchers have made sharp distinctions between different types of bilingualism (e.g., Ekstrand, 1978; Toukomaa & Skutnabb-Kangas, 1977). It is generally accepted that school instruction in a FL should be differentiated from the normal situation of an immigrant. As discussed in Chapter 1, this distinction has serious bearing on how we evaluate the effect of FL learning on the development of mother tongue skills.

When the FL is learned in an academic setting, it is usually treated just like another school subject. Even in a communicative classroom students and teacher are most of the time preoccupied with cognitive processes such as analysis, synthesis, evaluation, and recognition rather than with genuine communication. Natural-setting, lifelike activities make better sense and are emphasized more than in a classroom where students are deliberately and consciously rather than spontaneously exposed to speech situations. Eddy (1978) suggested that learning a FL in a communicative setting (such as in the street) may have almost no effect on a student's English language arts skills as measured by currently available tests. However, a FL learned in an academic environment might indeed result in higher scores in English language arts tests because of the special attention paid in the FL classroom to such things as vocabulary development and sentence structures. Hancock (1977) and Masciantonio (1977) also came to similar conclusions but from different perspectives. Hancock suggested that foreign language study "offers a facilitating experience through which learners use language as a medium for expressing perceptions, concepts, and inferences" (p. 29). Having surveyed U.S. research on the effects of Latin instruction, Masciantonio concluded that studying Latin supports the development of the vocabulary and reading skills of students of all backgrounds and abilities. Holmstrand (1979) surveyed Swedish elementary school children from Grade 1 through Grade 6. These students received English instruction from the second semester of Grade 1. The experiment investigated the effects of English on Swedish and mathematics in the first six grades. Holmstrand claimed that certain test results in Swedish indicated that the early commencement of English instruction may have a slightly stimulating effect on achievement in this subject.

Research has demonstrated that besides the factors already mentioned (i.e., adequate motivation and exposure as well as second threshold level command of the FL), there is one more variable that may be decisive in the FL → L1 effect—age. How do we know that? Studies focusing on children under the age of 12 years almost deny any positive or negative influence of the FL on the development of mother tongue skills (cf. Burstall, 1970; Burstall, Jamieson, Cohen, & Hargreaves, 1974; Potts, 1967; Smith, 1967). Even the Swedish immersion programs in Finland are no exception, although the presence of Swedish culture in Finland is considerable. Some studies and MA theses produced at the European Institute for Immersion Teaching, University of Vaasa, Finland (Bjorklund, 1995; Grandell, 1993, 1995; Hoglund, 1992; West, 1993) focused on testing the L1 skills of Finnish students immersed in Swedish in Finland. They compared the L1 skills (e.g., vocabulary, creativity, spoken language, reading comprehension, and retold stories) of third and fourth graders to the L1 skills of monolingual (Finnish) control groups. The experiments demonstrated that there is no significant difference between monolingual students and bilingual students. Immersion students, even though they learn to read and write in Swedish, did not lag behind the monolingual control groups and even achieved better results in some areas (e.g., creativity and more complex language). However, no significant influence of the L2 on the L1 could be demonstrated in the results of the experiments (Bjorklund, personal communication.)[1] A positive effect of FL learning was reported in studies that surveyed older students (Holmstrand, 1979;[2] T. Papp, 1991). This makes sense if we accept that conceptual knowledge, cognitive skills, and metalinguistic awareness, not linguistic elements, are transferred. All are connected with higher level cognitive operations that usually occur after age 10 or 11 years (Gagné, 1985; Piaget, 1929), and a firm conceptual base in the L1 is expected to develop by age 12 years (cf. Collier, 1989, 1992; Cummins, 1984).

Metalinguistic Awareness. Vygotsky (1962) was among the first who recognized that FL learning facilitates mastering the higher forms of the native language. He explained this facilitative role of the FL with the development of awareness in linguistic operations. Vygotsky thought that while studying a FL the learner discovers that his language is only one particular system among many systems and learns to see its phenomena under more general categories. What about the development of metalinguistic awareness in children who never study a FL? Does metalinguistic awareness depend upon FL learning? Of course not, although Goethe (cited in Vygotsky, 1962) said that "he who knows no foreign language does not truly know his own" (p. 109). The emphasis here must be on "truly" because the development of metalinguistic awareness is tied to L1 acquisition as a part of the child's overall cognitive and linguistic development and does not depend on FL learning.

Metalinguistic awareness may be defined as the ability to reflect upon and manipulate the structural features of spoken language, treating language itself as an object of thought, as opposed to simply using the language system to comprehend and produce sentences (Tunmer & Herriman, 1984). This cognitive control of linguistic processes is very important in school because students have to function in a cognitively demanding and context-reduced environment (Cummins, 1984). It has been argued by many (Bialystok, 1986; Bialystok & Ryan, 1985; Gass, 1983; O'Malley & Chamot, 1990; Ryan, 1975) that bilingual children develop a more analytic orientation

---

[1] I asked Bjorklund this question after her presentation at the 2nd European Conference on Immersion in Barcelona, Spain, in 1996.

[2] The relatively significant stimulating effect on achievement in Swedish is reported in the higher grades rather than the lower grades.

to language through organizing their two language systems. Several studies (Grandell, 1993, 1995; Holmstrand, 1979; Kecskes & Papp, 1995; T. Papp, 1991) have found that raising metalinguistic awareness results in more conscious and sophisticated use of the L1 system and can be supported through intensive FL learning as well. Consequently, the main point here is not that metalinguistic awareness is FL-learning dependent but that FL learning can facilitate the development of that feature.

Metalinguistic awareness is the ability to separate form from meaning and attend to and reflect on the structural features of language as well as evaluate these features (cf. Bialystok, 1986; Malakoff, 1992; Ryan, 1980; Thomas, 1992). Malakoff (1992) argued that metalinguistic awareness allows language users to step back from the comprehension or production of an utterance to consider the linguistic form and structure that underlies the meaning of the utterance. The development of basic metalinguistic abilities is connected with the first 11 or 12 years of human development (Birdsong, 1989; Ryan & Ledger, 1984), during which there is a gradual shift of attention from meaning to structure in tasks requiring deliberate control over language forms.[3] These basic abilities, such as judging synonymity, understanding structural ambiguity, judging grammaticalness and meaningfulness, segmenting sentences and words into their constituents, and manipulating forms by moving morpheme boundaries, develop as the result of interactions of linguistic, cognitive, and metacognitive skills. All these activities require students to have both an awareness of language as a system and the ability to access and manipulate knowledge about that system.

Bialystok and Ryan (1985) and Bialystok (1986) described metalinguistic awareness as a reflection of the growth of two skill components involved in language processing: *analyzed knowledge* and *control* over the selection and processing of specific linguistic information. According to their theory, metalinguistic problems entail high levels of analyzed knowledge and control. Writing (depending on the genre) requires changing amounts of analyzed knowledge and control procedures. Composition, for instance, belongs definitely to the domain of high-level analyzed knowledge and control. In contrast, writing a story based on a series of photos requires moderate amounts of analyzed knowledge and control. These differences were very clearly demonstrated in the Hungarian experiment.

Birdsong (1989) argued that individual differences in linguistic and metalinguistic abilities can be traced to the structuring of language users' linguistic knowledge. Certain language experiences contribute significantly to the growth of the dimension of analyzed knowledge because they require breaking down language into constituents and patterns. Such lan-

---

[3]That is why it makes sense to treat age as a variable in determining the nature of L2 influence on L1.

guage experiences are, for example, reading and writing. These activities are connected mainly with schooling. Bialystok (1986) emphasized the importance of schooling in the development of linguistic control and analyzed knowledge. She also referred to bilingualism as a contributing factor. Tunmer and Myhill (1984) came to the same conclusion. They hypothesized that increasing metalinguistic awareness is an important by-product of the development of two languages in bilinguals.

Our longitudinal experiment supports these claims. Students in the immersion class and the intensive class did a lot of language analysis. They often solved tasks that required analytic skills, and a considerable part of their language-learning process was governed by more bottom-up than top-down activities. Students beyond the second threshold (whose command of language was close to bilinguals) developed significant control over their procedural knowledge. They controlled the selection of appropriate structures, and most of their production showed careful planning that was partly the result of their monitoring the text production. The metalinguistic skills of students, combined with metacognitive strategies such as monitoring, produced good results during the surveys. Students transferred from the FL learning process not declarative but procedural knowledge, that is, metalinguistic ability that was used to manipulate structures according to communicative needs. This finding underscores the importance of the functional side of metalinguistic awareness, which implies the control of cognitive operations. There is nothing new in this evidence because several researchers including Sorace (1985), Odlin (1986), and Gass (1983) argued for a productive function for metalinguistic awareness in communication. Referring to the research by Huerta (1978), who found that bilinguals when code switching are aware of their lexical choices, Odlin (1986) provided evidence confirming that metalinguistic awareness has important productive functions in communication. Gass (1983) underlined the role of conscious repairs in preventing conversation from failing altogether when breakdowns occur. The difference between our survey and those mentioned here is that they focused on oral speech whereas our research investigated written speech.

Bialystok (1986) made an observation that is very important for our subject matter. She suggested that the notion metalinguistic ability could be replaced by "a description of continuing linguistic development in which analyzed concepts of language can be intentionally applied under a variety of contextual demands" (p. 508). This statement can be interpreted that linguistic development is not finished when the basic stage is completed around the age of 11 or 12 years but instead enters into a stage grounded on a qualitatively different, more complex language processing that has analyzed linguistic knowledge and control of linguistic processing as its basic components. At this stage metalinguistic awareness plays a decisive role.

In the Hungarian experiment we measured metalinguistic skills: how students manipulated their first language to meet their communicative goals and how sophisticated and controlled their language use was when solving language-production tasks. The experiment demonstrated that linguistic growth in the second stage depends to a great extent on the development of metalinguistic skills that students can use to facilitate their performance on text-production tasks. The transfer of metalinguistic skills developed on the material of one language to the production domain of another language is possible through the CUCB. The CUCB implies that experience with either language can promote the development of the conceptual and knowledge base underlying both languages, given adequate motivation and exposure to both in school or in the wider environment.

LINGUISTIC OPERATIONS AND MEMORY

Because multicompetent speakers have a high level of metalinguistic awareness they can control their language operations more than their monolingual counterparts or FL learners whose command of the FL is not good enough to pass the threshold that leads to the development of multicompetence. Based on this fact we hypothesized that students with a high command of a FL (resembling bilinguals in their language activities) are more bound to use linguistic operations in their mental activities than students with a low command of a FL; this boundedness to linguistic operations will influence their problem-solving strategies. In order to verify the validity of the hypothesis we examined the results of one task the students had to work on during the Hungarian longitudinal experiment. The task consisted of two parts. First the students were asked to describe in the FL what was happening in a series of pictures. They were expected to write a short story based on what they saw in the pictures. Then two pictures in the same series were slightly modified, and one picture that was in the FL version was removed. The second part of the task required the students to describe in the mother tongue what was happening in the pictures as well as to recall the missing picture (i.e., in the FL version but not in the mother tongue version) and describe it in Hungarian (Kecskes & Papp, 1995) It is important to underline that students were required to produce the two texts one immediately after the other. We sought explanations to three problems: To what extent are students bound to a particular language when doing different kinds of activities? To what degree are their mental processes language specific? What role do linguistic memory and visual memory play in memorization and mental planning? The answers to these questions are addressed in the next sections.

We expected that if students did the same task first in the L1 then in the FL, the FL production would be very similar to the one in the L1. However, this was usually not the case when they did the task first in the FL and then in the L1. Our findings demonstrated that the students used *three types of strategies* when describing the modified series of pictures in their mother tongue.

Some students followed their FL language production in the mother tongue version and gave a kind of reproduction of the text they developed in the FL. Not even the modified pictures could make them change their FL version of the story very much. They reproduced the motives as well as equivalent or similar sentence types in the mother tongue version.

Other students also followed the story line of their FL production but their mental planning was more language specific: They used sentence types other than the ones in their FL version. The motives in the story were similar, but the way they described them was different; for example, sentence structures were adjusted to the requirements of the language in use. In writing their compositions they utilized their mother tongue potential better than the first group of students did. The description of the modified pictures made an essential part of the story and bore little resemblance to the FL version. Although students produced the same story line in both languages, each production was quite well written and used the potential of the language in which the text was written.

The third group of students produced an entirely different story in the mother tongue, which only slightly or not at all resembled their FL production. Not only the sentence types but the motives were quite different. The analysis of data showed that in the immersion class, 8% of the L1 text was almost the same as the FL text, not only in motives but in sentence types as well. Additionally, 50% of the L1 text was a developed version of FL text—motives were similar, but description was different, and 42% of the L1 text entirely differed from the FL text. In the intensive class, 10% of the L1 text was almost the same as FL text, 19% was a developed version of the FL text, and 71% of the L1 text entirely differed from the FL text. In the control class, 4% of the L1 text was almost the same as the FL text, 10% was a developed version of the FL text, and 86% entirely differed from the FL text.

What do these numbers tell us? How do these results fit into the CUCB hypothesis? There is no problem explaining independent production, which has to do with the different levels of the two language channels. The FL texts produced by the control class students are quite primitive. When those students were asked to produce a text in their native tongue, they seemed to experience some kind of relief. Consequently, they came up with something that was entirely different from the low-level FL text. In this case hardly anything was transferred from the FL to the L1. However, those students' L1 productions were not on a very high level either. This finding seems to support the threshold hypothesis. There is hardly any multicompetence and CUCB until a particular level of fluency is achieved in the target language. The numbers seem to confirm this assumption. Students produced independent texts 86% of the time in the control class, 71% in the specialized class, and 42% in the immersion class.

The other extreme was the group that produced relatively equivalent texts, consisting of a small number of students from each class. We have to be very careful when trying to come up with some explanation for this type because individual problem-solving strategies also played an important role in the students' productions. A comparison of the texts in the L1 and the FL revealed that students worked very intensively on the FL version, which was, in spite of the serious student effort, full of mistakes. This intensivity was transferred to the L1 production, in which they tried to repeat the same kinds of linguistic operations and make a translation of their not-very-successful FL text. We attribute this type of production to personality factors rather than to some kind of strategy.

The most balanced productions are the variations. We found quite a lot of them (50%) in the immersion class but fewer in the other two classes (i.e., specialized class: 19%; control class: 10%). This result also seems to correlate with the level of language proficiency: The higher command of the FL students have the greater is the likelihood of their producing a variation. The optimal exploitation of CUCB means that most of its content can be used through both channels if both language systems are developed enough to reach the thresholds. With respect to our survey this translates as follows: High-level, proficient students do not articulate in their production how different the two languages are. Nor do they try to translate from one language to the other when they are asked to produce a text about the same story in two different languages. They rely on concept mediation rather than on word association. This finding was observed in the production of immersion students, many of whom produced variations. However, students with less language proficiency in the intensive and control classes did not produce like that. Their texts clearly appeared to be the sign of low command of the FL for the reasons explained previously.

The second task the students were asked to do was to recall the picture they saw in the first version of the series (when they were expected to write a composition in the FL) but that was missing in the second version of the series, when the students had to use the mother tongue. When evaluating the answers, we distinguished linguistic memory from visual memory. If linguistic memory was used by the students, they recalled the linguistic operations they applied when writing the text in the FL. Consequently, when the missing picture had to be recalled, the students who relied on linguistic memory tried to give a concept-mediated interpretation of that particular part of their FL text or produced only a slightly different version of the FL text. What they had in mind was the L2 version of the text, and they tried to develop its L1 equivalent, consciously focusing on the structural and lexical differences between the two languages. This concurs with Bialystok's (1986) understanding of metalinguistic awareness, which emphasizes the important role of analytic knowledge and control over the selection and processing of specific linguistic information. It is interesting to note, however, that concept mediation was not always possible, and students frequently fell back on the word-association mode, looking for the closest Hungarian equivalent of words used in the L2 text. This finding confirms what Kroll (1993) hypothesized about the two directions of translation. She claimed that the two directions of translation reflect two distinct processing sequences. Translation from the L2 into the L1 can be accomplished on a lexical basis, whereas translation in the opposite direction (from L1 into L2) requires concept mediation. When visual memory was used by the students, they recalled only the pictures themselves and did not remember the linguistic production in the FL; they usually produced a different description of events in the L1.

The analysis of data showed (Kecskes & Papp, 1995, p. 174) that in the immersion class, 63% of students used linguistic memory: 18% reproduced the FL text details and 45% recalled the plot. Additionally, 37% used visual memory. In the intensive class, 46% used linguistic memory, with 8% reproducing the FL text details and 38% recalling the plot, and 54% used visual memory. In the control class, 24% used linguistic memory, with 5% reproducing the FL text details and 19% recalling the plot, and 76% used visual memory.

These results demonstrated that linguistic memory is based on linguistic operations. In the immersion and intensive classes, linguistic operations primarily directed the verbal planning and problem solving of students, and visual impulses were of secondary importance. When the students saw the same picture series with a slight change they recalled the text they had produced in the foreign language, and according to the logical requirement of modification they continued developing the same story. This demonstrates that the difference in visual experience does not change the strategy students generally use when solving linguistic tasks. The findings of this study suggest that students studying FLs intensively are more bound to use linguistic operations in their mental activities than those who have less access to FL learning. This is a clear sign of strong metalinguistic awareness, an important component of multicompetence.

SUMMARY

High proficiency in a FL usually results in the development of a CUCB, which facilitates the transfer of skills obtained in Lx into Ly, and vice versa. This transfer can also support the internalization of a skill being developed in either language. Vygotsky (1962:109) suggested that foreign language learning can affect a child's mental development very positively: "In one's native language, the primitive aspects of speech are acquired before the more complex ones. The latter presuppose some awareness of phonetic, grammatical, and syntactic forms. With a foreign language, the higher forms develop before spontaneous, fluent speech. The intellectualistic theories of language, such as Stern's, which place a full grasp of the relationship between sign and meaning at the very beginning of linguistic development, contain a measure of truth in the case of a foreign language. The child's strong points in a foreign language are his weak points in his native language, and vice versa. In his own language, the child conjugates, and declines correctly, but without realizing it. He cannot tell the gender, the case, or the tense of the word he is using. In a foreign language, he distinguishes between masculine and feminine gender and is conscious of grammatical forms from the beginning." We do not necessarily agree with each statement of this quotation, but it certainly seems to be true that "the child's strong points in a foreign language are his weak points in his native tongue, and vice versa." This is why strong foreign language skills can support the internalization of mother tongue skills. In the Hungarian experiment the internalization of writing skills in the mother tongue was not yet completed when intensive FL learning began. This intensive FL learning process, through which learners used language as a medium for expressing perceptions, concepts, and inferences, increased the students' metalinguistic awareness. As a result, students studying a FL intensively or using the FL as medium of instruction developed better text-manipulation skills even in their mother tongue than students in the control class (where this exposure to the FL was not present) because they had significant control over their linguistic operations. Metalinguistic awareness allowed them to use the potentials of both languages for their communicative purposes in production through either language channel. Students in the immersion and intensive classes developed a special kind of conscious approach to language: They seemed to be able to plan the linguistic operations they needed to express their communicative goals. This concurs with Bialystok's (1986) hypothesis about bilingual children. She suggested that bilingual children have an advantage over monolingual children "in the acceleration of the control function involved in the solution to linguistic and metalinguistic problems" (p. 17).

Thomas (1985, 1988) mentioned two studies with bilinguals that resulted in findings similar to ours. She claimed that experience in a formal language learning environment had serious impact on the grammatical sensitivity and written communication of students (Thomas, 1992). In her study (Thomas, 1988) English–Spanish bilinguals were found to have advantages over monolingual English students when learning French in a formal classroom environment. They were especially good at grammar and composition if there was time for them to exploit their explicit or analyzed linguistic knowledge. In an earlier study based on error analysis of compositions, Thomas (1985) investigated differences among the errors of monolingual students, bilingual students acquiring Spanish informally at home, and bilingual students studying Spanish formally. Her findings revealed that students with at least minimal literacy in Spanish produced the lowest percentage of errors and attempted more structures than either of the two other groups. Thomas (1992) argued that bilingual students with formal Spanish instruction were "able to avoid interference, exploit positive transfer and develop more effective strategies for producing acceptable written communication due to their awareness of Spanish as a system" (p. 535). These studies seem to support the claim that a skill developed in Lx can be used in Ly, or a skill being developed in Lx can get support from Ly. General language manipulating skills may be facilitated by the intensive exposure to or extensive use of either channel. As we discuss in the next chapter, however, the linguistic and cultural relations between the two or more language systems that rely on a CUCB are critical.

CHAPTER

6

Language Distance and Multicompetence

For multicompetence to develop, the languages that constitute the language processing device (LPD) and their relation to each other are very important. Languages of the multilingual LPD share a common underlying conceptual base (CUCB) but have no shared representation in the constantly available interacting system (CAIS) where each language has its own separate formulator and lexicon. Language systems in the CAIS do not allow for shared processing mechanisms or strategies, however closely related they seem to be. The relation of the two (or more) languages is strongly affected by three variables: level of proficiency, typological closeness, and cultural distance. The level of proficiency is an obvious factor. A person who has taken French 101 will hardly develop a separate system for French. De Bot (1992) argued that the first language (L1) is usually flexible enough to add the emerging foreign language (FL) as an additional register to those already in existence.

In Chapter 3 we claimed that the development of multicompetence with a CUCB and CAIS is dependent on the level of the second language (L2), which has to reach a certain hypothetical threshold. The results of research conducted by Van Hell (1998) support this claim. She investigated whether FL knowledge influences performance in the native language or not, and to what extent proficiency in the FL plays a role in this influence. She examined performance of trilinguals (i.e., Dutch, English, French) on a word recognition task and in a word association task. She found performance in the L1 is facilitated by the knowledge of a FL only when proficiency in this FL is sufficiently high. Although Van Hell used techniques different from ours to measure this influence, her results support our findings: L2 effect is significant for language use only beyond a certain threshold.

It is not clear, however, how the organization of the two language systems develops as proficiency in the L2 increases. We assume that in order for multicompetence to begin to develop, the language learner has to use the language for real (i.e., not imitated or classroom-induced) communicative purposes. No problem should arise in the L2 environment because the target culture is present. In the FL environment, however, it is quite difficult to use the target language for real functions. The importance of exposure to the target culture was highlighted in Pavlenko's (1996) research: Learners' participation in the L2 culture was crucial for the development of multimodal conceptual representations. She concurred with Ushakova's (1994) opinion that with little or no exposure to a rich and meaningful variety of interactions with the members of the target culture, FL learning in the classroom is nothing but the learning of a new explicit code. This process usually leads to a subordinate organization of the two lexicons rather than to a CUCB. From this respect immersion programs in the FL environment are supposed to be very effective because the target language is used as the medium of instruction, which can compensate in one way or another for direct exposure with the target culture. Intensive programs also support the development of multicompetence by requiring much reading, writing, and media exposure in the target language as well as translation in both directions (Papp, 1991; Kecskes & Papp, 1995). These activities may result in the development of a multicompetent LPD. In the FL environment much depends on the individual effort of language learners. If they are willing to work on their language proficiency systematically they usually reach the threshold beyond which multicompetence begins to develop.

LANGUAGE DISTANCE

Language distance has an objective and a subjective side. The objective side is called *language typology* which focuses on classifying languages according to their structural characteristics. *Typological distance* or *closeness* usually goes together with cultural closeness or distance, but there is no one-to-one relationship between the two because culture is generally significantly influenced by geographical distance. Typologically Swedish (i.e., Indo-European, Germanic, configurational) and Finnish (i.e., Finno-Ugric, nonconfigurational) are farther from each other than Finnish and Estonian (i.e., Finno-Ugric, nonconfigurational). Culturally, however, Swedish is closer to Finnish than to Estonian.

The subjective side of language distance is constituted by the reflection of structural and cultural closeness in the human mind. Kellerman (1983) referred to the perception of language distance as *psychotypology*. Language typology builds on objective facts—structural differences and similarities between languages. Psychotypology tells us how multilingual speakers perceive those structural differences and similarities between their languages.

Our understanding of psychotypology differs at least at one point from Kellerman's interpretation. Kellerman suggested that transfer (he means mainly negative transfer) is seriously affected by the learner's perception of language distance. Transfer of a form from the L1 to the L2 partly depends on how likely the learner thinks it is to be acceptable in the other language. We assume that psychotypology plays a very important role in the development of multicompetence but not just the way Kellerman described. In Kellerman's framework transferability is a relative notion that depends on the perceived distance between the L1 and the L2 and the structural organization of the L1. From a multicompetence perspective psychotypology also depends on the perceived distance; however, it is not a one-way but a two-way process: It is not just the structural organization of the L1 that has a decisive role but the structural organization of the L2 as well. When, as a result of intensive FL learning, a CUCB starts to develop, the structural organization of the L2 has serious bearing on certain aspects of L1 use.

It is important to note that language learners are sensitive not only to structural differences between languages but to cultural and other differences as well. Kellermann also acknowledged the importance of these other differences. He referred to Widdowson (1980), who pointed out that differences other than typological, such as psychological and social, should be accounted for. Kellermann emphasized that those differences were beyond the scope of his study. We assume that in the mind of the language learner those differences, including structural, social, and cultural aspects, are inseparable, and they together have a cumulative effect on the decision-making process of the learner. It may well be that assumptions about cultural distance between languages direct the language learner not exactly as it is expected on the basis of language typology. For instance, English native speakers studying Finnish and Turkish probably feel that Finnish is closer to English than to Turkish, although both Finnish and Turkish differ from English to a great extent. They both have very complex morphology unlike English. Yet English speakers feel less distance to Finnish because they think Finnish culture is closer to them than Turkish culture.

The question is how language distance as a whole, with its objective and subjective sides, influences the acquisition process and the outcome of this process, multicompetence. What interests us is the nature, characteristics, and functioning of the multicompetent LPD.[1] The acquisition process is usu-

---

[1]We consider *interlanguage* a term that represents a monolingual view; therefore, we have tried to avoid using it in this book.

ally longer and more difficult if the two languages are remote both typologically and culturally. Native speakers of one language frequently believe that they will find certain other languages especially difficult to learn. They are guided by one of the main principles of learning, according to which learning difficulty is tied to the degree in which the object of learning resembles something already known. Odlin (1989) claimed that the cumulative effects of cross-linguistic and cross-cultural similarities and differences on the acquisition process can be assessed by the length of time needed to achieve a high degree of mastery of a language. Little research has been done to test the validity of this hypothesis. As an example, Odlin (1989) referred to the schedule of courses of the Foreign Service Institute (1985) of the U.S. State Department, which summarizes the lengths of language courses offered to the members of the U.S. diplomatic corps. Table 6.1 offers some examples from the list.

It can be questioned whether 44 weeks is enough for English speakers to acquire Arabic or Russian. For us, this issue is irrelevant. Languages in the first tier clearly differ from English both linguistically and culturally, whereas languages in the second tier are supposed to be much closer from both aspects. Typological differences, however, seem to play more of a role in course length than culture does. This can be demonstrated very well with some examples from the list. There is not much cultural difference between Finnish and Swedish for English native speakers, but linguistically Swedish is closer to English than Finnish. The same can be said about Rumanian and Hungarian with Rumanian being a neo-Latin language and Hungarian belonging to the Finno-Ugric language group with very complex morphology.

Analyzing language aptitude, Child (1998) referred to a more elaborated version of the language distance chart developed by the Foreign Service Institute. It focuses on three textual elements: a writing system as a representation of spoken language (A), a grammatical system as a framework for

TABLE 6.1
Distances of Foreign Languages From English

Near	Number of weeks	Remote	Number of weeks
Danish	24	Arabic	44
French	20	Bulgarian	44
German	20	Chinese	44
Italian	20	Czech	44
Norwegian	24	Finnish	44
Rumanian	24	Hungarian	44
Spanish	20	Japanese	44
Swedish	24	Korean	44
		Russian	44
		Turkish	44

communication (B), and a semantic system as the cultural outlook (C). These phenomena are then ordered in such a way as to indicate relative distance of FLs from English: near (1), middle (2), and remote (3). Using this system Child characterized German as A1/B2/C2, Turkish as A1/B3/C3, and Japanese as A3/B3/C3.

Once the hypothetical threshold in the FL is reached and a multicompetent LPD with a CUCB and CAIS begins to develop, the bidirectional transfer of skills and knowledge becomes possible no matter how remote the languages are typologically and culturally. However, this is just a possibility and not a necessity. Both subjective and objective variables play important roles in determining how this potential for transfer is used. We look at objective variables only. Subjective variables such as individual learner differences are discussed in Chapter 7.

Mace-Matluck, Hoover, and Calfee's (1984) study suggested that transfer of underlying cognitive skills occurred between Chinese and English despite strong surface structure dissimilarities. They examined how variables such as length of stay, level of L1 academic proficiency, and amount of reading instruction received influenced the L2 (English) oral and written proficiency of Chinese students in Seattle. Their findings demonstrated a consistent beneficial effect of bilingual instruction and of instruction in Chinese on the development of English literacy skills. However, very little research has been done to describe the effect of language distance in the symbiosis of two or more languages and whether differences and similarities have any impact on language production through either channel. What is better from the perspective of multicompetence? Should the two languages share similar typological and cultural features or the opposite—should they have hardly any features in common?

Most researchers emphasize that language learners are sensitive to encoding and decoding differences between their L1 and L2 or L*x*. One hypothesis of the longitudinal experiment described in Chapter 2 was that positive transfer from the FL to the L1 is expected to be especially intensive, marked, and beneficial if the L1 and the FL differ from each other in configurationality.[2] Learners are especially sensitive to differences in the structural configurations between the first language and the FL. Therefore, the setting of the configurationality parameter and the possible organization of sentences have decisive effects on bidirectional processes between the L1 and the FL. We hypothesized before the Hungarian experiment was conducted that the knowledge of languages that have different means to organize their phrase structures and express relations between words within those units (e.g., word order versus grammatical suffixes and endings)

---

[2]At the time of the experiment we focused only on this structural feature. Cultural distance between languages was not accounted for.

leads to the development of different discourse organization and learning and processing strategies. We also expected that the combination of different approaches to the organizing of linguistic materials (i.e., the knowledge of more than one language) will result in a firmly developed language operating system relying on two or more languages. However, in the experiment that was the weakest hypothesis for several reasons. First, this question has not been investigated yet, at least according to our knowledge. Further, the primary goal of the experiment was not the investigation of this issue. Consequently, when the environment and subjects were chosen, this hypothesis was taken into account as an issue of secondary importance. The analysis of the surveys directed our attention to very important questions, which, however premature a state they are in at this point, might be interesting for the linguistic and educational community, especially from the perspective of further research.

ORGANIZATION OF A SENTENCE

Grammatical Word Order Versus Pragmatic Word Order

Linguists have known about the important role of word order in language acquisition (cf. Frazier, 1985; Gass, 1987; Rutherford, 1989; Slobin, 1979; White, 1989). Depending on their perspective of investigation, discipline, and field of interest, researchers use specific terminology that refers to the same or similar phenomena. The universal grammar (UG) theory explains the dichotomy in the organization of phrase structures of languages by the two possible settings of the configurationality parameter (cf. White, 1989), which may take either a configurational (CON) or a nonconfigurational (NON-CON) setting. *Configurational languages* (e.g., English or French) have bound word order governed by grammatical rules. *Phrase structure configurations* encode the grammatical functions, and logical relations can only be computed at a virtual level of representation. *Non-configurational languages* (e.g., Russian or Hungarian) have complex morphology and a word order (White, 1989) governed by pragmatic rather than grammatical rules. Phrase structure expresses logical relations, and grammatical functions are encoded morphologically.

Kiss (1987) denied the existence of CON and NON-CON categories, arguing that all languages are configurational and claiming that languages differ primarily with respect to the type of information encoded in the phrase structure of their sentences. Berwick (1985) came to a similar conclusion: "there are no configurational or non-configurational languages, but simply languages that exhibit a range of adjacency requirements for one or another type of phrase" (p. 285). We agree with Kiss and with Berwick that human languages are all configurational, but configurationality is governed by two different rule types that play decisive roles in organizing and processing information.

Language data demonstrate that word order movements in languages are governed by grammatical or pragmatic rules. Word order freedom at sentence level is conditioned by pragmatic rules that are sensitive to old versus new information, topic-comment, focus, and so on. Although the grammatical word order (GWO) and pragmatic word order (PWO) features are scalar tendencies, this dichotomy must be maintained because it is based on essential differences between languages. If we want to highlight or emphasize something in English (which is a GWO language) or wish to sound more emotive, we need to use a new configuration, a new structure governed by grammatical rules.

Neutral: Peter has broken the window.
Emphatic/Emotive: It is Peter who has broken the window.

Neutral: I know so little about you.
Emphatic/Emotive: So little do I know about you.

In PWO languages such as Hungarian or Russian, there is usually no need for a new configuration to make a certain piece of information emphatic in the sentence. Reordering of the same words within the sentence according to pragmatic rules results in a shift in emphasis as in the Hungarian sentences below.

Neutral: Péter betörte az ablakot.
Peter in broke the window.
(Peter broke the window.)

Emphatic: Az ablakot Péter törte be.
The window Peter broke in.
(It was Peter who broke the window.)

Referring to the same phenomenon, Li and Thompson (1976) distinguished between *topic-prominent* and *subject-prominent* languages. English is a subject-prominent language in which the fundamental relation is that of subject-predicate. Subject prominence requires GWO in which the position of canonical constituents (e.g., subject, verb, object) is constrained by syntactic rules (Thompson, 1978). Therefore, languages such as English are said to be syntactically dominant (Gass, 1987). Topic-prominent languages, on the other hand, are characterized by the relation of topic-comment (i.e., positioning of old and new information). Topic prominence usually goes together with PWO in which discourse factors determine the order of canonical constituents in the sentence. Consequently, languages with PWO, such as Finnish, Italian, Russian, or Hungarian, are often referred to as pragmatically (or semantically) dominant languages (Gass, 1987). For instance, the English sentence, *Peter found a small dog in the garden of the house* can have in Russian many equivalents that differ from one another mainly in topic–comment placement. Grammatical relations between words in the sentence are expressed by morphological markers so the movement of phrase structures does not result in a change in sentence meaning. Consider some of the possible permutations of one Russian sentence:

Петр нашел малеькую собаку в саду дома.
(Peter found a small dog in the garden of the house.)

В саду дома Петр нашел маленькую собаку.
Маленькую собаку Петр нашел в саду дома.
Маленькую собаку нашел в саду дома Петр.
В саду дома маленькую собаку Петр нашел.

Dichotomies such as *subject prominent versus topic prominent, GWO versus PWO, configurational versus nonconfigurational,* and *syntactically dominant versus semantically (or pragmatically) dominant* are similar. To stick to our cognitive-pragmatic theoretical framework and make further discussions more transparent, we use GWO and PWO to denote the differences between the two types of languages. However, differences between GWO and PWO can be best understood as a continuum on which languages with strong GWO dominance are positioned on the left and languages with strong PWO dominance are placed on the right. On a continuum with English left and Finnish right, we can put the following languages (from left to right): English, French, German, Japanese, Italian, Russian, Hungarian, and Finnish. Japanese takes the middle position among these languages on the continuum because it marks case morphologically but has a rigid verb-final position, a typical GWO characteristic. Phrase structures can be moved according to pragmatic requirements, but the verb always stays in the same position—at the end of the sentence. For instance, the equivalents of the English sentence, *Peter found a small dog in the garden of the house* can be the following in Japanese:

Peter wa uchi no niwa de chiisai inu o mitsukemasita.
Uchi no niwa de Peter wa chiisai inu o mitsukemasita.

Chiisai inu o Peter wa uchi no niwa de mitsukemasita.
Peter wa chiisai inu o uchi no niva de mitsukemasita.

Peter wa	= Peter + topic marker
chiisai inu o	= small dog + object marker
uchi no niwa de	= in the garden of the house
mitsukemasita	= found

Transfer of Sentence Organization

Research demonstrates a significantly easier adjustment to the requirements of the target language when the direction of multilingual development is from GWO to PWO rather than the other way. Negative transfer seems to be more likely if students with a PWO L1 study a GWO language as a FL (e.g., Hungarian native speakers studying English). Several researchers (Rutherford, 1983, 1989; Schacter & Rutherford, 1979; Yip & Matthews, 1995) argued that the discourse organization of topic-prominent languages could undergo transfer. Investigating the degree of candidacy for L2 transfer of L1 phenomena identified in terms of the canonical word order (CWO)[3] and GWO/PWO typologies Rutherford (1989) claimed that "the syntax-definable construct known as L1 CWO would not of itself leave traces in IL syntax, whereas a discourse-definable propensity of L1 to permute its canonical constituents would leave traces" (p. 169). In other words, the CWO will not undergo transfer if the L1 of the learner is a GWO language. In the opposite case, when the L1 is a PWO language and has several permutations of the CWO, transfer is expected to occur. After investigating the characteristic features of Chinese–English interlanguage, Yip and Matthews (1995) came to a similar conclusion. They argued that topic and subject prominence and GWO/PWO that are definable in discourse and not strictly syntactic terms will exert a measurable effect on the interlanguage. Typological generalizations of this type based on empirical observation should be considered with caution because individual language learners have no access to such generalizations (Tomlin, 1994). Some other studies (e.g., Jin, 1994, on the acquisition of Chinese by English speakers) claimed that transfer occurs in the other direction too: Subject-prominent features can also undergo transfer.

Gass (1987) investigated the interaction of syntax, semantics, and pragmatics from the perspective of functional constraints on sentence processing. As a theoretical framework she used the competition model of Bates and MacWhinney (1981, 1987), who argued that the acoustic-articular chan-

---

[3]Canonical word order means the arrangement of subject (S), object (O), and verb (V) within a sentence.

nel has limited resources to determine the relations among language elements in the incoming language data to be processed. Natural languages have four means to determine such relations: lexical items, morphological markers (e.g., suffixes and endings), word order, and prosody. When the language user has to determine the form aligned with each function, all four means are not equally used for interpretation; rather, they compete for dominance. In English, for instance, word order has the greatest weighting, overriding all the other possible factors (Gass, 1987). In Russian, however, the dominant factor in interpretation is morphology (Kecskes, 1995). Gass' study focused on how language learners "move from one organizational system to another" (p. 332). Participants were native speakers of Italian learning English and native speakers of English learning Italian. Gass explained her choice of language learners with the difference in sensitivity between the two languages; that is, Italian is sensitive to semantics and pragmatics for interpretation, and English is sensitive to syntax for interpretation. Gass (1987) concluded that it is easier to cancel syntax as a primary interpretation strategy in favor of other factors such as semantics and pragmatics than it is to go from semantics to syntax. In other words, syntactic constraints on word order usually cause problems for language learners whose L1 does not have those constraints. Using Gass's example, Italian learners of English have more difficulty acquiring English word order than do English learners of Italian. How decisive is this difference in bidirectional learnability? Does this really mean that English speakers learn Italian easier than Italian speakers learn English? Gass answered this question positively, but more research needs to be done with other languages before the question can be answered convincingly. Word order functions (grammatical or pragmatic) are very important features of languages and demonstrate how thought is organized and interpreted in a particular language.

CULTURAL DISTANCE AND VOCABULARY

Learners' Judgments

Several researchers (cf. Andersen, 1982; Weltens & Grendel, 1993) argued that the less a particular language resembles the mother tongue, the harder it will be to acquire that language. However, as mentioned previously, the objective estimation of distance does not always concur with the learner's subjective judgment. In several cases the subjective estimation of distance by the learner can override an objective measure. Odlin (1989) discussed the importance of learner judgment in connection with transfer. He said that based on subjective estimation the learner consciously or unconsciously decides if a particular structure in a previously learned language is similar to a certain structure in the target language. Transfer will most likely result from this judgment.

Odlin was referring to L1 structural interference, but not only in structure does the objective estimation of language distance differ from the subjective estimation. From this respect it is interesting to look at vocabulary acquisition. The Germanic and Romance branches of the Indo-European language family share a massive vocabulary stock consisting of words of science, art, and abstract thought that are mainly of Latin and Greek origin. This vocabulary is said to constitute the core of Western culture. Consequently, an English or Spanish native speaker will not experience much difficulty acquiring this particular part of French vocabulary because in most cases the words are the same in their languages but are pronounced differently or the concept is the same but each language uses a different word to denote it. For example, French *factage* is similar to English *carriage* (and delivery), and French *eloigne* is similar to English *far away, distant.* In linguistically and culturally close languages we can usually find quite a number of cognates. Cognate relations cannot only be of help but also cause several problems in language learning, although those problems are usually quite easy to overcome.

The farther the culture is, the more difficult it is for the learner to acquire new concepts and to reconceptualize L1 words. Some European languages, such as Estonian, Finnish, and Hungarian, belong to the Finno-Ugric language family. These cultures are more remote to English native speakers than Germanic or Romance cultures. Consequently, English native speakers have more difficulty in acquiring the vocabulary of those languages, although they can still rely on some Latin word stock. Language learners have to be careful because some of the Latin words that are well known for them can have entirely different meanings in Finno-Ugric languages. Compare, for example, English *person* and Hungarian *perszóna*, or English *administration* and Hungarian *adminisztráció*.[4] Arabic, Chinese, and Japanese cause even more problems for English native speakers because the remote and exotic cultures are represented in words denoting concepts that do not exist in Western cultures or need reconceptualization.

We assume that multicompetence constituted by a Germanic or Romance language plus another language that represents a remote culture and a different way of thinking and discourse organization can result in a very positive form of multilingualism. In a very limited way the Hungarian experiment seems to demonstrate that the influence of L2 was stronger and more beneficial in the cases of Hungarian–English and Hungarian–French speakers than in the case of Hungarian–Russian speakers. In the symbiosis of two or more languages, the more remote L*x* is, the more articulated its influence is on the dominant language, if the proficiency threshold is reached

---

[4]In Hungarian *perszóna* is used only for a woman in a negative sense. *Adminisztráció* refers to paperwork.

in multilingual development. However, at this point this speculation warrants future investigation and requires empirical support.

The subjective estimation of language distance also has a very important bidirectional influence on the vocabulary use. Kellerman (1977, 1978) studied the vocabulary use of Dutch-English bilinguals and found some interesting evidence that supports the importance of learner judgment on language distance. Dutch students acquired the English vocabulary somewhat easily because they could rely on the many cognates the two languages have. In acceptability tests they gave a systematic preference to transparent uses, when the sense of a word was closer to the core meaning.[5] It seems obvious that the notion of transparency presupposes universal form-meaning relations. This idea was supported by research (Kellerman, 1983; Osgood et al., 1975; Slobin, 1985).

Student judgments about idioms and metaphors are different. Kellerman (1977, 1978) found that students were reluctant to transfer idioms, even if the idioms were quite transparent. Dutch students frequently refused to accept idioms that are parallel in Dutch and English. Kellerman (1977) concluded that there are strong constraints on what is transferable from one language to the other and that "idioms are one class of language items that are generally not transferred" (pp. 101-102). To understand why, we return to the CUCB. Transfer of senses close to the core meaning of a word and the intransferability of idioms supports our hypothesis about the partial language specificity of the CUCB. Core meanings usually represent universal concepts that exist in most languages. These concepts are usually language neutral in the CUCB and easily transferable and useable through both language channels. Idioms and metaphors, however, are language specific. They are the representatives of a particular culture and demonstrate how people in that culture understand the world around them. Even if idioms are transparent and easy to comprehend (which is usually not the case), language learners are reluctant to transfer them.

According to the traditional view, idioms are simply a matter of language and have nothing to do with the conceptual system. They are regarded as a special set of the larger category of words. In this approach linguistic meaning is cut off from the conceptual system and encyclopedic knowledge shared by speakers of a particular language.

In contrast, Kövecses and Szabó (1996) argued that "most idioms are products of our conceptual system, and not simply a matter of language (i.e. a matter of the lexicon)" (p. 330). Idioms are not linguistic but conceptual in nature: They arise from our general knowledge of the world embodied in our conceptual system. The meanings of idioms are motivated and not arbitrary (Gibbs, 1990, 1994; Kövecses & Szabó, 1996; Lakoff, 1987, 1993). Semantic moti-

---

[5]The core meaning was determined through an experimental procedure.

vation is based on a cognitive mechanism that connects domains of knowledge to idiomatic meanings. Lakoff (1987) claimed that metaphor, metonymy, and conventional knowledge are the cognitive mechanisms responsible for the motivation of idioms. We do not have space here to discuss how these mechanisms function, but Kövecses and Szabó (1996) provided an excellent description. Based on Lakoff and Johnson (1980) and Lakoff (1993), they argued that conceptual metaphors link two domains of knowledge: one a familiar physical domain (i.e., source domain) and the other a less familiar abstract domain (i.e., target domain). The source domain is used to provide understanding about the target domain. Further, they explained how conceptual metaphors provide semantic motivation for the occurrence of particular words in idioms. In the idiom *spit fire*, the domain of fire is the source domain used to understand the target domain, anger. The conceptual metaphor here is the ANGER IS FIRE; that is, the concept of anger is supposed to be understood through the concept of fire. The conceptual metaphor serves as a link between an abstract domain and a more physical domain. To demonstrate that conceptual metaphors linking special idiomatic meaning and conceptual knowledge really exist and that metaphors are indeed conceptual in nature, Kövecses and Szabó collected several idioms in which the ANGER IS FIRE conceptual metaphor is represented:

After the row, he was spitting fire.
Smoke was coming out of his ears.
He is smoldering with anger.
She was fuming.
Boy, am I burned up!

L2 learners and bilinguals are probably reluctant to transfer idioms because cognitive mechanisms that motivate those idioms are not universal. To put it another way, only a part of conceptual metaphors, metonymies, and conventional knowledge can be found in most languages. The other part of these cognitive mechanisms is language specific. Students' reluctance may arise because they usually do not know which mechanism is language specific. From this respect it is interesting to discuss the results of our experiment that measured metaphorical density in texts produced by different types of foreign language learners (Kecskes & Papp, 2000).

Metaphorical Density in Multilingual Language Production

Earlier we suggested three procedures that can be used to measure the influence of foreign language learning on the mother tongue: structural well-formedness, use of linguistic memory versus visual memory, and metaphor-

TABLE 6.2
Metaphorical Density Surveys

First Survey (Composition: "My Home")

Class	Boys	Girls
Immersion Class	48%	36%
Intensive Class	40%	30%
Control Class	34%	35%

Second Survey (Picture-series)

Class	Boys	Girls
Immersion Class	56%	42%
Intensive Class	35%	32%
Control Class	38%	30%

ical density. We have already presented the results of the first two surveys in Chapter 2 (structural well-formedness) and Chapter 5 (linguistic memory vs. visual memory). At a later point texts produced by the Hungarian students in the longitudinal experiment were also analyzed for metaphorical density (Kecskes & Papp, 2000). An index of metaphorical density (MD) was computed for each written production in the foreign language and the mother tongue. This index simply measured the number of metaphorical sentences in the writings of the students as a percentage of the total number of sentences written. If, for instance, a text consisting of 9 sentences contained 3 metaphorical expressions the MD index was 3/9 = 0.33 = 33%. It was irrelevant for this count whether metaphorical expressions occurred in one sentence only or in several sentences. The method was the same as Danesi (1992) used in his study. A metaphorical sentence in his survey was defined as "a token or instantiation of the underlying culturally-appropriate conceptual system: e.g., an orientation metaphor, an entity metaphor, etc." (p. 496). We did not count repeated instantiations of a conceptual metaphor because these can be considered simply as elaborations. An average metaphorical density (AMD) was then computed for each group and test. The two surveys gave the following results in the L1 (see Table 6.2).

Metaphorical Density (MD)

$$\frac{\text{Number of Metaphorical Expressions}}{\text{Total number of sentences}} = \frac{ME}{TS}$$

The MD values in the table are for the students' L1, Hungarian. The Immersion Class is already slightly ahead of the two other classes in the first survey. This insignificant difference is very similar to what we saw in the structural well-formedness analysis in Chapter 2. It can be explained by two factors, one of which was already given in Chapter 2: students in the Immersion Class were selected based on the results of a logical test. This may have put them ahead of the other two groups. However, based on some extralinguistic factors a more convincing explanation can be given. Immersion students had to leave their homes to study in that dual language school. For the first time in their lives they were away from their families because they had to live in dormitories. This was not the case with the intensive and control classes, which were in a town where most of the students lived. There were few commuters among them. The topic of the composition (i.e., "My home") and the change in their living conditions may have pushed the children to reevaluate their relation with their home. They may have learned to value their home more than earlier, and that value showed in their compositions. Many of them emphasized the change in their understanding of what "home" really means for them. For instance:

"Nekem az otthon fogalma különösen mostanában kapott szerepet az életemben..." (For me the concept of home has recently received a higher priority in my life . . .)

"Mióta elköltoztem otthonról, teljesen megváltozott ennek a szónak a jelentése . . ." (Since I left home, the meaning of this word [home] has entirely changed for me.)

These students seem to have experienced a serious change in their lives that inspired them to describe their feelings about their home. Their approach resulted in a frequent use of metaphors and rather complex sentences. This may explain why they were slightly ahead of their peers in both indexes (i.e., structural well-formedness and metaphorical density) in the first survey; this difference can hardly be due to the effect of their previous FL experience.

The second survey demonstrated that the immersion class is way ahead of the other two classes but there is no significant difference between the intensive class and the control class. The 1-year period was enough only for the immersion class to become a clear leader both in the structural well-formedness and the MD indexes. It has been pointed out several times that we compared results within each test and did not try to compare results of different tests because of the different nature of tasks and the goal of the experiment. Writing a composition on "My home" and a story based on a series of pictures are two different tasks. A composition may be expected to elicit more metaphors than a picture-based story, but remarkably the MD index of the immersion class is better in the picture story than in

TABLE 6.3
MD Indexes in FL and L1

Immersion class

Students	French	L1 (Hungarian)
Boys	20%	56%
Girls	17%	42%

Standard deviation: 8 (boys L2)
8.35 (girls L2)

Intensive class

Students	English	Russian	L1 (Hungarian)
Boys	20%	13%	35%
Girls	16%	5%	32%

Standard deviation: 9.94 (girls L2, English)

Control class

Students	English/Russian	L1
Boys	no minimum data	38%
Girls	no minimum data	30%

the composition. However, there is no increase whatsoever in the two other classes' numbers. The results are even more interesting if we compare MD indexes in the FL and the L1 (Table 6.3).

High MD indexes in the L1 do not usually mean high MD indexes in the FL. The high level of metaphorical thinking in one language hardly results in better metaphorical competence in the other language, according to these data. Conceptual fluency is dominated by the L1, but proficiency in the FL usually has a positive influence on the monolithic conceptual base, resulting in more sophisticated conceptual thinking in the target language. From this respect it is interesting to examine some samples from the students' production written about the same series of pictures first in the target language and then in their L1.

The influence of L1 metaphorical thinking is obvious when students used target language words and phrases as carriers of their native language concepts. Our data show a clear connection between proficiency in the target language and the effect of L1 conceptual thinking. The less proficient a student was in the target language, the more he or she relied on L1-dominated metaphorical thinking. This was very common in the Russian productions of the specialized class and was not scarce in the English and French trilingual production either:[6]

"Он искал деньги."   (Equivalent of Hungarian :
                            "Pénzt keresett.")
                       "He was making money."
"I would like know with you."   (L1: "Szeretnék megismerkedni
                                veled.")
"Pierro semble trés léger."   (L1: "Pierro nagyon könnyednek
                                tünik.")
                  "Pierro seemed to be very relaxed."

There were some counterexamples where the student liked the FL phrase so much that he or she tried to use an equivalent in the L1 even if it did not exist or sounded a bit strange in the L1. This occurred in the French texts only.

"J'ai invité"   "invitálom"
"petite amie"   "kis barátnöjét"

In the intensive class productions were some cases where students clearly tried to use an equivalent of the FL metaphor in the L1 but were not sure if it was correct in the mother tongue. They crossed it out and used something that sounded better for them in the L1:

". . . a beautiful girl, with long fair hair caught his eyes."
"(Megpillantott) Szembe jött vele egy csinos szöke lány."

There were also some instances for concept mediation when a student included a metaphor in the FL text and looked for an equivalent in the L1. Several times students used conceptual metaphors that were alike in both languages:

"Je suis tombé sur une ancienne amie. . . ."   "Belebotlottam egy rég nem látott barátnömbe."
                   "I came across an old friend of mine."

Real concept mediation, however, occurred when metaphors lexicalized differently were used in both languages:

"Je devais aller chez moi"   "Haza kellett ugranom."

---

[6]In the examples no error correction was made. Student productions are quoted as they appear in the texts.

"I had to 'jump' home."

". . . and his eyes caught on a very pretty girl"
". . . észrevett egy feltünöen csinos lányt"

This survey supports the structural well-formedness analysis. After 9 months the immersion class preceded the other two classes in all indexes, but this period of time was too short for the intensive class to gain a significant advantage over the control class in the AMD index. Only if a certain threshold has been reached will the effect of a foreign language be significant enough to bring about changes in the use of mother tongue.

SUMMARY

Level of proficiency, typological closeness, and cultural distance are variables that affect the interrelation of languages in the multilingual LPD. All three have some kind of psychological reality for speakers; therefore, linguistic actions are seriously influenced by these variables. It is hard to say what is better for language learners, if their languages show typological and cultural closeness or distance. The Hungarian experiment suggested that if typological and cultural distance accompany a high level of proficiency in the L2, multicompetence can be expected to be slightly better than in the opposite case, when typological and cultural closeness pair with high-level L2 proficiency. However, the outcome of multilingual development is discussed here, not the developmental process itself. Multilingual development is usually longer and more difficult for language learners if their languages and cultures are distant because they need to make several changes in the CUCB. New concepts must be developed, and the existing ones have to be modified significantly to accommodate the new language and culture. This is usually not the case if the two languages are typologically close and there is not much distance between the cultures either.

Studies discussed in this chapter tend to point to two different tendencies. Theoretically, typological and cultural distance of languages may be expected to result in the development of a very flexible CUCB that brings two remote conceptual systems together. However, extralinguistic factors such as social identity, relations of power, anxiety, and motivation of the individual may seriously influence this process, especially in an L2 environment. We do not have a comprehensive theory that integrates the language learner, the language-learning context, and the language-learning process. A deeper understanding of the constantly changing social identity and its impact on language acquisition processes would help us better understand the ups and downs of multilingual development.

Both the syntactic well-formedness index (Chapter 2) and the metaphorical density index (this chapter) of Hungarian learners of foreign languages pointed to the same direction: students with a multilingual Language Processing Device (CUCB+CAIS) outperform their counterparts who do not have a multilingual LPD, or are just in the process of developing it. Similar conclusions were reported by Kessler and Quinn (1987) who used measuring devices similar to ours. They investigated the effects of bilingualism on the linguistic and cognitive creativity of language minority children proficiently bilingual in Spanish and English. Their research addressed the cognitive processes of divergent and convergent thinking and the linguistic process of metaphorising in the context of formulating scientific hypotheses. They viewed the linguistic and cognitive processes together as manifesting aspects of a common underlying creativity. Their subjects were 6th-grade students, age 11, in two intact classrooms, one with monolingual English-speaking majority children and the other with Spanish–English bilingual minority children. Both groups took part in an inquiry-based science programme in which they learned to formulate scientific hypotheses in a problem-solving setting (Kessler & Quinn, 1987). After the problem presentation sessions students were asked to write as many hypotheses as possible in a 12-minute period. Students' papers were then scored on three criteria: Quinn's Hypothesis Quality Scale (1972), the Syntactic Complexity Formula developed by Botel, Dawkins, and Granowsky (1973), and the Metaphor Index (Quinn & Kessler, 1986) created to assess semantic creativity. Kessler and Quinn (1987) reported that although the monolinguals were superior to bilinguals on a standardized test of reading in English, the bilingual children outperformed monolinguals in three scores: they generated high quality scientific hypotheses, used syntactically complex language and produced far more metaphors. Their findings on complex language use and metaphors concur with our results in the Hungarian experiment.

CHAPTER

7

Pragmatic Knowledge of Multilinguals

THE NATURE OF POSITIVE TRANSFER

Bialystok (1995) argued that language learning is a unique process: It is never exactly like learning anything else, "no matter how much general cognitive apparatus is shared" (p. 60). Language skills such as communicating, reading, understanding, and writing are special skills, distinguished at least as much by their uniqueness as by their generality. If we are not ready to acknowledge that these are special skills different from all other nonverbal activities, we will never be able to understand how any of these processes develop and function in humans.

In the Preface we referred to the double nature of transfer. In foreign language (FL) learners transfer is usually considered to be structural, phonological, and lexical with a negative overtone until the multicompetence threshold is reached. When, however, multicompetence is established in the mind, transfer usually becomes positive, with emphasis on knowledge and pragmatic skills that can be observed in the language use of multilingual speakers—in better language manipulating skills, metalinguistic awareness, good interaction style, broader knowledge base, and multicultural attitude. This assumption is supported not only by the Hungarian experiment but also by Verhoeven's (1994) study that addressed the linguistic interdependence hypothesis (Cummins, 1986), which states that in bilingual development, language and literacy skills can be transferred from one language to another. Verhoeven worked with Turkish children living in the Netherlands since infancy. During the longitudinal experiment he monitored the development of lexical, morphosyntactic, pragmatic, phonological, and literacy abilities in both the first language (L1; Turkish) and second language (L2; Dutch) of the children. Verhoeven's findings demonstrated almost no transfer at the level of lexicon and syntax. However, he found positive evidence for the interdependence in bilingual development at the level of pragmatic skills and literacy skills. It is important to note that these were multilingual speakers who were exposed to the L2 since infancy so it was essential that they developed a multicompetent language processing device (LPD) with a common underlying conceptual base (CUCB). Verhoeven's experiment confirmed that positive transfer usually occurs after multicompetence has developed, and for the existence of CUCB we can find evidence at the level of pragmatic skills and literacy skills.

We know very little about this positive transfer, that is, about pragmatic behaviors or other knowledge displays consistent across L1, L2, and the developing multicompetent LPD. Kasper and Blum-Kulka (1993) argued that this phenomenon has received little attention from researchers because positive transfer usually results in successful communication and therefore is less exciting to study. The other reason for neglect may be a methodological problem. It is difficult to distinguish positive transfer from universal pragmatic knowledge and generalization on the basis of pragmatic knowledge available in the developing multicompetent LPD.[1] In this chapter we discuss the interplay of pragmatic skills in written and spoken discourse in multicompetent speakers as well as the effect of sociocultural environment and background knowledge on this interplay. Further, we examine if this interplay also concerns FL learners who have managed to reach the proficiency threshold beyond which a CUCB is to develop.

Role of Sociocultural Environment

According to Bruner (1966), the sociocultural environment plays a major role in the child's cognitive growth once the symbolic stage is reached. Culture then serves as a catalyst for cognitive growth. It is therefore crucial to focus on the cultural environment—with its values, beliefs, world views, and presuppositions—in which multilingual development occurs and to understand its role in the development of multicompetence. Lambert (1977) introduced the notion of an interdependence hypothesis at the level of the internalization of social cultural values and language statuses: It is the relative status between the two languages and its internalization that determines the nature of biliguality. Evidence stemming from research on immersion programs (Bjorklund, 1995; Genesee, 1984, 1987; Swain & Lapkin, 1982) suggests that when a child is a member of a dominant ethnolinguistic group, for whom L1 is valorized in the community, schooling through the medium

---

[1]Kasper and Blum-Kulka discussed *available interlanguage pragmatic knowledge*.

of L2 may be a way for the child to develop high bilinguistic skills, possibly with positive cognitive effects.

A FL environment presents a unique challenge to the language learners because they have to enhance background knowledge and sociocultural competence without direct contact with the target language environment and culture. As a result FL students with a high command of linguistic competence in the target language often suffer culture shock when traveling or living in the country where their FL is spoken as a first language. Why does this happen? What do these FL students miss? Stalnaker (1991) argued that shared mutual beliefs and assumptions are essential in communication and comprehension. Several researchers (cf. Gonzalez, 1987; Schachter, 1983; Schmidt, 1993; Strevens, 1987) found that world views, beliefs, pragmatic assumptions, and values are almost always transferred from the L1 to the L2 environments. Willingness, motivation and ability of individual learners to assume L2 sociocultural beliefs and norms seem to play a decisive role in multilingual development. Consequently, an advanced non-native speaker cannot be expected "simply to abandon his/her own cultural world" (Barro, Byram, Grimm, Morgan, & Roberts, 1993, p. 56). Adamson (1988) pointed out that non-native speakers are often reluctant to accept and share the values, beliefs, and presuppositions of the L2 community even if they have been living there for a long period of time and can speak the language quite well. Language proficiency is, of course, a crucial factor, but not the only factor. Bardovi-Harlig (1996) observed that the range of success among students with a high level of grammatical proficiency is quite wide. Kecskes (1998) argued that this variety in pragmatic proficiency can partly be explained by individual learner differences. Students seem to have more control over their pragmatic development than their grammatical development. They frequently learn pragmatic units and develop pragmatic attitude by choice, which they usually cannot do when learning grammar. Acton and Walker de Felix (1986) claimed that until proficient non-native speakers reach an advanced acculturation stage, their language production is usually based on their L1 world view and its sociocultural framework. Hinkel (1995) demonstrated how cultural values are reflected in the use of modal verbs in the language production of non-native speakers of English. All these findings seem to point to one important conclusion: L2 language production is heavily influenced by the L1-dominated conceptual base until the language learner reaches an advanced acculturation threshold. Successfully reaching this acculturation threshold depends not only on the development of L2 language proficiency but also the willingness of the speaker to acquire the new sociocultural frameworks and make them a functional part of their CUCB.

From this perspective it is interesting to note the evidence that this motivation and willingness sometimes appears to be more intensive in the case of FL learners than in the case of L2 learners. This "socially motivated transfer" (Beebe, 1988, p. 56) occurs when the foreign language is highly valorized in the given society (e.g., English in Hungary). FL learners transfer certain parts of the sociocultural competence developed in the target language to the first language, which can make their communicative behavior rather odd in an environment where the FL is not spoken outside the classroom. The oral encounters with the students during the Hungarian experiment revealed several interesting things. Although none of those phenomena was specifically investigated by us, we find it important to mention some of them. Students from the immersion and intensive classes sometimes used intonation in their L1 production clearly transferred from their L2 and mixed words from the L2 into their L1 speech when there was no particular reason for it. Linguistic means were transferred from the L2 to the L1 without any linguistic or communicative need. The use of intonation patterns and L2 words in the L1 production of the participants of the Hungarian experiment can be considered negative transfer. It was conscious and controlled by the speakers and, in our opinion, it appeared to be a way of showing off before schoolmates and other people who did not have the privilege to be a part of an immersion or intensive program.[2] These same students, however, showed a positive transfer of pragmatic skills and knowledge in conversation through both language channels. They addressed issues from a broader perspective than their counterparts whose FL training was less intensive, and their linguistic behavior in conversations demonstrated careful planning. Their linguistically well-organized, situationally appropriate, carefully planned, intelligent answers and approach to topics raised during our conversations may partly be due to the beneficial effect of their multicompetent CUCB, although there is no direct evidence for that.[3]

Another interesting example for pragmatic transfer is the intercultural style hypothesis (Kasper & Blum-Kulka, 1993). It refers to a unique development of the CUCB in multilingual people. According to this hypothesis (Blum-Kulka, 1991; Blum-Kulka & Sheffer, 1993; Kasper & Blum-Kulka, 1993), speakers fully competent in two languages may create an intercultural style of speaking that is both related to and distinct from the styles prevalent in the two substrata, a style on which they rely regardless of the language being used (Kasper & Blum-Kulka, 1993). Kasper and Blum-Kulka claimed that the hypothesis is supported by many studies of cross-cultural communication, especially those focusing on interactional sociolinguistics (e.g., Gumperz, 1982; Tannen, 1985), and research into the pragmatic behavior of

---

[2]In Eastern European countries it is still considered to be a kind of privilege or great achievement to enroll in dual language schools or programs where a western language is studied intensively.

[3]There is no evidence that their oral production was positively influenced by the knowledge of the L2. We demonstrated, however, that their written production had clear signs of the beneficial effect of the L2.

immigrant populations across generations (e.g., Clyne, Ball, & Neil, 1991). Our experience with the immersion class and the specialized class in Hungary (Kecskes & Papp, 1991) and some findings of the Finnish immersion program (Bjorklund, 1995) also seem to indicate that native speakers develop some kind of intercultural style while learning a FL intensively or studying content area subjects in the FL.

THOUGHT AND DISCOURSE

The sociocultural interdependence in the multicompetent LPD is reflected most clearly in the relation of thought and discourse. In the previous chapters we examined the relations of thought and word and thought and sentence. Here our target is thought and discourse. The discourse organization of multilingual speakers demonstrates the beneficial effect of subsequent languages on the language processing and production of multilingual speakers (Papp, 1991; Pavlenko, 1996). The question is how this beneficial effect comes about when languages show great differences in their discourse organization. A firmly established multicompetent LPD seems to balance these differences and lead to better skills in using either system according to the multilingual person's communicative needs. Research on the nature of cross-linguistic variation in discourse has demonstrated that there are great differences in the discourse organization in different cultures, and these differences are dependent upon two main variables: sociocultural norms and conventions of the community and language typology.

Oral Discourse

Norms of Conversation. Richards (1980) argued that when non-native speakers violate norms of conversation in their L2, the violations are potentially much more serious than errors in pronunciation and syntax because such violations can affect what is usually called the presentation of self. The usual bottom-up and unit-by-unit approach to FL learning does not support the development of multicompetence. Students do not have much opportunity to learn about coherence of discourse in the target language community. Odlin (1989) argued that the notion of coherence is applicable to conversations and monologues in every society, but relations between linguistic means expressing this coherence can vary to a great extent in the discourse patterns of different languages. Because the conceptual base of non-native speakers is governed by the discourse patterns of their native tongue until the multicompetence threshold is passed, cross-linguistic differences in discourse can affect production as well as comprehension. Non-native speakers may sound rude or inappropriate when they use their own L1-based discourse patterns and norms in the target language (Kecskes, 1998). In the case of multicompetent speakers, however, the development of an intercultural style and the ability to use different discourse patterns is essential. Speakers with a multicompetent LPD are expected to know what is appropriate and inappropriate to say in certain situations. Kasper and Blum-Kulka (1993) argued that at a conceptual level negative pragmatic transfer does not always reflect lack of competence in the pragmatics of the target language community. Although multilingual speakers know the rules, they may choose not to act accordingly. The degree of sociocultural accommodation to the culture of the L2 (or Lx) may be as well a matter of choice as of ability.

There are several variables that regulate multicompetent speakers' decisions about keeping or violating the pragmatic rules of either of their languages. First is context dependency. Takahashi (1992) investigated the transferability of conventionally indirect requests from Japanese to English and found that although learners' proficiency and familiarity with the situation are also important, the context has the decisive effect on the choice of Japanese students. Second is linguistic and cultural distance. The specificity or closeness of pragmalinguistic or sociopragmatic patterns in the two (or more) languages also regulates pragmatic transfer (Kasper & Blum-Kulka, 1993).

Third, is non-native perception of L2 sociopragmatic norms. Sometimes multicompetent speakers are fully aware of the content of a specific concept existing in only one of their languages, but they are not able to perceive it as the native speakers do. A typical example is the concept of "potluck dinner," which is very popular in American culture. There is a good explanation for it: Americans like socializing and being in the company of others, but they do not necessarily want to pick up the expenses (or all expenses) of these get-togethers. Therefore everyone is expected to contribute to the party with food or drinks. This approach is almost unacceptable for a Russian, Japanese, or Hungarian, whose culture requires a host to be responsible for the guests. Although bilingual speakers of English and Japanese, English and Russian, or English and Hungarian understand this sociocultural phenomenon as an outsider, they usually do not as an insider no matter how high the level of their multicompetence is. This is especially the case with multilingual speakers who started to develop their multicompetence as adults. Finally, convergence or divergence with the speech community affects linguistic decisions. Appropriate use of sociopragmatic patterns is considered a marker of cultural identity and depends on individual choice in each situation.

Use of Pragmatic Routines. According to Kasper and Blum-Kulka (1993), "one area where insufficient control of pragmalinguistic knowledge is particularly obvious is that of pragmatic routines" (p. 9). We conducted an experiment (Kecskes, 1999) focusing on situation-bound utterances (SBUs), which constitute a particular group of formulaic expressions. SBUs are highly conventionalized, prefabricated units whose occurrence is tied to more or less standardized communicative situations (Coulmas, 1981; Fónagy, 1982; Kecskes, 1997; in press; Kiefer, 1985). If, according to their obligatoriness and predictability in social situations, formulaic expressions are placed on a continuum where obligatoriness increases to the right, SBUs will take the rightmost place because their use is highly predetermined by the situation.

The cross-sectional experiment aimed at investigating two closely related research questions concerning the use of SBUs by non-native speakers of English (NNSs): What are the variables that affect the use of SBUs by NNSs? Why, in a given situation, of all possible SBUs that can be used, only certain SBUs are used by NNSs? Eighty-eight NNS students and 33 native speakers of English (NS) were given three different types of test: two discourse completion tests, a problem-solving test, and a dialogue interpretation test. All participants of the experiment had started to learn English as a FL (i.e., designated EFL). This fact seriously affected their use of SBUs. EFL learners always have a more conscious approach to language production than learners who acquire the language in a naturalistic environment with or without instruction. This FL learning strategy is characterized by an analytic, bottom-up approach to language production, less automatic use of unanalyzed chunks, more L1 pragmatic dependency, and a more dominant role of individual learner strategy (Kecskes, 1999).

In order to answer the research questions, data were analyzed for several variables that could affect the use of SBUs. Regarding the nature of SBUs, we looked at semantic transparency and compositional structure, relative frequency, and cultural specificity. For individual learner differences, we looked at individual learner strategy and length of stay.

Here we focus only on these two latter variables. An important finding of the survey was that individual learner strategies dominated the selection and use of SBUs. Because SBUs are learned rather than evolve in the L2 speakers play an active role in selecting which SBU or SBUs to acquire for particular situations. Their like or dislike of certain expressions and situations was demonstrated in their verbal behavior. Students often picked some expressions from their inventory and started to use them in a formulaic way. The increase of L2 knowledge seems to lead away from target-oriented verbal behavior to a phase of creative but sometimes pragmatically inadequate verbalizations (Bahn, Burmeister, & Vogel, 1986). Cognitive mechanisms responsible for SBUs can differ to a great extent in the L1 and L2. Pragmatic transfer, however, is motivated not only by L1 influence but also by individual learner like and dislike of pragmatic units. Length of stay in the target language country was relevant only if combined with previous exposure to the target language. There was no significant difference between the production of students who had lived in the United States for 1 year and those who had lived in the United States 3 years. Better pragmatic skills were noticeable, however, when students studied the target language as a foreign language for a longer period of time in their home country and had lived in the United States for at least 1 year. Three or four years of study of the target language as a FL and more than 1 year exposure to the target culture seem to be sufficient for multicompetence to start to develop.

Written Discourse

In an attempt to categorize the ESL writings of students from various countries with different cultural backgrounds, Kaplan (1966) compared the written productions of students in terms of different types of lines. He claimed that "the foreign-student paper is out of focus because the foreign student is employing a rhetoric and a sequence of thought which violate the expectations of the native reader" (p. 4). This violation of discourse organization of English can be explained by the fact that the rhetoric and sequence of thought of foreign students reflect the discourse and thought patterns of their own cultures. According to Kaplan, writing in English resembles a straight line because it is supposed to be direct and straight to the point. The same cannot be said about writing in Russian or in Oriental languages. Kaplan suggested that Russian writing resembles a zigzag, whereas writing in Oriental languages is something like a "widening gyre" (p. 4).

There is not enough evidence to generalize these claims, but several other studies have led to similar conclusions. Comprehension of written discourse depends on two important variables: familiarity with the culture and presentation of information. Each can seriously jeopardize the understanding of the coherence and content of a discourse. Kintsch and Greene (1978) argued that narratives have culturally specific patterns, and cultural differences in the format of narratives can cause problems in comprehension. According to Carrell (1982), coherence of discourse is dependent upon the coherence of content, rather than on the formal structure of discourse. The coherence of content is the reflection of thought processes underlying any discourse form. The problem is that coherence that is closely related to the notions of logic and relevance can hardly be reached without the use of appropriate linguistic means. It appears that both discourse organization and means of coherence in a particular language are highly conventionalized and dependent on typological features and cultural phenomena. These unique features of writing in different languages are traceable both at sentence level and discourse level.

Rutherford (1983) reported that his experiment revealed strong typological transfer in the English written production of Mandarin, Japanese, and Korean speakers. These students were especially sensitive to topic versus subject prominence and pragmatic versus grammatical word order differences. However, there was no sign of transfer of canonical arrangements of S, V, and O. Rutherford concluded that transferable typologies—topic prominence and pragmatic word order—are discourse phenomena, whereas the untransferable S, V, O configurations are a syntactic phenomenon. Based on this observation Rutherford made a very important statement: "I take these observations as evidence that it is therefore discourse and not syntax that gives gross overall shape to interlanguage" (p. 368).

Although Rutherford made this statement from an interlanguage perspective, it still can fit into our cognitive-pragmatic framework. This claim strongly supports Verhoeven's (1994) findings and our observation about multicompetence that has been emphasized several times in this book: The beneficial effects of multicompetence appear at conceptual rather than at grammatical or lexical level. Rutherford noted that the interlanguages of learners whose mother tongue and target language contrast typologically usually manifest unique features that can be explained by this typological intersection. This is exactly what we found in the LPD of FL students with multicompetence. Rutherford (1983) was also right when he wrote that these characteristic features "do not appear as discrete entities, nor are they amenable to traditional cross-language surface comparison. They are rather abstractions and, as such, have much wider generalizability" (p. 368). Our findings (Kecskes, 1998; Kecskes & Papp, 1995; T. Papp, 1991) also demonstrated that bidirectional interdependence results in unique abstractions that are traceable to the CUCB rather than to the two (or more) channels of CAIS. The other important factor accompanying these unique abstractions is bidirectionality. Rutherford spoke only about L1 → L2 influence, but in the L1 production of speakers with multicompetence the L2 influence also appears in unique abstractions that are traceable in structural well-formedness of sentences, the use of linguistic versus visual memory, and metaphorical density.

The differences between writing in English and writing in other languages become especially articulated in English composition classes where NNSs are expected to learn how to write American academic essays. A study by Purves (1986) examined this issue very thoroughly. Purves reported that NNSs struggle when they are expected to organize a text according to the requirements of American cultural conventions but this problem is expected to disappear when students get over the multicompetence threshold. Purves participated in 5 years of research for the International Association for the Evaluation of Education Achievement (IEA), which examined the writing of students from 15 countries in their native language. Purves concluded that within each culture or society at least one if not several rhetorical communities exist. The term *rhetorical community* is used in the same sense as Fish's (1980) *interpretive community*. During the research students were asked to write in class on the topic "My native town," a topic selected to be as nondirective as possible. If the compositions were not written in English, they were translated from the original language. The translators were asked to retain the style and flavor of the original texts. All translations were checked by bilingual teachers for fidelity to the original. Purves found "a striking difference between countries and a striking similarity within countries" (p. 40). The research focused on both formal and stylistic features of texts.

Like Hofstede (1980) and Glenn and Glenn (1981), Purves assumed that national writing styles reflect important differences in the values and cognition styles of the given culture, and therefore these differences among national communities will be likely to be sharper as students progress through the educational system. For educators this may mean that the later a student comes to study in another country, the more difficult it will be to modify his or her writing style based on education in the L1.[4] When students enter another system, they are expected to participate as full-fledged members of that new system without fully knowing what its rules and conditions might be (Purves, 1986). This usually does not work until students have reached the threshold in their L2 proficiency and have had practice in the required presentation format. As mentioned earlier, language production not only is influenced by sociocultural conventions but also is dependent upon the way in which the language of that particular linguistic-cultural community is organized. A language that is a subject-prominent, configurational, syntactically dominant, GWO language such as English will definitely have a presentation format different from that of a language that is topic-prominent, nonconfigurational, pragmatically dominant, and PWO, such as Russian. The question is how this organizational difference is reflected in the presentation style. Rhetorical differences are multidimensional and usually include factors such as the inductive–deductive dimension, linear–nonlinear organization, and topic-centered versus topic-associating style.

Having reviewed the findings of several researchers (Fish, 1980; Glen & Glen, 1981; Y. Kachru, 1982, 1986; Kaplan, 1966; Kintsch & Greene, 1978; Odlin, 1989; Purves, 1986; Sato, 1989) concerning presentation formats in different cultures, we conclude that the further a language can be placed to the right on the configurational or GWO versus nonconfigurational or PWO typological continuum, the greater the chance that this language will have an inductive, nonlinear, and topic-associating presentation format. However, this hypothesis needs further investigation because at present it is merely speculation. Based on its configurational, subject-prominent, GWO, and syntactically dominant structure, the English presentation style appears to be more deductive, linear, and topic centered than inductive, non-

---

[4]The level of proficiency, however, is a very important variable in this case.

linear, and topic associating. *Deductive* and *linear* do not need to be explained, but *topic-centeredness* does. According to our knowledge the dichotomy of topic centered and topic-associating presentational styles was first used by Michaels (1981, 1986), detailing a contrast in the discourse patterns of Black English Vernacular-speaking students and their Caucasian teacher. Michaels described the topic-centered style of White students in the class as "tightly organized, centering on a single topic or series of closely related topics, with thematic development accomplished through lexical cohesion, and a linear ordering of events, leading quickly to a punch line resolution" (p. 102). On the other hand, he argued that the African American students' topic-associating presentation style represented "a series of segments or episodes which are implicitly linked in highlighting some person or theme" (p. 103).

Michaels discussed oral presentation styles in an entirely different context than the one discussed here. We, however, think that the topic-centered versus topic-associating dichotomy has its validity when languages are compared according to their presentation styles. It is enough to compare an article written on a linguistic topic in English by a NS of English to another article written on a linguistic topic in Russian by a NS of Russian. In the English article the point is made at the very beginning of the article, and then come the facts that support the argument, with a summary at the end functioning like a conclusion. In the Russian article, however, first comes a list of facts that are about the topic, but it is not yet clear exactly how those facts are connected. Close to the end of the article the loosely connected facts are united in an inseparable whole supporting the main point that is just becoming clear for the reader. This presentation style, used by a NS of Russian writing an essay, composition, or article in English, can easily upset a NS of English who is not familiar with that kind of organization of text.

The language and culture dependency of presentation styles receives a particular overtone in countries where a language functions like a lingua franca for the whole population. India, with its own variety of English, is a good example. Y. Kachru (1986) argued that non-native varieties are variations in their own right. People learn a lingua franca in order to fulfill their communicative needs, which may not coincide with the needs of the NSs of the target language. The language use of these speakers differs from that of the NSs of the target language because their cultures and ways of thinking are different. This difference is reflected in the variety of the target language that the new speakers develop according to their communicative needs and based on their perceptions of the world around them. Y. Kachru (1982) argued that in Indian English texts, the writers usually transfer the discourse structure of Hindi texts. Because the discourse structure in the Indic tradition is cyclical, spiral, and nonsequential rather than straight and sequential as in English, texts written in English by Hindi-speaking writers are difficult for NSs of English to understand. According to Y. Kachru, differences in the discourse organization of the two languages are the reflections of typological and cultural differences. She underlined that in L2 learning an increased awareness of different strategies of coherence and cohesion facilitates interpretation of texts in the target language.

SUMMARY

In written discourse the sociocultural experience of language learners appears to be even more decisive than in spoken discourse. The individual language learner has less control over the use of discourse patterns carved into the mind by the L1 development and education. Comparing native speakers of English with non-native speakers Kaplan (1990) concluded: "The non-native English speaker is likely to have a different notion of what constitutes evidence, of the optimal order in which evidence ought to be presented, and of the number of evidentiary instances that need to be presented in order to induce conviction in the reader" (p. 10). Length of stay in the target language country functions more like a variable than it does in the case of oral discourse. Until multicompetence occurs, a typical language learner will think in the L1, following previously established patterns, norms, and sequences of activation and will look for words and possible forms in the L2 that seem appropriate to fulfill the required communicative task. Grabois (1996) argued that in order for the L2 to become an embodied means of cognizing the world, a sufficient richness and intensity of experience needs to be mediated by the L2. The rigidity of mapping onto the L1 will begin to break down, and the L2 will no longer be an encased system embedded in the L1. This breakdown means that a multilingual LPD begins to develop with a CUCB that makes it possible for the L2 channel to function as a mediational tool. Grabois asked a question similar to the one we asked at the beginning of this book: Can multicompetence develop in a FL environment? In Grabois' words, "can students use the L2 as a mediational tool in a classroom setting?" (p. 10). Grabois was not optimistic, noting that the classroom would need to approximate the richness and intensity of life, which is usually not the case. Our experiment, in contrast, demonstrated that this development is not impossible in immersion classes and classes where the language is studied with sufficient intensity. We agree with Grabois that it is not learning discourse that counts but participating in it, because "true participation in a discourse requires not only negotiating meaning, but also situating oneself in relation to the other participants (p. 20)." In fact, discourse is a procedure: One has to be engaged in it in order to learn it. This makes the development of multicompetence difficult (but not impossible) in a classroom setting. Even if students situate themselves in relation to other participants, the other participants are usually not NSs but language learners. We also cannot expect multilingual speakers to act like NSs because although they can inhabit discourse patterns and behavior norms, their linguistic behavior and discourse activities will always depend on more variables than the NS's actions are governed by.

In this chapter we also pointed out something important about the changing nature of transfer. In the first period of the multilingual development transfer is usually characterized by structural and lexical features, and the process is very rarely affected directly by the learner's preferences. The learner plays a passive role with sensitivity to differences and similarities in structure and lexicon. When, however, the CUCB starts to develop and transfer becomes mainly pragmatic and knowledge transfer, individual learners begin to play a more decisive and conscious role in the process. Beebe and Giles (1984) emphasized the extreme importance of speakers' subjective feelings, values, and motives that play a crucial role in determining discourse behavior. This observation was supported by further research in cross-cultural and interlanguage pragmatics (cf. Bardovi-Harlig, 1996; Cenoz & Valencia, 1996; Kasper & Blum-Kulka, 1993; Kecskes, 1998).

Conclusion

In this book we have attempted to present the state of the art in our present knowledge about the effect of foreign language (FL) learning on the development and use of mother tongue skills. Throughout our discussion it has been obvious that the issues and the problems raised by this phenomenon are of a degree of complexity such that we are only beginning to appreciate the magnitude of the task. All along we have emphasized that the effect of L2→L1 can be best explained from a multilingual perspective, and stressed the need for an interdisciplinary approach when studying this complex issue. Neither bilingual research nor second language (L2) research can account for all processes that go on in the mind of a multilingual speaker. We need the mutual effort of many disciplines such as psycholinguistics, theoretical linguistics, sociolinguistics, cognitive linguistics, communication studies, etc. to consider the totality of the phenomenon and describe the multicompetent language processing device. We have attempted in this book to bring together findings from these fields in order to explain multilingual language development.

Following the Lambertian tradition (Lambert, 1974) in our theoretical framework we have integrated the cognitive and the sociocultural dimensions. Although we have tried to keep this theoretical framework as a leading principle, several times we were compelled to turn to other theories and models for the sake of better presentation of the problem in question. This has never meant, however, that we have given up our original theoretical approach. Universal Grammar (UG) theory, connectivism, theory of communication and other areas only helped us introduce the issue, which, after all, was interpreted within the confines of the cognitive–pragmatic approach.

Relying on Grosjean's (1982, 1985, 1992) wholistic view of bilingualism Cook (1991b, 1992) postulated the theory of multicompetence as an alternative to the mainly UG-based monolingual approach to propose the idea that because more than 50% of the inhabitants of the earth speak more than one language, the main question of linguistics should be "what constitutes knowledge of languages?" rather than "what constitutes knowledge of language." Following Grosjean and Cook we have developed our model of the multilingual Language Processing Device with a Common Underlying Conceptual Base and two or more Constantly Available Interacting Systems which can accommodate not only the L1→L2 effect but the L2→L1 effect as well. In multicompetent speakers the interplay of the two or more languages has a positive result not in the CAIS but in the CUCB. Consequently, this effect is cognitive, cultural and pragmatic in nature rather than structural or lexical. One of the most difficult problems of the research on the L2→L1 effect is that this influence is hard to demonstrate because its processes are difficult to quantify using the research methodology that is presently available for us. The task is not impossible but there is no doubt that we are only at the beginning of this investigation, and much more research is needed to reveal the nature of processes characterizing the operation of the CUCB and the language behavior of multilingual speakers.

Our main focus in this book has been on one particular type of multicompetence: the multicompetence of language learners acquiring their foreign language in a classroom setting. This perspective had a serious impact on the selection of problems highlighted here and the research methodology applied to support the points made. Some methods we used proved to be effective. The analysis of structural well-formedness, use of linguistic versus visual memory and measuring metaphorical density in language production helped us demonstrate that there is some influence of the FL on the state of L1 knowledge in foreign language learners but only when a certain threshold in FL proficiency has been reached. This claim has been supported by the results of other research (Van Hell, 1998) that has not yet been published. Van Hell (1998) argued that "native language performance of bi(multi)linguals can be influenced by foreign language knowledge, but only when the person is sufficiently fluent in the foreign language." Whether a FL learner reaches this fluency threshold or not, depends on three variables: exposure, age, and motivation, each is very important for the development of a multicompetent LPD.

The interactive functioning of two or more languages and the beneficial effect of the L2 on the L1 through the CUCB has several implications for both linguistic and language education research. As mentioned in the Preface, few people listened to Roman Jacobson (1953) when he suggested that bilingualism is the fundamental problem of linguistics. For many years in both theoretical linguistics and bilingualism research we have had a strong monolingual view that has categorically denied any kind of linguistic relativism. The climate, however, seems to have been changing in both disciplines in the last decade. There have been attempts to rethink and revise linguistic relativity (cf. Gumperz & Levinson, 1996; Kecskes, 1998; Pavlenko, forthcoming). The multilingual perspective allows us to look inside the real 'deep structure' of language which is not just a collection of rules and words but an extremely complex and unique phenomenon in which human mind and the outside world meet. If that outside world requires the use of more than one language the human mind is capable of doing the adjustment. Linguistic theory should address the nature of this adjustment. We know very little yet about the multilingual mind as opposed to the monolingual one, but we know two things for sure: A multilingual is not two or more monolinguals in one body, and the acceptance of a "weak" version of linguistic relativism seems to be essential in any research that aims at explaining the relationship of language and cognition in multilinguals. The multilingual CUCB is not neutral: it contains language and culture specific elements because concept development is not restricted to only one language in the multilingual mind. This claim requires us to rethink several major issues of bilingual or multilingual research such as the relationship of two or more systems in the mind, multilingual language processing, the conceptual–linguistic interface, code switching and code mixing, and the output of the multilingual system. We also need new research methods to investigate the output of the multilingual system in comparison to each monolingual system represented in a unique way in the multilingual LPD. This book has focused mainly on written speech. Spoken language was addressed only when the subject matter under discussion required us to do so. We would need to know more about multilingual oral production; how does it differ from monolingual oral production, and how can the signs of multicompetence be traced in spoken language?

For educators this book has three important conclusions. First, it was claimed that the CUCB is language and culture specific, and is always dominated by one of the languages of the multilingual. When children enter school language becomes the main regulator of thinking (Vygotsky, 1962). This means that we have to be very careful when deciding which language to make the medium of instruction in bilingual programs. Children need to have a strong conceptual system to succeed in education. Only fully developed abstract concepts acquired through one of the language channels can be modified for use through any language channels of the multilingual LPD if the given channel is proficient enough to "carry" those concepts. The development of abstract concepts and the ability to use language metaphorically are based on strong concrete concepts that are gradually shaped by experience in the sociocultural environment. Multilingualism leads to success in educational achievements if the CUCB consists of fully development concrete and abstract concepts no matter which language channel has been responsible for their development in a given period of time.

Second, testing procedures developed for monolinguals are almost useless to measure multilingual skills and knowledge (cf. Oller, 1997). Even if we take an extreme case the result may not be very favorable for the multilingual: Suppose a multilingual person has excellent proficiency in one of his or her languages and is tested in that particular language. In this case the CUCB is expected to function as a monolingual conceptual base, which is hardly possible since the CUCB has been filled through more than one language channel. "Monoglottosis" as Oller (1997, p. 467) calls it, is not without danger for multilingual development. Oller (1997, p. 468) argued that "people who are monolingual (monodialectal) are naturally language/dialect blind. It is not at all obvious to them that they even require a language/dialect for thinking, conceptualizing, and expressing information." This is quite a strong claim which we cannot discuss here. One thing, however, is sure: tests for multilinguals have to be prepared by multilinguals.

Third, we call educators' attention to the idea, that foreign language is not just another school subject. FL learning requires and develops a complexity of skills that can have very beneficial effects on the general development of every student. FLs should be taught not just for themselves but for the general educational enhancement and development of students. The U.S. educational system has no national standards in language arts. Requirements change state by state, and there are no common syllabi. Students are given much freedom and flexibility in their language use. In the elementary and middle school they are not drilled to acquire the specific code of their written language. There is more emphasis on vocabulary acquisition than on the development of written speech. Individual learner differences do not disappear but become more articulated. FL instruction is almost nonexistent in most places in the country at elementary and middle school level. The development of national standards in language arts, the introduction of compulsory foreign language studies at least at the high school level, and the coordination of mother tongue and FL education would lead to a more conscious and creative use of the English language in written speech. Several good foreign language programs supporting multilingual development have been reported in the literature (Allen, Anderson, & Narvaez, 1993; Mitchell & Redmond, 1993; Richard-Amato, 1988; Verhoeven, 1991), but only some pay attention to the problem of how to coordinate FL instruction with mother tongue education. Most programs want to cease the curricular isolation of foreign language learning and emphasize the "FL across the curriculum" approach (cf. Watkins, 1990). Language arts is only one of several content area subjects that these programs want FL instruction to be connected with: there is no special part of these programs aiming at coordinating mother tongue education with foreign language teaching. Based on the research discussed in this book, we assume that a special coordination of mother tongue education and FL teaching could be very beneficial for the overall language and cognitive development of students.

References

Acton, W., & Walker de Felix, J. (1986). Acculturation and mind. In J. Valdes (Ed.), *Culture bound* (pp. 20–32). Cambridge, England: Cambridge University Press.

Adamson, H. D. (1988). *Variation theory and second language acquisition.* Washington, DC: Georgetown University Press.

Adamson, H. D. (1993). *Academic competence.* New York: Longman.

Aitchison, J. (1994). *Words in the mind.* Oxford, England: Basil Blackwell.

Allen, W., Anderson, K., & Narvaez, L. (1993). Foreign language across the curriculum. In J. W. Oller, Jr. (Ed.), *Methods that work* (pp. 149–159). Boston, MA: Heinle & Heinle.

Andersen, R. W. (1982). Determining the linguistic attributes of language attrition. In R. D. Lambert & B. F. Freed (Eds.), *The loss of language skills* (pp. 83–118). Rowley, MA: Newbury House.

Andersen, R. W. (1983). Transfer to somewhere. In S. Gass & L. Selinker (Eds.), *Language transfer in language learning* (pp. 177–201). Rowley, MA: Newbury House.

Anderson, J. R. (1983). *The architecture of cognition.* Cambridge, MA: Harvard University Press.

Anderson, J. R. (1985). *Cognitive psychology and its implications.* New York: Freeman.

Applegate, J. L., & Delia, J. G. (1980). Person-centered speech, psychological development, and the contexts of language use. In R. St. Clair & H. Giles (Eds.), *The social and psychological contexts of language* (pp. 245–282). Hillsdale, NJ: Lawrence Erlbaum Associates.

Bahn, J., Burmeister, H., & Vogel, T. (1986). The pragmatics of formulas in L2 learner speech: Use and development. *Journal of Pragmatics, 10,* 693–723.

Baker, C. (1996). *Foundations of bilingual education and bilingualism.* Clevedon, England: Multilingual Matters.

Bardovi-Harlig, K. (1996). Pragmatics and language teaching: Bringing pragmatics and pedagogy together. *Pragmatics and Language Learning, 7,* 21–41.

Barro, A., Byram, M., Grimm, H., Morgan, C., & Roberts, C. (1993). Cultural studies for advanced language learners. In D. Graddol, L. Thompson, & M. Byram (Eds.), *Language and culture* (pp. 55–70). Clevedon, England: Multilingual Matters.

Bates, E., & MacWhinney, B. (1981). Functionalist approaches to grammar. In E. Wanner & L. Gleitman (Eds.), *Language acquisition: The state of the art.* New York: Cambridge University Press.

REFERENCES

Bates, E., & MacWhinney, B. (1987). Competition, variation, and language learning. In B. MacWhinney (Ed.), *Mechanism of language acquisition* (pp. 173–217). Hillsdale, NJ: Lawrence Erlbaum Associates.

Beebe, L. (1987). Five sociolinguistic approaches to second language acquisition. In L. Beebe (Ed.), *Issues in second language acquisition* (pp. 43–77). New York: Newbury House.

Beebe, L., & Giles, H. (1984). Speech-accommodation theories: A discussion in terms of second-language acquisition. *International Journal of the Sociology of Language, 46*, 5–32.

Benyon, J., & Tooney, K. (1991). Heritage language education in British Columbia: Policy and programs. *Canadian Modern Language Review, 47*, 606–616.

Ben-Zeev, S. (1977). The influence of bilingualism on cognitive strategy and cognitive development. *Child Development, 48*, 1009–1018.

Berko Gleason, J. (1993). *The development of language.* New York: Macmillan.

Berlin, B. (1971). *Speculations on the growth of ethnobotanical nomenclature* (Working Paper No. 39). Berkeley: University of California Language Behavior Research Laboratory.

Berns, M. (1990). 'Second' and 'foreign' language acquisition/foreign language learning: A sociolinguistic perspective. In B. VanPatten & J. F. Lee (Eds.), *Second language acquisition/foreign language learning* (pp. 3–13). Clevedon, England: Multilingual Matters.

Bernstein, B. (1962). Social class, linguistic codes and grammatical elements. *Language and Speech, 5*, 31–46.

Bernstein, B. (1964). Elaborated and restricted codes: Their social origins and consequences. *American Anthropologist, 6*(6), 55–69.

Bernstein, B. (1973). *Class, codes and control.* London: Routledge & Kegan Paul.

Berwick, R. (1985). *The acquisition of syntactic knowledge.* Cambridge, MA: MIT Press.

Bialystok, E. (1986). Factors in the growth of linguistic awareness. *Child Development, 57*, 498–510.

Bialystok, E. (1988). Levels of bilingualism and levels of linguistic awareness. *Developmental Psychology, 24*, 560–567.

Bialystok, E. (1991). *Language processing in bilingual children.* Cambridge, England: Cambridge University Press.

Bialystok, E. (1995). Why we need grammar: Confessions of a cognitive generalist. In L. Eubank, L. Selinker, & M. Sharwood Smith (Eds.), *The current state of interlanguage* (pp. 55–63). Amsterdam: Benjamins.

Bialystok, E., & Ryan, E. B. (1985). Toward a definition of metalinguistic skill. *Merrill-Palmer Quarterly, 31*, 229–251.

Bierwisch, M., & Schreuder, R. (1992). From concepts to lexical items. *Cognition, 42*, 23–60.

Bild, E. R., & Swain, M. (1989). Minority language students in a French immersion programme: Their French proficiency. *Journal of Multilingual and Multicultural Development, 10*, 255–274.

Birdsong, D. (1989). *Metalinguistic performance and interlinguistic competence.* New York: Springer-Verlag.

Biró, Z. (1984). *Beszéd és környezet.* Bukarest: Kriterion Könyvkiadó.

Bjorklund, S. (1995). Views on the pilot immersion classes in Vaasa: Lexical development through context. In M. Buss, & C. Lauren (Eds.), *Language Immersion* (pp. 152–168). Vaasa: University of Vaasa.

Blumer, H. (1969). *Symbolic interactionalism: Perspective and method.* Englewood Cliffs, NJ: Prentice-Hall.

Blum-Kulka, S. (1991). Interlanguage pragmatics: The case of requests. In R. Phillipson, E. Kellerman, L. Selinker, M.Sherwood Smith, & M. Swain (Eds.), *Foreign/second language pedagogy research* (pp. 255–272). Clevedon, England: Multilingual Matters.

Blum-Kulka, S., & Sheffer, H. (1993). The metapragmatic discourse of American–Israeli families at dinner. In G. Kasper & S. Blum-Kulka (Eds.), *Interlanguage pragmatics* (pp. 196–224). New York: Oxford University Press.

Botel, M. J., Dawkins, J., & Granowsky, A. (1973). A syntactic complexity formula. In W. H. MacGinitie (Ed.), *Assessment problems in reading*. Newark, DE: International Reading Association.
Bouton, L. (1994). Can NNS skill in interpreting implicatures in American English be improved through explicit instruction?—A pilot study. In L. Bouton & J. Kachru (Eds.), *Pragmatics and language learning* (Vol. 5, pp. 88–110). Urbana: University of Illinois Press.
Brooks, L. (1978). Nonanalytic concept formation and memory for instances. In E. Rosch & B. B. Lloyd (Eds.), *Cognition and categorization* (pp. 65–79). Hillsdale, NJ: Lawrence Erlbaum Associates.
Bruner, J. S. (1966). *Towards a theory of instruction*. New York: Norton.
Burstall, C. (1970). *French in the primary school. Attitudes and achievement*. Slough: NFER.
Burstall, C., Jamieson, M., Cohen, S., & Hargreaves, M. (1974). *Primary French in the balance*. Slough: NFER.
Caramazza, A., Gordon, J., Zurif, E., & DeLuca, D. (1976). Right hemisphere damage and verbal problem solving behaviour. *Brain and Language, 3*, 41–46.
Carrell, P. (1982). Cohesion is not coherence. *TESOL Quarterly, 16*, 479–488.
Carroll, J. (1960). Vectors of prose style. In T. A. Sebeok (Ed.), *Style in language* (pp. 283–292). New York: Wiley.
Caskey-Sirmons, L. A., & Hickson, N. P. (1977). Semantic shift and bilingualism: Variation in the color terms of five languages. *Applied Linguistics, 19*, 358–367.
Cenoz, J., & Valencia, J. F. (1996). Cross-cultural communication and interlanguage pragmatics: American vs. European requests. *Pragmatics and Language Learning, 7*, 41–55.
Chaudron, C. (1988). *Second language classrooms: Research on teaching and learning*. New York: Cambridge University Press.
Chen, H. C., & Leung, Y. S. (1989). Patterns of lexical processing in a nonnative language. *Journal of Experimental Psychology: Memory and Cognition, 15*, 316–325.
Child, J. R. (1998). Language aptitude testing. *Applied Language Learning, 9*, 1–10.
Chomsky, N. (1986). *Knowledge of language: Its nature, origins, and use*. New York: Praeger.
Chomsky, N. (1987). Language in a psychological setting. *Sophia Linguistica (Tokyo), 22*, 1–73.
Chomsky, N. (1989). Some notes on economy of derivation and representation. In R. Freiden (Ed.), *Principles and parameters in comparative grammar* (pp. 417–454). Cambridge, England: Cambridge University Press.
Clahsen, H. (1992). Learnability theory and the problem of development in language acquisition. In J. Weisenborn, H. Goodluck, & T. Roeper (Eds.), *Theoretical issues in language acquisition* (pp. 53–76). Hillsdale, NJ: Lawrence Erlbaum Associates.
Clark, H. H., & Clark, E. V. (1977). *Psychology and language*. New York: Harcourt Brace Jovanovich.
Clarkson, P. C. (1992). Language and mathematics: A comparison of bilingual and monolingual students of mathematics. *Educational Studies in Mathematics, 23*, 417–429.
Clarkson, P. C., & Galbraith, P. (1992). Bilingualism and mathematics learning: Another perspective. *Journal for Research in Mathematics Education, 23*(1), 34–44.
Clyne, M., Ball, M., & Neil, D. (1991). Intercultural communication at work in Australia: Complaints and apologies in turns. *Multilingua, 10*, 251–273.
Collier, V. P. (1989). How long? A synthesis of research on academic achievement in a second language. *TESOL Quarterly, 23*(3), 509–531.
Collier, V. P. (1992). The Canadian bilingual immersion debate: A synthesis of research findings. *Studies in Second Language Acquisition, 14*, 87–97.
Cook, V. (1991a). The poverty-of-the-stimulus argument and multicompetence. *Second Language Research, 7*(2), 103–117.
Cook, V. (1991b). *Second language learning and language teaching*. London/New York: Edward Arnold.
Cook, V. (1992). Evidence for multicompetence. *Language Learning, 42*, 557–591.
Cook, V. (1993). *Linguistics and second language acquisition*. New York: St. Martin's Press.

REFERENCES

Cook, V. (1997). *Inside language.* New York: St. Martin's Press.
Coppetiers, R. (1987). Competence differences between native and near-native speakers. *Language, 6,* 545–573.
Corder, S. P. (1983). A role for the mother tongue. In S. Gass & L. Selinker (Eds.), *Language transfer in language learning* (pp. 85–97). Rowley, MA: Newbury House.
Coulmas, F. (Ed.). (1981). *Conversational routine: Explorations in standardized communicative situations and prepatterned speech.* The Hague: Mouton.
Cruse, D. A. (1990). Prototype theory and lexical semantics. In S. L. Tsohatzidis (Ed.), *Meaning and prototypes: Studies in linguistic categorization* (pp. 382–402). London: Routledge.
Cruse, D. A. (1992). Antonymy revisited: Some thoughts on the relationship between words and concepts. In A. Lehrer & E. F. Kittay (Eds.), *Frames, fields, and contrasts* (pp. 289–309). Hillsdale, NJ: Lawrence Erlbaum Associates.
Cummins, J. (1976). The influence of bilingualism on cognitive growth: A synthesis of research findings and explanatory hypotheses. *Working Papers on Bilingualism, 9,* 1–43.
Cummins, J. (1979). Cognitive/academic language proficiency, linguistic interdependence, the optimum age question and some other matters. *Working Papers on Bilingualism, 19,* 121–129.
Cummins, J. (1984). *Bilingualism and special education: Issues in assessment and pedagogy.* San Diego: College-Hill.
Cummins, J. (1986). Empowering minority students: A framework for intervention. *Harvard Educational Review, 56*(1), 18–36.
Cummins, J. (1989). Language and literacy acquisition. *Journal of Multilingual and Multicultural Development, 10,* 17–31.
Cummins, J. (1991). Conversational and academic language proficiency. *AILA Review, 8,* 75–90.
Cummins, J., & Swain, M. (1986). *Bilingualism in education.* New York: Longman.
Danesi, M. (1992). Metaphorical competence in second language acquisition and second language teaching: The neglected dimension. In J. E. Alatis (Ed.), *Georgetown University round table on languages and linguistics* (pp. 489–500). Washington, DC: Georgetown University Press.
De Bot, K. (1992). A bilingual production model: Levelt's 'speaking' model adapted. *Applied Linguistics, 13,* 1–24.
De Bot, K., & Schreuder, R. (1993). Word production and the bilingual lexicon. In R. Schreuder & B. Weltens (Eds.), *The bilingual lexicon* (pp. 191–215). Amsterdam/Philadelphia: John Benjamins.
De Groot, A. (1992). Bilingual lexical representation: A closer look at conceptual representations. In R. Frost & L. Katz (Eds.), *Orthography, phonology, morphology and meaning* (pp. 389–412). Amsterdam: Elsevier.
De Groot, A. (1993). Word-type effects in bilingual processing tasks: Support for a mixed-representational system. In R. Schreuder & B. Weltens (Eds.), *The bilingual lexicon* (pp. 27–52). Amsterdam: John Benjamins.
De Houwer, A. (1990). *The acquisition of two languages from birth: A case study.* Cambridge, England: Cambridge University Press.
Dewaele, J.-M. (1999). Word order variation in French interrogative structures. *ITL. Review of Applied Linguistics,* 125–126: 161–180.
Dik, S. C. (1980). *Studies in functional grammar.* London: Academic Press.
Dodson, C. J., & Thomas, S. E. (1988). The effect of total L2 immersion education on concept development. *Journal of Multilingual and Multicultural Development, 9,* 467–485.
Dressler, W. U., & Barbaresi, L. M. (1994). *Morphopragmatics.* Berlin/New York: Mouton de Gruyter.
Duff, P. A. (1991). Innovations in foreign language education: An evaluation of three Hungarian–English dual-language programs. *Journal of Multilingual and Multicultural Development, 12,* 459–476.
Duff, P. A. (1995). An ethnography of communication in immersion classrooms in Hungary. *TESOL Quarterly, 29,* 505–536.

Durgunoglu, A. Y., & Roediger, H. L. (1987). Test differences in accessing bilingual memory. *Journal of Memory and Language, 26*, 377–391.

Eddy, P. (1978). *The effect of foreign language study on verbal ability in the native language: A review of evidence.* Paper presented at the Fifth International Conference of Applied Linguistics, Montreal, Canada.

Ekstrand, L. H. (1978). *Bilingualism and bicultural adaption.* Unpublished doctoral dissertation, Institute of International Education, University of Stockholm.

Ellis, D. (1992). Syntactic and pragmatic codes in communication. *Communication Theory, 2*, 1–23.

Ellis, R. (1985). *Understanding second language acquisition.* New York: Oxford University Press.

Ervin, S. M., & Osgood, C. E. (1954). Second language learning and bilingualism. *Journal of Abnormal Social Psychology, Supplement,* Vol. 11, 139–146.

Ferguson, C. A. (1982). Foreword. In Braj Kachru (Ed.), *The other tongue: English across cultures* (pp. vii–ix). Urbana, IL: University of Illinois.

Fischer, C., Gleitman, H., & Gleitman, L. (1991). On the semantic content of subcategorization frames. *Cognitive Psychology, 23*, 331–392.

Fish, S. (1980). *Is there a text in this class? The authority of interpretive communities.* Cambridge, MA: Harvard University Press.

Flege, J. E. (1987). Effects of equivalence classification on the production of foreign language speech sounds. In A. James & J. Leather (Eds.), *Sound patterns in second language acquisition* (pp. 9–39). Dordrecht: Foris.

Fónagy, I. (1982). *Situation et signification. Pragmatics and beyond.* Amsterdam: John Benjamins.

Frazier, L. (1985). Syntactic complexity. In D. Dowty, L. Kartunen, & A. Zwicky (Eds.), *Natural language parsing.* Cambridge, England: Cambridge University Press.

Gagné, E. D. (1985). *The cognitive psychology of school learning.* Boston: Little, Brown.

Gagné, R. M. (1977). *The conditions of learning and theory of instruction.* New York: Holt, Rinehart & Winston.

Gass, S. (1983). The development of L2 intuition. *TESOL Quarterly, 17*, 273–291.

Gass, S. (1987). The resolution of conflicts among competing systems: A bidirectional perspective. *Applied Psycholinguistics, 8*, 329–350.

Gass, S. (1990). Second language and foreign language learning: Same, different or none of the above? In B. VanPatten & J. F. Lee (Eds.), *Second language acquisition/foreign language learning.* Clevedon, England: Multilingual Matters.

Gass, S., & Selinker, L. (Eds.). (1983). *Language transfer in language learning.* Rowley, MA: Newbury House.

Genesee, F. (1984). French immersion programs. In S. Shapson & V. D'Oyley (Eds.), *Bilingual and multicultural education: Canadian perspective.* Clevedon, England: Multilingual Matters.

Genesee, F. (1987). *Learning through two languages: Studies of immersion and bilingual education.* Cambridge, MA: Newbury House.

Genesee, F. (1989). Early bilingual development: One language or two? *Child Development, 16*, 161–179.

Gentner, D., & Gentner, D. R. (1982). *Flowing waters or teeming crowds: Mental models of electricity* (Report No. 4981, prepared for the Office of Naval Research Personnel and Traning Research Programs). Boston: Bolt, Beranek & Newman.

Gibbs, R. W. (1990). Psycholinguistic studies on the conceptual basis of idiomaticity. *Cognitive Linguistics,* 1–4, 417–451.

Gibbs, R. W. (1994). *The poetics of mind.* Cambridge, England: Cambridge University Press.

Giora, R. (1997). Understanding figurative and literal language: The graded salience hypothesis. *Cognitive Linguistics, 8-3*, 183–206.

Gleitman, L. (1990). The structural sources of verb meaning. *Language Acquisition, 1*, 3–55.

Gleitman, L., & Landau, B. (Eds.). (1994). *The acquisition of the lexicon.* Cambridge, MA: MIT Press.

Glenn, E. S., & Glenn, C. G. (1981). *Man and mankind: Conflict and communication between cultures.* Norwood, NJ: Ablex.

REFERENCES

Gonzalez, A. (1987). Poetic imperialism or indigenous creativity. In L. Smith (Ed.), *Discourse across cultures* (pp. 141–156). Englewood Cliffs, NJ: Prentice Hall.

Grabois, H. (1996). Distributed cognition and participation in second language discourse. In A. Pavlenko & R. Salaberry (Eds.), *Cornell Working Papers in Linguistics* (Vol. 14, pp. 1–25). Ithaca, NY: Cornell University Press.

Grandell, C. (1993). *Kielikylpylasten aidinkielen kehitys—toisella luokalla olevien lasten toistokertomusten tarkkailua.* Unpublished master's thesis, Vaasa, University of Vaasa.

Grandell, C. (1995). First language development in Swedish immersion. In M. Buss and C. Lauren (Eds.), *Language immersion.* Vaasa: University of Vaasa.

Green, D. W. (1986). Control, activation and resource. *Brain and Language, 27*, 210–223.

Green, D. W. (1993). Towards a model of L2 comprehension and production. In R. Schreuder & B. Weltens (Eds.), *The bilingual lexicon* (pp. 243–279). Amsterdam/Philadelphia: John Benjamins.

Gregory, M. E., & Mergler, N. L. (1990). Metaphor comprehension: In search of literal truth, possible sense, and metaphoricity. *Metaphor and Symbolic Activity, 5*(3), 151–173.

Grimshaw, J. (1994). Lexical reconciliation. In L. Gleitman & B. Landau (Eds.), *The acquisition of the lexicon* (pp. 128–143). Cambridge, MA: MIT Press.

Grosjean, F. (1989). Neurolinguistics, beware! The bilingual is not two monolinguals in one person. *Brain and Language, 36*, 3–15.

Grosjean, F. (1992). Another view of bilingualism. In R. J. Harris (Ed.), *Cognitive processing in bilinguals* (pp. 51–62). Amsterdam: North-Holland.

Gumperz, J. J. (1982). *Discourse strategies.* Cambridge, England: Cambridge University Press.

Gumperz, J. J., & Hymes, D. (1972). *Directions in sociolinguistics: The ethnography of communication.* New York: Holt.

Gumperz, J. J., & Levinson, S. C. (1996). *Rethinking linguistic relativity.* Cambridge, England: Cambridge University Press.

Hammerly, H. (1991). *Fluency and accuracy. Toward balance in language teaching and learning.* Clevedon, England: Multilingual Matters.

Hancock, C. R. (1977). Second language study and intellectual development. *Foreign Language Annals, 10*, 75–79.

Haugen, E. (1953). *The Norwegian language in America.* Philadelphia: University of Pennsylvania Press.

Hinkel, E. (1995). The use of modal verbs as a reflection of cultural values. *TESOL Quarterly, 29*, 325–343.

Hofstede, G. (1980). *Culture's consequences: International differences in work-related values.* London: Sage.

Hoglund, H. (1992). *Lasforstaelse i svenska och finska hos spakbadselever.* Unpublished master's thesis, Vaasa, University of Vaasa.

Holmstrand, L. S. E. (1979). *The effects on general school achievement of early commencement of English instruction.* (Uppsala Reports on Education, No. 4). Uppsala: University of Uppsala, Department of Education.

Horvath, A. (1990). Tradition and modernization: Educational consequences of changes in Hungarian society. *International Review of Education, 36*, 207–217.

Hudson, R. (1984). *Word grammar.* Oxford: Basil Blackwell.

Huerta, A. (1978). *Code-switching among Spanish–English bilinguals: A sociolinguistic perspective.* Unpublished doctoral dissertation, Austin: University of Texas.

Humboldt, W. von (1903–1936). *Wilhelm von Humboldts Werke* (Vols. 1–17, A. Leitzmann, Ed.). Berlin: B. Behr.

Hunt, E., & Agnoli, F. (1991). The Whorfian hypothesis: A cognitive psychology perspective. *Psychological Review, 98*, 377–389.

Hyltenstam, K., & Viberg, A. (Eds.). (1993). *Progression and regression in language. Sociocultural, neuropsychological and linguistic perspectives.* Cambridge, England: Cambridge University Press.

Irujo, S. (1993). Steering clear: Avoidance in the production of idioms. *IRAL, XXXI/3*, 205–219.

Jackendoff, R. (1990). *Semantic structures.* Cambridge, MA: MIT Press.

Jackendoff, R. (1991). Parts and boundaries. *Cognition, 41*, 9–45.

Jacobson, R. (1953). Results of the conference of anthropologists and linguists. *IJAL Supplement*, Memoir 8, 19–22.

Jarvis, S. (1997). *The role of L1-based concepts in L2 lexical reference.* Unpublished doctoral dissertation, Bloomington: Indiana University.

Jarvis, S. (in press). *Conceptual transfer in the interlingual lexicon.* Bloomington: Indiana University Press.

Jin, H. -G. (1994). Topic prominence and subject-prominence in L2 acquisition: Evidence of English-to-Chinese typological transfer. *Language Learning, 44*, 101–122.

John-Steiner, V. (1985). The road to competence in an alien land: A Vygotskian perspective on bilingualism. In J. V. Wertsch (Ed.), *Culture, communication and cognition: Vygotskian perspectives* (pp. 348–372). Cambridge, England: Cambridge University Press.

Johnson, M. (1987). *The body in the mind.* Chicago: University of Chicago Press.

Kachru, B. (1983). *The Indianization of English: The English language in India.* Delhi: Oxford University Press.

Kachru, Y. (1982). Linguistics and written discourse in particular languages: contrastive studies: English and Hindi. *Annual Review of Applied Linguistics, 3*, 50–75.

Kachru, Y. (1986). Applied linguistics and foreign language teaching: A non-Western perspective. *Studies in the Linguistic Sciences, 16*(1), 35–51.

Kamhi, A. G., & Lee, R. F. (1988). Cognition. In M. A. Nippold (Ed.), *Later language development* (pp. 127–159). Boston: Little Brown.

Kaplan, R. (1966). Cultural thought patterns in intercultural education. *Language Learning, 16*, 1–20.

Kaplan, R. (1990). Writing in a multilingual/multicultural context: What's contrastive about contrastive rhetoric? *The Writing Instructor*, Fall 1990, 7–18.

Kaskela-Nortamo, B. (1995). An overview of teaching practices in Swedish immersion in Finland. In M. Buss & C. Lauren (Eds.), *Language immersion.* Vaasa: University of Vaasa.

Kasper, G. (1996). The development of pragmatic competence. In E. Kellerman, B. Weltens, & T. Bongaerts (Eds.), *EUROSLA 6: A selection of papers, 55*(2), 103–120.

Kasper, G., & Blum-Kulka, S. (Eds.). (1993). *Interlanguage pragmatics.* Oxford: Oxford University Press.

Kecskes, I. (1994). Conceptualization in foreign language learning. *Hands On Language, 6*, 55–64.

Kecskes, I. (1995). Concept formation of Japanese EFL/ESL students. In M. Ahmed, T. Fujimura, Y. Kato, & M. Leong (Eds.), *Second language research in Japan* (pp. 130–149). Yamato-matchi: International University of Japan.

Kecskes, I. (1997, March). *A cognitive-pragmatic approach to situation-bound utterances.* Paper presented to the Chicago Linguistic Society, University of Chicago.

Kecskes, I. (1998). The state of L1 knowledge in foreign language learners. *WORD, 49*, 321–341.

Kecskes, I. (1999). The use of situation-bound utterances from an interlanguage perspective. In J. Verscheuren (Ed.), *Pragmatics in 1998: Selected papers from the 6th International Pragmatics Conference, Vol. 2* (pp. 299–310). Antwerp: International Pragmatics Association.

Kecskes, I. (in press). A cognitive-pragmatic approach to situation-bound utterances. *Journal of Pragmatics, 36*.

Kecskes, I., & Papp, T. (1991). *Elméleti nyelvészet, alkalmazott nyelvészet, nyelvoktatás. (Theoretical linguistics, applied linguistics, language teaching).* Budapest: Ts-Programiroda.

REFERENCES

Kecskes, I., & Papp, T. (1995). The linguistic effect of foreign language learning on the development of mother tongue skills. In M. Haggstrom, L. Morgan, & J. Wieczorek (Eds.), *The foreign language classroom: Bridging theory and practice* (pp. 163–181). New York/London: Garland.

Kecskes, I., & Papp, T. (2000). Metaphorical competence in trilingual language production. In J. Cenoz & U. Jessner (Eds.), *Acquisition of English as a third language* (pp. 99–120). Clevedon: Multilingual Matters.

Keil, F. (1986). Conceptual domains and the acquisition of metaphor. *Cognitive Development, 1,* 73–96.

Keil, F. (1989). *Concepts, kinds, and cognitive development.* Cambridge, MA: MIT Press.

Kellerman, E. (1977). Toward a characterisation of the strategy of transfer in second language learning. *Interlanguage Studies Bulletin, 2,* 58–145.

Kellerman, E. (1978). Transfer and non-transfer: Where we are now. *Studies in Second Language Acquisition, 2,* 37–57.

Kellerman, E. (1983). Now you see it, now you don't. In S. Gass & L. Selinker (Eds.), *Language transfer in language learning* (pp. 112–133). Rowley, MA: Newbury House.

Kellerman, E. (1995). Crosslinguistic influence: Transfer to nowhere. *Annual Review of Applied Linguistics, 15,* 125–150.

Kellerman, E., & Sharwood-Smith, M. (Eds.). (1986). *Cross-linguistic influence in second language acquisition.* Elmsford, NY: Pergamon.

Kessler, C., & Quinn, M. E. (1987). Language minority children's linguistic and cognitive creativity. *Journal of Multilingual and Multicultural Development, 8*(1&2), 173–186.

Kiefer, F. (1985). How to account for situational meaning? *Quaderni di semantica, 2/85,* 288–295.

Kintsch, W., & Greene, E. (1978). The role of culture-specific schemata in the comprehension and recall of stories. *Discourse Processes, 1,* 1–13.

Kiss, K. E. (1987). *Configurationality in Hungarian.* Dordrecht: D. Reidel.

Klein, E. C. (1995). Second versus third language acquisition: Is there a difference? *Language Learning, 45*(3), 419–465.

Kövecses, Z., & Szabó, P. (1996). Idioms: A view from cognitive semantics. *Applied Linguistics, 17,* 326–355.

Kroll, J. (1993). Accessing conceptual representations. In R. Schreuder & B. Weltens (Eds.), *The bilingual lexicon* (pp. 53–83). Amsterdam/Philadelphia: John Benjamins.

Kroll, J., & Curley, J. (1988). Lexical memory in novice bilinguals: The role of concepts in retrieving second language words. In M. M. Gruneberg, P. E. Morris, & R. N. Sykes (Eds.), *Practical aspects of memory: Current research and issues* (Vol. 2, pp. 389–395). Chichester: John Wiley.

Kroll, J., & Stewart, E. (1990, November). *Concept mediation in bilingual translation.* Paper presented at the 31st Annual Meeting of the Psychonomic Society, New Orleans, LA.

Kroll, J., & Stewart, E. (1992). *Category inference in translation and picture naming: Evidence for asymmetric connections between bilingual memory representations.* Unpublished manuscript, Mount Holyoke College, South Hadley, MA.

Kroll, J., & Stewart, E. (1994). Category interference in translation and picture naming: Evidence for asymmetric connections between bilingual memory representations. *Journal of Memory and Language, 33,* 149–174.

Labov, W. (1972). *Language in the inner city: Studies in the black English vernacular.* Philadelphia: University of Pennsylvania Press.

Lado, R. (1957). *Linguistics across cultures.* Ann Arbor, MI: University of Michigan Press.

Lakoff, G. (1972). Hedges: A study in meaning criteria and the logic of fuzzy concepts. *Papers of the Eighth Regional Meeting.* Chicago: Chicago Linguistic Society. 183–228.

Lakoff, G. (1987). *Women, fire and dangerous things.* Chicago: University of Chicago Press.

Lakoff, G. (1993). The contemporary theory of metaphor. In A. Ortony (Ed.), *Metaphor and thought* (2nd ed., pp. 132–148). Cambridge, England: Cambridge University Press.

Lakoff, G., & Johnson, M. (1980). *Metaphors we live by.* Chicago: University of Chicago Press.

Lambert, W. (1974). Culture and language as factors in learning and education. In F. E. Aboud & R. D. Meade (Eds.), *Cultural factors in learning*. Bellingham: Western Washington State College.
Lambert, W. (1977). Effects of bilingualism on the individual. In P. A. Hornby (Ed.), *Bilingualism: Psychological, social and educational implications*. New York: Academic Press.
Lambert, W. (1990). Persistent issues in bilingualism. In B. Harley, P. Allen, J. Cummins, & M. K. Swain (Eds.), *The development of second language proficiency* (pp. 201–218). Cambridge, England: Cambridge University Press.
Langacker, R. W. (1987). *Foundations of cognitive grammar* (Vol. 1: Theoretical prerequisites). Stanford: Stanford University Press.
Langacker, R. W. (1990). *Concept, image, and symbol: The cognitive basis of grammar*. Berlin/New York: Mouton de Gruyter.
Lantolf, J. P., & Appel, G. (Eds.). (1994). *Vygotskian approach to second language research*. Norwood, NJ: Ablex.
Larsen-Freeman, D., & Long, M. H. (Eds.). (1991). *An introduction to second language acquisition research*. London and New York: Longman.
Lauren, U. (1991). A creativity index for studying the free written production for bilinguals. *International Journal of Applied Linguistics, 1*, 198–208.
Lawton, D. (1970). *Social class, language and education*. London: Routledge and Kegan Paul.
Lawton, D. (Ed.). (1986). *School curriculum planning*. London: Hodder and Stroughton.
Lehrer, A., & Kittay, E. F. (Eds.). (1992). *Frames, fields, and contrasts*. Hillsdale, NJ: Lawrence Erlbaum Associates.
Leibniz, G. W. (1704/1903). *Opuscules et fragments inedits de Leibniz*. L. Couturat (Ed.). Paris: Presses Universitaires de France. Repr. 1961. Hildesheim: Georg Olms.
Lengyel, Z. (1981). *A gyermeknyelv (Child language)*. Budapest: Gondolat.
Lenneberg, E. (1953). Cognition in ethnolinguistics. *Language, 29*, 463–471.
Levelt, W. J. M. (1989). *Speaking: From intention to articulation*. Cambridge, MA: MIT Press.
Levin, B., & Pinker, S. (1991). Introduction to the special issue of cognition on lexical and conceptual semantics. *Cognition, 41*, 1–7.
Li, C., & Thompson, S. (1976). Subject and topic: A new typology of language. In C. Li (Ed.), *Subject and topic* (pp. 158–169). New York: Academic Press.
Limber, J. (1973). The genesis of complex sentences. In T. E. More (Ed.), *Cognitive development and the acquisition of language*. New York: Academic Press.
Loban, W. (1954). *Literature and social sensitivity*. Champaign, IL: National Council of Teachers of English.
Loban, W. (1963). *The language of elementary school children* (N.C.T.E. Research Report No. 1). Champaign, IL: NCTE.
Loban, W., Ryan, M., & Squire, J. R. (1961). Teaching language and literature grades 7-12. In W. B. Spalding (Ed.), *Teaching language and literature*. New York: Harcourt, Brace, and World
Locke, J. (1690/1959). *An essay concerning human understanding*. A. C. Fraser (Ed.). Reprinted (1959), Oxford, England: Clarendon.
Luria, A. R. (1982). *Language and cognition*. New York: Wiley.
Mace-Matluck, B. J., Hoover, W. A., & Calfee, R. C. (1984). *Teaching reading in bilingual children. Final report*. Austin, TX: Southwest Educational Development Laboratory.
MacWhinney, B. (1992). Transfer and competition in second language learning. In R. J. Harris (Ed.), *Cognitive processing in bilinguals* (pp. 371–390). Amsterdam/London/New York: North-Holland.
Magiste, E. (1979). The competing linguistic systems of the multilingual: A developmental study of decoding and encoding processes. *Journal of Verbal Learning and Verbal Behavior, 18*, 79–89.
Malakoff, M. (1992). Translation ability: A natural bilingual and metalinguistic skill. In R. J. Harris (Ed.), *Cognitive processing in bilinguals*. Amsterdam: North-Holland.

REFERENCES

Marcellesi, J. B., & Gardin, B. (1974). *Introduction a la sociolingistique.* Paris: Librairie Larousse.

Martin-Jones, M., & Romaine, S. (1987). Semilingualism: A half-baked theory of communicative competence. *Applied Linguistics, 7,* 26–38.

Masciantonio, R. (1977). Tangible benefits of the study of Latin: A review of research. *Foreign Language Annals, 10,* 375–382.

Meara, P. (1983). Introduction. In P. Meara (Ed.), *Vocabulary in a second language* (pp. ii–iv). London: CILTR.

Michaels, S. (1981). "Sharing time": Children's narrative style and differential access to literacy. *Language in Society, 10,* 423–442.

Michaels, S. (1986). Narrative presentations: An oral preparation for literacy with first graders. In J. Cook-Gumperz (Ed.), *The social construction of literacy* (pp. 84–116). Cambridge, England: Cambridge University Press.

Mitchell, J. T., & Redmond, M. L. (1993). The FLES methods course: The key to K–12 certification. In J. Oller, Jr. (Ed.), *Methods that work* (pp. 113–118). Boston: Heinle & Heinle.

Monti-Belkaoui, J., & Belkaoui, A. (1983). Bilingualism and the perception of professional concepts. *Journal of Psycholinguistic Research, 12*(2), 111–127.

Morris, W. (1976). *The American Heritage Dictionary of the English Language.* Boston: Houghton Mifflin.

Nathan, G. S. (1987). On second-language acquisition of voiced stops. *Journal of Phonetics, 15,* 313–322.

Neufeld, G. (1976). The bilingual's lexical store. *International Review of Applied Linguistics in Language Teaching, 14,* 15–35.

Nuyts, J. (1992). *Aspects of a cognitive-pragmatic theory of language.* Amsterdam/Philadelphia: John Benjamins.

Odlin, T. (1986). On the nature and use of explicit knowledge. *International Review of Applied Linguistics in Language Teaching, 24,* 123–144.

Odlin, T. (1989). *Language transfer.* Cambridge, England: Cambridge University Press.

Oksaar, E. (1990). Language contact and culture contact: Towards an integrative approach in second language acquisition research. In H. Dechert (Ed.), *Current trends in European second language acquisition research* (pp. 230–243). Clevedon: Multilingual Matters.

Oller, J. W., Jr. (1997). Monoglottosis: What's wrong with the idea of the IQ meritocracy and its racy cousins? *Applied Linguistics, 18,* 467–507.

O'Malley, J. M., & Chamot, A. U. (1990). *Learning strategies in second language acquisition.* Cambridge, England: Cambridge University Press.

Osgood, C., May, W., & Miron, M. (1975). *Cross-cultural universals of affective meaning.* Urbana: University of Illinois Press.

Paivo, A., & Desrochers, A. (1980). A dual-coding approach to bilingual memory. *Canadian Journal of Psychology, 34,* 390–401.

Papp, T. (1991). *Az anyanyelvi tudás és az eredményes idegennyelv tanulás összefüggései egy többszintű longitudinális vizsgálat alapján.* [The study of the interrelation of the mother tongue development and foreign language learning in a multi-level longitudinal experiment]. Unpublished dissertation for the candidate degree, The Hungarian Academy of Sciences, Budapest.

Papp, M., & Pléh, C. (1975). A szociális helyzet és a beszéd összefüggései az iskoláskor kezdetén [The interdependence of social situation and speech at the beginning of schooling]. *Valóság,* XV évf. 2, 52–58.

Paradis, M. (1979). Language and thought in bilinguals. In H. J. Izzo & W. E. McCormack (Eds.), *The sixth LACUS forum* (pp. 393–419). Columbia, SC: Hornbeam.

Paradis, M. (1985). On the representation of two languages in one brain. *Language Sciences, 7,* 1–40.

REFERENCES

Paradis, M. (1994). Neurolinguistic aspects of implicit and explicit memory: Implications for bilingualism and SLA. In N. Ellis (Ed.), *Implicit and explicit learning of languages* (pp. 393–419). New York: Academic Press.

Paradis, M. (Ed.). (1995). *Aspects of bilingual aphasia.* London: Pergamon.

Paradis, M. (1997). The Cognitive neuropsychology of bilingualism. In A. De Groot & J. Kroll (Eds.), *Tutorials in bilingualism: Psycholinguistic perspective* (pp. 331–354). Mahwah, NJ: Lawrence Erlbaum Associates.

Pavlenko, A. (1996). Bilingualism and cognition: Concepts in the mental lexicon. In A. Pavlenko & R. Salaberry (Eds.), *Papers in second language acquisition and bilingualism* (pp. 49–85). Ithaca: Cornell University Press.

Pavlenko, A. (1998a). Second language learning by adults: Testimonies of bilingual writers. *Issues in Applied Linguistics, 9,* 3–19.

Pavlenko, A. (1998b). New approaches to concepts in the bilingual mental lexicon. *Bilingualism: Language and Cognition.* Manuscript submitted for publication.

Peal, E., & Lambert, W. E. (1962). The relationship of bilingualism to intelligence. *Psychological Monographs, 76*(27), 1–23.

Penfield, W., & Roberts, L. (1959). *Speech and brain mechanisms.* New York: Atheneum.

Perecman, E. (1989). Language processing in the bilingual: Evidence from language mixing. In K. Hyltenstam and L. Obler (Eds.), *Bilingualism across the lifespan* (pp. 227–244). Cambridge, England: Cambridge University Press.

Phillipson, R. (1992). *Linguistic imperialism.* Oxford, England: Oxford University Press.

Piaget, J. (1929). *The child's conception of the world.* London: Routledge & Kegan Paul.

Piaget, J. (1968). *Six Psychological Studies.* London: University of London Press.

Pinker, S. (1989). *Learnability and cognition: The acquisition of argument structure.* Cambridge, MA: MIT Press.

Pinker, S. (1994). How could a child use verb syntax to learn verb semantics? In L. Gleitman & B. Landau (Eds.), *The acquisition of the lexicon* (pp. 201–223). Cambridge, MA: MIT Press.

Potter, M., So, K., Von Eckardt, B., & Feldman, L. (1984). Lexical and conceptual representation in beginning and proficient bilinguals. *Journal of Verbal Learning and Verbal Behavior, 23,* 23–38.

Potts, M. (1967). The effect of second language instruction on the reading proficiency and general school achievement of primary grade children. *American Educational Research Journal, 1,* 367–373.

Poulisse, N. (1993). A theoretical account of lexical communication strategies. In R. Schreuder & B. Weltens (Eds.), *The bilingual lexicon* (pp. 157–191). Amsterdam/Philadelphia: John Benjamins.

Preston, M. S., & Lambert, W. E. (1969). Interlingual interferences in a bilingual version of the Stroop color-word task. *Journal of Verbal Learning and Verbal Behavior, 8,* 295–301.

Purves, A. C. (1986). Rhetorical communities, the international student, and basic writing. *Journal of Basic Writing, 5*(1), 38–51.

Putnam, H. (1975). The meaning of 'meaning.' In K. Gunderson (Ed.), *Language, mind and knowledge. Minnesota Studies in the Philosophy of Science* (Vol. 7, pp. 157–169). Minneapolis: University of Minneapolis Press.

Quinn, M. E. (1972). Hypothesis formation can be taught. *The Science Teacher, 39*(6), 30–31.

Quinn, M. E., & Kessler, C. (1986). Bilingual children's cognition and language in science learning. In J. J. Gallagher & G. Dawson (Eds.), *Science Education & Cultural Environments in the Americas: Inter-American Seminar on Science Education* (pp. 32–39). Washington, DC: National Science Teachers Association.

Redliger, W. E., & Park, T. (1980). Language mixing in young bilinguals. *Journal of Child Language, 7,* 337–352.

Rehorick, S. (1991). The new meaning of creativity in the foreign language classroom: A Canadian perspective. In G. L. Ervin (Ed.), *International Perspective on Foreign Language Teaching* (pp. 108–120). Lincolnwood, IL: National Textbook Co.

REFERENCES

Ricciardelli, L. A. (1992). Creativity and bilingualism. *Journal of Creative Behavior, 26*, 242–254.
Richard-Amato, P. A. (1988). *Making it happen: Interaction in the second language classroom.* New York: Longman.
Richards, J. (1980). Conversation. *TESOL Quarterly, 14*, 413–432.
Rosch, E. (1977). Human categorization. In N. Warren (Ed.), *Studies in cross-cultural psychology* (pp. 78–92). New York: Academic Press.
Ross, J. (1992). Semantic contagion. In A. Lehrer & E. F. Kittay (Eds.), *Frames, fields, and contrasts* (pp. 143–171). Hillsdale, NJ: Lawrence Erlbaum Associates.
Rutherford, W. E. (1983). Language typology and language transfer. In S. Gass & L. Selinker (Eds.), *Language transfer in language learning* (pp. 358–370). Rowley, MA: Newbury.
Rutherford, W. E. (1989). Interlanguage and pragmatic word order. In S. Gass and J. Schachter (Eds.), *Linguistic perspectives on second language acquisition* (pp. 163–183). Cambridge, England: Cambridge University Press.
Ryan, E. B. (1975, July). *Metalinguistic development and bilingualism.* Paper presented at the Summer Conference on Language Learning, Queens College, Flushing, NY.
Ryan, E. B. (1980). Metalinguistic development and reading. In L. Waterhouse, K. Fischer, & E. Ryan (Eds.), *Language awareness and reading* (pp. 38–59). Newark, DE: International Reading Association.
Ryan, E. B., & Ledger, G. W. (1984). Learning to attend to sentence structure: Links between metalinguistic development and reading. In J. Downing & R. Valtin (Eds.), *Language awareness and learning to read* (pp. 149–171). New York: Springer Verlag.
Sante, L. (1997). Living in tongues. In I. Frazier, A. Frazier, & R. Atwan (Eds.), *The best American essays* (pp. 121–133). New York: Houghton Mifflin.
Sapir, E. (1921). *Language.* New York: Harcourt, Brace and World.
Sato, C. J. (1989). A nonstandard approach to standard English. *TESOL Quarterly, 23*, 259–283.
Schachter, J. (1983). A new account of language transfer. In S. Gass & L. Selinker (Eds.), *Language transfer in language learning* (pp. 98–111). Rowley, MA: Newbury House.
Schachter, J. (1988). Second language acquisition and its relationship to Universal Grammar. *Applied Linguistics, 9*, 219–235.
Schachter, J., & Rutherford, W. (1979). Discourse function and language transfer. *Working Papers in Bilingualism, 19*, 1–12.
Schmidt, A. (1985). *Young people's Dyirbal.* Cambridge, England: Cambridge University Press.
Schmidt, R. (1993). Consciousness, learning and interlanguage pragmatics. In G. Kasper & S. Blum-Kulka (Eds.), *Interlanguage pragmatics* (pp. 21–42). Oxford, England: Oxford University Press.
Searle, J. (1969). *Speech acts: An essay in the philosophy of language.* Cambridge, England: Cambridge University Press.
Selinker, L. (1972). Interlanguage. *IRAL, X*(3), 209–231.
Sinclair, J. M. (Ed.). (1987). *Looking up.* London: Collins.
Sinclair, J. M. (1991). *Corpus, concordance, collocation.* Oxford, England: Oxford University Press.
Skutnabb-Kangas, T., & Phillipson, R. (1989). 'Mother tongue': The theoretical and sociopolitical construction of a concept. In U. Ammon (Ed.), *Status and function of languages and language variety* (pp. 23–38). New York: De Gruyter.
Slobin, D. I. (1973). Cognitive prerequisites for the development of grammar. In C. A. Ferguson & D. I. Slobin (Eds.), *Studies of child language development.* New York: Holt, Rinehart & Winston.
Slobin, D. I. (1978). A case study of early language awareness. In A. Sinclair, R. J. Jarvella, & W. J. M. Levelt (Eds.), *The child's conception of language.* New York: Springer-Verlag.
Slobin, D. (1979). *Psycholinguistics.* Glenview, IL: Scott, Foresman.
Slobin, D. (1985). The child as a linguistic icon-maker. In J. Haiman (Ed.), *Iconocity in syntax.* Amsterdam: John Benjamins.
Slobin, D. (1991). Learning to think for speaking: Native language, cognition, and rhetorical style. *Pragmatics, 1*, 7–25.

Slobin, D. (1996). From 'thought and language' to 'thinking for speaking.' In J. J. Gumperz & S. Levinson (Eds.), *Rethinking linguistic relativity* (pp. 70–97). Cambridge, England: Cambridge University Press.

Sorace, A. (1985). Metalinguistic knowledge and language use in acquisition-poor environments. *Applied Linguistics, 3*, 239–254.

Sridhar, S. N., & Sridhar, K. K. (1980). The syntax and psycholinguistics of bilingual code mixing. *Canadian Journal of Psychology, 34*, 407–416.

Stalnaker, R. (1991). Pragmatic presuppositions. In S. Davis (Ed.), *Pragmatics* (pp. 471–484). Oxford, England: Oxford University Press.

Stern, H. H. (1981). The formal–functional distinction in language pedagogy: A conceptual clarification. In J. G. Savard & L. Laforge (Eds.), *Proceedings of the 5th Congress of L'Association internationale de linguistique appliquee* (pp. 112–124). Quebec: Les Presses de l'Universite Laval.

Stockwell, R., Bowen, J., & Martin, J. (1965). *The grammatical structure of English and Spanish.* Chicago: University of Chicago Press.

Strevens, P. (1987). Cultural barriers to language learning. In L. Smith (Ed.), *Discourse across cultures* (pp. 169–178). New York: Prentice-Hall.

Swadesh, M. (1971). *The origin and diversification of language.* Chicago: Aldine.

Swain, M. (1977). Bilingualism, monolingualism and code acquisition. In W. Mackey & T. Andersson (Eds.), *Bilingualism in early childhood* (pp. 57–72). Rowley, MA: Newbury House.

Swain, M., & Lapkin, S. (1982). *Evaluating bilingual education: A Canadian case study.* Clevedon, England: Multilingual Matters.

Swain, M., Lapkin, S., Rowen, N., & Hart, D. (1991). The role of mother tongue literacy in third language learning. In S. P. Norris & L. M. Philips (Eds.), *Foundations of literacy policy in Canada* (pp. 185–206). Calgary: Detselig Enterprises.

Swan, M. (1985a). A critical look at the communicative approach (1). *ELT Journal, 39*, 2–11.

Swan, M. (1985b). A critical look at the communicative approach (2). *ELT Journal, 39*, 76–87.

Sweetser, E. (1990). *From etymology to pragmatics.* Cambridge, England: Cambridge University Press.

Takahashi, S. (1992). Transferability of indirect request strategies. *University of Hawaii Working Papers in ESL, 11*, 69–124.

Talmy, L. (1985). Lexicalization patterns: Semantic structure in lexical forms. In T. Shopen (Ed.), *Language typology and syntactic description: Grammatical categories and the lexicon* (pp. 57–149). Cambridge, England: Cambridge University Press.

Tannen, D. (1985). Cross-cultural communication. In T. A. Van Dijk (Ed.), *Handbook of discourse analysis* (Vol. 4, pp. 203–215). London: Academic.

Taylor, J. R. (1993). Some pedagogical implications of cognitive linguistics. In R. A. Geiger & B. Rudzka-Ostyn (Eds.), *Conceptualizations and mental processing in language* (pp. 200–223). Berlin/New York: Mouton de Gruyter.

Thomas, J. (1985). The role played by prior linguistic experience in second and third language learning. In R. Hall, Jr. (Ed.), *The Eleventh Linguistic Association of Canada and United States Forum* (pp. 56–72). Columbia, SC: Hornbeam Press.

Thomas, J. (1988). The role played by metalinguistic awareness in second and third language learning. *Journal of Multilingual and Multicultural Development, 9*, 235–247.

Thomas, J. (1992). Metalinguistic awareness in second- and third-language learning. In R. J. Harris (Ed.), *Cognitive processing in bilinguals* (pp. 531–545). Amsterdam: North-Holland.

Thomason, S., & Kaufman, T. (1988). *Language contact, creolization, and genetic linguistics.* Berkeley: University of California Press.

Thompson, S. A. (1978). Modern English from a typological point of view: Some implications of the function of word order. *Linguistische Berichte, 54*, 19–35.

REFERENCES

Tomlin, R. (1994). Functional grammars, pedagogical grammars, and communicative language teaching. In T. Odlin (Ed.), *Perspectives on pedagogical grammar* (pp. 140–178). Cambridge, England: Cambridge University Press.

Toukomaa, P., & Skutnabb-Kangas, T. (1977). *The intensive teaching of the mother tongue to migrant children at pre-school age* (Research Report No. 26). Tampere: University of Tampere, Department of Sociology and Social Psychology.

Tunmer, W. E., & Herriman, M. L. (1984). The development of metalinguistic awareness: A conceptual overview. In W. E. Tunmer, C. Pratt, & M. L. Herriman (Eds.), *Metalinguistic awareness in children*. Berlin: Springer-Verlag.

Tunmer, W. E., & Myhill, M. (1984). Metalinguistic awareness and bilingualism. In W. Tunmer, C. Pratt, & M. Herriman (Eds.), *Metalinguistic awareness in children* (pp. 169–187). Berlin: Springer-Verlag.

Ushakova, T. (1994). Inner speech and second language acquisition: An experimental–theoretical approach. In J. P. Lantolff & G. Appel (Eds.), *Vygotskian approaches to second language research* (pp. 135–156). Norwood, NJ: Ablex.

Valeva, G. (1996). On the notion of conceptual fluency in a second language. In A. Pavlenko & R. Salaberry (Eds.), *Cornell working papers in linguistics* (Vol. 14, pp. 22–38). Ithaca: Cornell University Press.

Van Hell, J. (1998). *Does foreign language knowledge influence native language performance?* Paper presented at the 43rd Annual Conference of International Linguistics Association, New York.

Van Hell, J., & de Groot, A. (1998). *Conceptual representation in bilingual memory: Effects of concreteness and cognate status in word association.* Manuscript submitted.

VanPatten, B., Dvorak, T. R., & Lee, J. F. (Eds.). (1987). *Foreign language learning: A research perspective.* Rowley, MA: Newbury House.

VanPatten, B., & Lee, J. F. (Eds.). (1990). *Second language acquisition/Foreign language learning.* Clevedon: Multilingual Matters.

Verhoeven, L. (1991). Predicting minority children's bilingual proficiency: Child, family and institutional factors. *Language Learning, 41*, 205–233.

Verhoeven, L. (1994). Transfer in bilingual development: The linguistic interdependence hypothesis revisited. *Language Learning, 44*, 381–415.

Verschueren, J. (1987). The pragmatic perspective. In J. Verschueren & M. Bertuccelli-Papi (Eds.), *The pragmatic perspective* (pp. 10–22). Amsterdam: John Benjamins.

Vygotsky, L. S. (n.d.) *On language acquisition.* Manuscript.

Vygotsky, L. S. (1934). *Myslenie i rech.* Moskva: Sotsekriz.

Vygotsky, L. S. (1962). *Thought and language.* Cambridge, MA: MIT Press.

Vygotsky, L. S. (1978). *Mind in society: The development of higher psychological processes.* Cambridge, MA: Harvard University Press.

Watkins, B. T. (1990, November 20). Program at St. Olaf College offers students incentives to make foreign languages more than a requirement. *The Chronicle of Higher Education* pp. A19, A21.

Weinreich, U. (1953/1968). *Languages in contact.* The Hague: Mouton.

Weisenborn, J., Goodluck, H., & Roeper, T. (1992). Introduction. In J. Weisenborn, H. Goodluck, & T. Roeper (Eds.), *Theoretical issues in language acquisition* (pp. 1–24). Hillsdale, NJ: Lawrence Erlbaum Associates.

Weltens, B., & Grendel, M. (1993). Attrition of vocabulary knowledge. In R. Schreuder & B. Weltens (Eds.), *The bilingual lexicon* (pp. 135–157). Amsterdam/Philadelphia: John Benjamins.

Wertsch, J. V. (1985). *Culture, communication and cognition: Vygotskian perspectives.* Cambridge, England: Cambridge University Press.

West, M. (1993). *Kielikypylasten ja soumenkielisten vertailulasten aidinkielen tutkimusta—puheen tutkimus.* Unpublished master's thesis, Vaasa, University of Vaasa.

White, L. (1989). *Universal grammar and second language acquisition.* Amsterdam/Philadelphia: John Benjamins.

Whorf, B. L. (1956a). The relation of habitual thought and behavior to language. In J. B. Caroll (Ed.), *Language, thought, and reality* (pp. 134–159). Cambridge, MA: MIT Press.

Whorf, B. L. (1956b). Science and linguistics. In J. B. Carroll (Ed.), *Language, thought, and reality* (pp. 207–219). Cambridge, MA: MIT Press.

Widdowson, H. (1980). Models and fictions. *Applied Linguistics, 1,* 165–170.

Wierzbicka, A. (1990). 'Prototypes save': On the uses and sbuses of the notion of 'prototype' in linguistics and related fields. In S. L. Tsohatzidis (Ed.), *Meanings and prototypes: Studies in linguistic categorization* (pp. 347–367). London: Routledge & Kegan Paul.

Wierzbicka, A. (1992). *Semantics, culture, and cognition.* Oxford, England: Oxford University Press.

Wierzbicka, A. (1993). A conceptual basis for cultural psychology. *Ethos, 21,* 205–231.

Winner, E. (1982). *Invented worlds: The psychology of the arts.* Cambridge, MA: Harvard University Press.

Yip, V., & Matthews, S. (1995). I-interlanguage and typology: The case of topic-prominence. In L. Eubank, L. Selinker, and M. Sharwood-Smith (Eds.), *The current state of interlanguage* (pp. 17–31). Amsterdam/Philadelphia: John Benjamins.

Yoshida, K. (1990). Knowing vs. behaving vs. feeling: Studies on Japanese bilinguals. In L. A. Arena (Ed.), *Language proficiency* (pp. 19–40). New York: Plenum.

Zurif, E., & Blumstein, S. (1978). Language and the brain. In M. Halle, J. Bresnan, & G. Miller (Eds.), *Linguistic theory and psychological reality* (pp. 211–228). Cambridge, MA: MIT Press.

Author Index

A

Acton, W., 108, 124
Adamson, H. D., xxiii, 48, 108, 124
Agnoli, F., 42, 129
Aitchison, J., 58, 124
Allen, W., 122, 124
Andersen, R. W., xiii, 96, 124
Anderson, J. R., 74, 76, 122, 124
Anderson, K., 122, 124
Appel, G., 76, 132
Applegate, J. L., xxii, 124

B

Bahn, J., 112, 124
Baker, C., 48, 49, 124
Ball, M., 110, 126
Barbaresi, L. M., 58, 127
Bardovi-Harlig, K., 108, 118, 124
Barro, A., 108, 124
Bates, E., 95, 124, 125
Beebe, L., 6, 109, 118, 125
Belkaoui, A., 42, 133
Ben-Zeev, S., 73, 76, 125
Berko Gleason, J., 16, 125
Berlin, B., xxii, 125
Berns, M., 6, 125
Bernstein, B., xx, xxi, xxii, 18, 22, 30, 125
Berwick, R., 92, 93, 125
Bialystok, E., xviii, 49, 52, 76, 78, 79, 80, 84, 85, 106, 125
Bierwisch, M., 45, 56, 125
Bild, E. R., 76, 125
Birdsong, D., 79, 125

Biró, Z., xxi, xxii, 23, 32, 125
Bjorklunk, S., 4, 77, 78, 107, 110, 125
Blum-Kulka, S., x, xvi, 33, 55, 71, 107, 109, 111, 118, 125, 130
Blumer, H., xxi, 125
Blumstein, S., 41, 138
Botel, M. J., 105, 126
Bouton, L., 13, 126
Bowen, J., xiii, 136
Brooks, L., 61, 126
Bruner, J. S., 107, 126
Burmeister, H., 112, 124
Burstall, C., 77, 126
Byram, M., 108, 124

C

Calfee, R. C., 91, 132
Caramazza, A., 41, 126
Carrell, P., 113, 126
Caskey-Sirmons, L. A., xii, 126
Cenoz, J., 118, 126
Chamot, A. U., 75, 78, 133
Chaudron, C., 6, 126
Chen, H. C., 65, 126
Child, J. R., 90, 126
Chomsky, N., x, 38, 41, 58, 126
Clahsen, H., 58, 126
Clark, E. V., 23, 126
Clark, H. H., 23, 126
Clarkson, P. C., 52, 126
Clyne, M., 110, 126
Cohen, S., 77, 126
Collier, V. P., 16, 78, 126
Cook, V., ix, x, xiii, xiv, xviii, 37, 38, 39, 46, 51, 59, 120, 126, 127
Coppetiers, R., 5, 38, 127

Corer, S. P., xvi, 127
Coulmas, F., 112, 127
Cruse, D. A., 59, 60, 127
Cummins, J., x, xi, xx, 17, 47, 48, 51, 52, 78, 106, 127
Curley, J., 65, 131

D

Danesi, M., x, 9, 10, 11, 12, 127
Dawkins, J., 105, 126
De Bot, K., 40, 41, 56, 57, 87, 127
De Groot, A., xviii, 45, 54, 65, 127, 137
De Houwer, A., xi, 37, 127
Delia, J. G., xxii, 124
DeLuca, D., 41, 126
Desrochers, A., 38, 133
dewaele, J. -M., xii, 127
Dik, S. C., 58, 127
Dodson, C. J., 49, 50, 127
Dressler, W. U., 58, 127
Duff, A. P., 20, 27, 31, 76, 127
Durgunoglu, A. Y., 37, 128
Dvorak, T. R., 6, 137

E

Eddy, P., 77, 128
Ekstrand, L. H., 76, 128
Ellis, D., xx, xxii, xxiii, 128
Ellis, R., x, 128
Ervin, S. M., 65, 128
Feldman, L., 8, 134
Ferguson, C. A., 1, 2, 128
Fish, S., 114, 115, 128
Fisher, C., 63, 128
Flege, J. E., 47, 128
Fónagy, I., 112, 128
Frazier, L., 92, 128

G

Gagné, E. D., 75, 78, 128
Gagné, R. M., 61, 128

Galbraith, P., 52, 126
Gardin, B., 29, 133
Gass, S., x, xiii, xv, 5, 6, 7, 8, 14, 38, 78, 80, 92, 93, 94, 95, 96, 128
Genesee, F., xviii, 37, 107, 128
Gentner, D. R., 42, 128
Gentner, D., 41, 128
Gibbs, R. W., 11, 12, 98, 128
Giles, H., 117, 125
Giora, R., 11, 12, 128
Gleitman, H., 63, 128
Gleitman, L., 58, 59, 63, 128
Glenn, C. G., 115, 128
Glenn, E. S., 115, 128
Gonzalez, 108, 128
Goodluck, H., 58, 137
Gordon, J., 41, 126
Grabois, H., 117, 128
Grandell, C., 77, 79, 128
Granowsky, A., 105, 126
Green, D. W., 40, 41, 46, 55, 128
Greene, E., 113, 115, 131
Gregory, M. E., 12, 128
Grendel, M., 96, 137
Grimm, H., 108, 124
Grimshaw, J., 59, 63, 64, 129
Grosjean, F., ix, xiv, xviii, 37, 38, 120, 129
Gumperz, J. J., xxi, 109, 121, 129

H

Hammerly, H., 2, 3, 6, 129
Hancock, C. R., 33, 77, 129
Hargreaves, M., 77, 126
Hart, D., 52, 136
Haugen, E., xvii, 129
Herriman, M. L., 78, 137
Hickson, N. P., xii, 126
Hinkel, E., 108, 129
Hoglund, H., 77, 129
Holfstede, G., 115, 129
Holmstrand, L. S. E., xii, 77, 78, 79, 129
Hoover, W. A., 91, 132
Horvath, A., 31, 129

AUTHOR INDEX

Hudson, R., 58, 129
Huerta, A., 80, 129
Humboldt, W. von, 42, 43, 44, 129
Hunt, E., 41, 129
Hyltenstam, K., xiv, 130
Hymes, D., xxi, 129

J

Jackendoff, R., 56, 130
Jacobson, R., x, 120, 130
Jamieson, M., 77, 126
Jarvis, S., xv, 130
Jin, H. -G., 95, 130
John-Steiner, V., 17, 130
Johnson, M., 11, 42, 59, 99, 130, 131

K

Kachru, B., 6, 115, 116, 130
Kahru, Y., 6, 7, 130
Kamhi, A. G., 16, 130
Kaplan, R., 1, 2, 113, 115, 117, 130
Kaskela-Nortamo, B., 4, 130
Kasper, G., x, xvi, xxiii, 33, 55, 71, 107, 109, 111, 118, 130
Kaufman, T., xvii, 136
Kecskes, I., ix, x, xiv, xv, xix, 5, 6, 16, 18, 20, 22, 24, 31, 43, 48, 49, 51, 52, 53, 55, 60, 63, 68, 70, 79, 81, 84, 88, 96, 108, 110, 111, 112, 114, 118, 121, 130, 131
Keil, F., 46, 131
Kellerman, E., xiii, xv, xvi, 88, 89, 98, 131
Kessler, C., 105, 131
Kiefer, F., 112, 131
Kintsch, W., 113, 115, 131
Kiss, K. E., 92, 93, 131
Kittay, E. F., 58, 59, 132
Klein, E. C., 58, 131
Kövecses, Z., xx, 10, 13, 98, 99, 131
Kroll, J., xviii, 131
Kroll, J., xviii, 8, 65, 66, 84, 131

L

Labov, W., xxi, 131
Lado, R., xiii, 131
Lakoff, G., 11, 42, 59, 62, 98, 99, 131
Lambert, W., 37, 47, 73, 107, 119, 132, 134
Landau, B., 58, 59, 63, 128
Langacker, R. W., xx, 7, 58, 132
Lantolf, J. P., 76, 132
Lapkin, S., 52, 107, 136
Larsen-Freeman, D., x, xi, 132
Lauren, U., 73, 132
Lawton, D., 18, 22, 23, 132
Ledger, G. W., 79, 135
Lee, J. F., 6, 16, 139
Lee, R. F., 16, 130
Lehrer, A., 58, 59, 132
Leibniz, G. W., 44, 132
Lengyel, Z., 24, 132
Lenneberg, E., 43, 132
Leung, Y. S., 65, 126
Levelt, W. J. M., 39, 40, 41, 46, 56, 57, 132
Levin, B., 56, 132
Levinson, S. C., 121, 129
Li, C., 93, 132
Limber, J., 23, 132
Loban, W., 18, 22, 132
Locke, J., 42, 132
Long, M. H., x, xi, 132
Luria, A. R., xxiii, 132

M

Mace-Matluck, B. J., 91, 132
MacWhinney, B., xvi, 95, 124, 125, 132
Magiste, E., 47, 132
Malakoff, M., 73, 79, 132
Marcellesi, J. B., 29, 133
Martin, J., xiii, 136
Masciantonio, R., 33, 77, 133
Matthews, S., 95, 138
May, W., 43, 133
Meara, P., ix, 133

Mergler, N. L., 12, 128
Michaels, S., 116, 133
Miron, M., 43, 133
Mitchell, J. T., 122, 133
Monti-Belkaoui, J., 42, 133
Morgan, C., 108, 124
Morris, W., 58, 133
Myhill, M., 80, 137

N

Narvaez, L., 122, 124
Nathan, G. S., 47, 133
Neil, D., 110, 126
Neufeld, G., 37, 133
Nuyts, J., xx, 58, 133

O

O'Malley, J. M., 75, 78, 133
Odlin, T., xi, xiii, xv, xvii, 80, 90, 96, 110, 115, 133
Oksaar, E., x, 133
Oller, J. W., Jr., 122, 133
Osgood, C. E., 43, 44, 65, 98, 128, 133

P-Q

Paivo, A., 38, 133
Papp, M., xxi, xxii, 133
Papp, T., x, xiii, xix, xxiii, 5, 15, 16, 18, 20, 22, 24, 31, 51, 53, 78, 79, 81, 84, 88, 99, 110, 114, 130, 133
Paradis, M., 37, 38, 41, 133, 134
Park, T., xviii, 37, 134
Pavlenko, A., xv, 42, 46, 65, 63, 88, 110, 121, 134
Peal, E., 73, 134
Penfield, W., 47, 134
Perecman, E., 37, 41, 46, 47, 134
Phillipson, R., 1, 3, 134, 135
Piaget, J., 54, 78, 134
Pinker, S., 44, 56, 59, 63, 132, 134
Pléh, C., xxi, xxii, 133
Potter, M., 8, 64, 65, 134
Potts, M., 77, 134

Poulisse, N., 39, 40, 41, 134
Preston, M. S., 47, 134
Purves, A. C., 114, 115, 134
Putnam, H., 62, 134
Quinn, M. E., 131, 134

R

Redlinger, W. E., xviii, 37, 134
Redmond, M. L., 122, 133
Rehorick, S., 31, 134
Ricciardelli, L. A., 73, 76, 134
Richard-Amato, P. A., 31, 122, 134
Richards, J., 110, 134
Roberts, C., 108, 124
Roberts, L., 47, 134
Roediger, H. L., 37, 128
Roeper, T., 58, 137
Rosch, E., 59, 70, 135
Ross, J., 59, 62, 135
Rowen, N., 52, 136
Rutherford, W. E., 92, 95, 113, 114, 135
Ryan, E. B., 18, 78, 79, 125, 135
Ryan, M., 18, 132

S

Sante, L., 2, 52, 135
Sapir, E., 40, 42, 43, 135
Sato, C. J., 115, 135
Schachter, J., 5, 38, 95, 108, 135
Schmidt, R., xvi, xvii, 135
Schreuder, R., 40, 41, 45, 56, 125, 127
Searle, J., 43, 135
Selinker, L., x, xiii, xiv, xv, 128, 135
Sharwood-Smith, M., xvi, 131
Sheffer, H., 109, 125
Sinclair, J. M., 58, 62, 135
Skutnabb-Kangas, T., 1, 52, 76, 135, 136
Slobin, D. I., 23, 44, 46, 76, 92, 98, 135
So, K., 8, 134
Sorace, A., 80, 135

AUTHOR INDEX

Squire, J. R., 18, 132
Sridhar, K. K., 37, 136
Sridhar, S. N., 37, 136
Stalnaker, R., 108, 136
Stern, H., 3, 5, 136
Stewart, E., xviii, 8, 65, 131
Stockwell, R., xiii, 136
Strevens, P., 108, 136
Swadesh, M., xxii, 136
Swain, M., xviii, 37, 48, 52, 76, 107, 125, 127, 136
Swan, M., 8, 136
Sweetser, E., xx, 42, 43, 58, 59, 70, 71, 136
Szabó, P., xx, 10, 13, 98, 99, 131

T

Takahashi, S., 111, 136
Talmy, L., 56, 136
Tannen, D., 109, 136
Taylor, J. R., 7, 136
Thomas, J., 73, 79, 85, 86, 136
Thomas, S. E., 49, 50,127
Thomason, S., xvii, 136
Thompson, S., 93, 132
Tomlin, R., 95, 136
Toukomaa, P., 52, 76, 136
Tunmer, W. E., 78, 80, 137

U

Ushakova, T., 64, 68, 88, 137

V

Valencia, J. V., 118, 126
Valeva, G., 11, 139
Van Hell, J., 54, 87, 120, 137
VanPatten, B., 6, 137
Verhoeven, L., 106, 107, 114, 122, 137
Verschueren, J., xx, 137
Viberg, A., xiv, 130
Vogel, T., 112, 124
Von Eckardt, B., 8, 134
Vygotsky, L. S., x, xviii, xix, xxiii, 5, 16, 17, 57, 58, 59, 61, 75, 78, 85, 121, 137

W

Walker de Felix, J., 108, 124
Watkins, B. T., 122, 137
Weinreich, U., xi, xiv, xvii, 52, 64, 137
Weisenborn, J., 58, 137
Weltens, B., 96, 137
West, M., 77, 137
White, L., 31, 92, 137
Whorf, B. L., 40, 43, 137
Widdowson, H., 89, 137
Wierzbicka, A., 43, 44, 63, 138
Winner, E., 11, 138

Y-Z

Yip, V., 95, 138
Yoshida, K., x, 33, 55, 71, 138
Zurif, E., 41, 126, 138

Subject Index

B

Bidirectional
  influence, 38, 43, 98
  interaction, 53
  interdependence, 53, 114
  learnability, 96
  relation, 43
Bidirectionality, 114
Bilingual speech production, 40
Borrowing, 45

C

Central operating system, 47, 48
Code
  elaborated, 30, 32
  restricted, 30, 32
  mixing, 47, 51
  switching, 47, 51
Cognitive-pragmatic
  approach, 120
  framework, 94, 114
  perspective, 7, 39
Cognitive
  approach, 7
  linguistics, 7
  mechanisms, 10, 13, 99
  synonyms, 60
Common Underlying Conceptual
  Base (CUCB), 38, 40, 43, 47-53,
  55, 73, 82, 87, 98, 107, 120
Community
  interpretive, 114
  linguistic-cultural, 115
  rhetoric, 114
Competence
  communicative, 11, 12, 29
  conceptual, 59
  grammatical, 7, 12
  metaphorical competence, 11, 12
  monolingual, 38
  nativelike, 5
  sociocultural, 109
Compound
  bilinguals, 65
  model, 41
  system, 42, 64, 65
Concept formation, 61, 62, 67
Concept mediation model, 65-67,
  71, 72, 83
Concepts
  abstract, 61, 121
  concrete, 61, 121
  culture-specific, 46
  decompositional, 45, 67
  knowledge-based, 46
  one-language, 45, 67
  scientific, 17
  universal, 44, 45, 67
Conceptual
  base, 7-11, 40, 41, 48, 49, 52, 64,
    72, 108, 110
  content, 59, 61
  domain, 46, 61
  fluency, 9-13
  knowledge, 10, 48, 99
  level, 67-69
  metaphors, 99, 100
  primitives, 56
  structures, 14
  system, 14, 42, 49, 58, 59, 64, 66,
    69, 98, 100, 104, 121
  thinking, 102
Conceptualization, 8, 40, 46, 55, 57,
  59, 61, 71

Conceptual-linguistic interface, 55-58
Configurational languages, 31, 91-95, 115
Configurationality, 31, 91-95
Constantly Available Interacting Systems (CAIS), 38, 87, 120
Conventionalized conceptualizations, 7, 8
Coordinate system, 42, 64, 65
Cultural distance, 96-99, 104, 111
Culture specificity, 41, 45, 50, 53, 71
Culture specific, 41, 49, 53, 54

D

Developmental level, 26
Development
  bilingual, 37, 107
  cognitive, 5, 18, 54, 71, 72, 78, 123
  conceptual, 53, 66
  grammatical, 5
  lexical, 66
  linguistic, 5, 78, 80, 85
  mental, 85
  multilingual, 37, 66, 71, 95, 104
  potential, 75
  zone of proximal, 75, 76
Discourse organization, 97, 110, 113, 117

E

Environment
  academic, 77
  context-reduced, 78
  cultural-historical, 5
  foreign language, 2
  formal classroom, 86
  linguistic, 48
  second language, 2, 3

F

Figurative language, 11, 12
Formulaic implicatures, 13

G

Graded-salience hypothesis, 11, 12
Grammatical word-order languages, 20, 92-95, 114

H

Hypercorrection, 29

I

Intercultural style, 71, 109, 110
Interdependence hypothesis, 47, 48, 51, 106, 107
Intertranslatability postulate, 43, 54

K

Knowledge
  analytic, 84
  analyzed, 79, 86
  background, 4, 59, 61, 107
  communicative, 10, 11
  conceptual, 48, 78
  conventional, 99
  declarative, 39, 40, 42, 74
  encyclopedic, 98
  grammatical, 7-11
  language-specific, 54
  pragmatic, 106-118
  procedural, 39, 74, 80
  sociolinguistic, 7
  syntactic, 7

L

Language
  aptitude, 90, 91
  distance, 31, 87-105
  proficiency, 83, 88, 108
  specific, 41, 43, 49, 53, 54, 59, 67, 82
  specificity, 45, 50, 53, 67, 98
  subject-prominent, 93, 95, 115
  topic-prominent, 93, 95, 115
  typology, 31, 88-96

SUBJECT INDEX

Language Processing Device (LPD), 37, 38, 40, 44, 46, 47, 56, 58, 87, 104, 105, 107, 120
Lexical
  learning hypothesis, 58
  level, 69-71
  plurality, 70
Linguistic general relativity, 62, 63
Linguistic relativism, 42, 44
Literal meaning, 11

M

Mental lexicon, 42, 64-71
Memory
  linguistic, 16, 81-84, 99, 114, 120
  visual, 16, 81-84, 99, 114, 120
Metalinguistic
  advantages, 76
  awareness, 78-81, 106
Metaphorical
  competence, 11-13, 102
  density, 12, 16, 19, 99-105, 114, 120
  expressions, 100
  structure, 66, 69
  system, 43, 44
  thinking, 102
Monocompetence, 9, 38, 39, 56
Monolingual
  approach, 2, 43
  perspective, 56
  system, 30, 39, 49, 53, 55, 121
  view, 38, 42
Mother tongue, 1, 2, 16, 18, 22, 32
  development, 18, 47
  education, 30, 122
  potential, 82
  skills, 15-17, 30, 74, 85, 119
  use, 22
  version, 82
Multicompetence, 2, 9, 14, 16, 30, 38, 48, 49, 51-53, 56, 83, 87, 89, 97, 114, 117, 120
Multilingual
  development, 44, 67, 107, 108
  language production, 99-104

perspective, 45, 121
system, 39, 121
view, 39, 45, 56

N

Neutralization, 46, 50, 66, 71
Nonconfigurational languages, 31, 92-95, 115

O

Operations
  cognitive, 80
  linguistic, 81-84

P

Polysemy, 70
Pragmatic ambiguity, 71
Pragmatic word-order languages, 20, 92-95, 114
Preverbal
  thought, 40
  message, 56
Proficiency
  bilingual, 47, 48
  close-to-native, 11
  common underlying, 47, 48, 52
  level, 87
  nativelike, 5, 6, 11
  threshold, 98, 107
Prototype theory, 59, 70
Psychotypology, 89

R

Reconceptualization, 9, 10, 46, 66-68, 97
Relabeling, 70
Representation
  conceptual, 49, 53-55, 61, 67
  formal, 49
  lexical, 44, 63-65, 69, 70
  mental, 42
  symbolic, 49

S

Sapir-Whorf theory, 40, 43
Situation-bound utterances, 6, 112
Sociocultural
 background, 13, 48
 competence, 108
 conventions, 115
 development, 56
 dimensions, 119
 environment, 2, 3, 6, 7, 57, 61, 107, 122
 framework, 108
 interdependence, 110
 norms, 108
Speech production model, 39, 40
Structural well-formedness, 16, 19, 33, 100, 101, 104, 105, 114, 120
Subordinate
 clauses, 23, 24, 27
 level, 59
Subordination, 23-28
Subordinative type of relation, 52, 65
Superordinate level, 59
Style
 discourse, 71, 109, 110
 intercultural, 71, 109, 110
 presentation, 116

T-U

Topic-associating, 115, 116
 topic-centered, 115, 116
Threshold, 33, 52, 91, 98, 104, 106, 108, 114, 120
Thresholds theory, 52, 83, 87, 88
Thought-word relation, 57, 58
Transfer, 19, 20, 47, 48, 52, 89-91, 96-99, 118
 of sentence organization, 95, 96
 of skills, 73-86
 positive, 86, 106-110
 negative, 95
Typological
 closeness, 88-95, 104
 differences, 31
 distance, 88-95, 104
Universal grammar (UG), 92, 119, 120

W

Word order, 92-95
Word association model, 65, 83
Word-specific semantic properties, 60, 61, 67, 70
Word-specific pragmatic properties, 67, 70
Written speech, 16-19, 30